TRANSLATION AND ETHNOGRAPHY

TRANSLATION AND ETHNOGRAPHY

The Anthropological Challenge of Intercultural Understanding

Tullio Maranhão and Bernhard Streck, editors

Leland Searles, editorial consultant

The University of Arizona Press

Tucson

The University of Arizona Press

© 2003 The Arizona Board of Regents

First Printing

All rights reserved

♾ This book is printed on acid-free, archival-quality paper.

Manufactured in the United States of America

08 07 06 05 04 03   6 5 4 3 2 1

Library of Congress Cataloging-in-Publication Data

Translation and ethnography: the anthropological challenge
of intercultural understanding / Tullio Maranhão,
Bernhard Streck, editors.

p.   cm.

Includes index.

ISBN 0-8165-2303-7 (cloth: alk. paper)

1. Ethnology—Methodology.   2. Intercultural
communication.   3. Cross-cultural studies.

I. Maranhão, Tullio.   II. Streck, Bernhard.

GN345.6 T72   2003

305.8–dc21   2003006707

British Library Cataloguing-in-Publication Data

A catalogue record for this book is available from the British Library.

*To my colleague and friend Tullio Maranhão, who has done so much for bridging
gaps: between Latin- and Anglo-America, between New and Old World
anthropology, and between forest and town ways of thinking. Unfortunately
he could not wait until this book was ready. He has gone now to see behind all
those bridges we were only talking about. Perhaps by reading his thoughts about
translation and the responses to them we can keep contact with him, one of the
unforgettable pontifices anthropology has provided to this world in pieces.*

—*B.S.*

Tullio Persio de Albuquerque Maranhão

1944–2002

Contents

Acknowledgments

We would like to acknowledge financial support from the Institute for Ethnology of the University of Leipzig, as well as from the Deutsche Forschungsgemeinschaft. We would like to recognize Maren Rössler and Johannes Ries, students at the University of Leipzig, for their unflinching efforts in the organization of the conference. We would like to express our deepest appreciation to Leland Searles for careful editing and for helping with the project in Tullio's untimely absence.

Introduction

Tullio Maranhão

The papers included in this anthology were presented at an international conference entitled "*Translationes*—A Conference on Intercultural Understanding," at the Institut für Ethnologie of the University of Leipzig, in Germany, in September of 2000, and sponsored by the Deutsche Forschungsgemeinschaft. At a first approximation, the subject, "translation," seems to be unequivocally specific, perhaps like a technical discipline the procedures and goals of which are unquestionable. There is also a broader sense of the word "translation," however, in which it can refer to not only linguistic but also cultural and inter- and intrasemiotic systems. Many disciplines, such as anthropology, belong to the science of translation. Even within the confines of a given language, expressing something such as pain (see Jackson, this volume) or articulating the practice of self-cultivation (see Basso) already poses Gargantuan problems of translation, because language is an attempt at translating proto-intended meanings. This anthology does not aim at questioning the practice of translation of things written or said in one language (the source) into another (the target). However, as Crapanzano argues (this volume), the metaphorical and the strict senses of translation cannot often be told apart. Indeed, it seems that the language game of the *traduttore/traditore* ("translator/traitor") consists precisely in playing with the broad and narrow conceptions of translation. In spite of the apparent coherence of the practice of translation, the articles in this anthology point to a wide variety of directions and raise issues capable of shaking up the most obdurate objectivist translator. As a brief introduction, the topics of the articles in the anthology include as follows:

- postcolonial translation/transculturation from the perspective of colonized languages as in the Zapatista movement in Mexico (Mignolo and Schiwy);
- scientistic and mimetic regimes of translation in anthropology (Rottenburg);
- the games played by juridical hermeneutics with translation in strict and metaphorical senses (Crapanzano);

- anthropological mistranslations of Amerindian conceptions and practices in the Amazon as an illustration of the subversive potential of anthropology as a science of translation (Maranhão);
- the Asian notion of self-cultivation as practiced by the Kalapalo Indians of Brazil as translation of tentative identifications in postnational contexts (Basso);
- forgetting, rather than interpretation, as perhaps the most important mediation process in translation, as in a pedagogy of hope (Münzel);
- the similarities between the works of the philologist and of the ethnographer as translators in bringing language out of the domain of native competence (Heeschen);
- oracles in a trance translating divine messages for the open-ended interpretation of believers in a cult in Ethiopia (Palmisano);
- dreams and clowns as translation processes among the Gamk of Sudan (Okazaki);
- the difficulties of translation of the pain experience into verbal reports (Jackson); and
- postmodern translation in its Babylonic and theological roots—translators and practitioners of the sciences of man as pontifices—that is, bridge makers, carrying on this tradition of biblical beginnings (Streck).

Translation is the second-best choice after the dream of a perfect language that would resolve religious and political conflict introduced by the Tower of Babel. The systematic failure in the efforts to adopt a universal language—a pursuit of almost two thousand years that is well documented by Eco (1995)—has put translation in the position of the next best and more realistic choice for dealing with linguistic diversity that otherwise would be a source of strife. However, the supposedly pacifist mission of translation has not always been accepted as a plausible solution. In ancient times, both polytheistic and cosmotheistic religions had already underscored ethno- and religio-centric divisions between selfsameness and alterity, and they had tried to counterbalance the asymmetries with the institution of translation, as is argued by the Egyptologist Jan Assmann (1996). In the scenario of the ancient era created by the great religious traditions, the other's resistance to translation was declared to be abomination. Translation was (and of course still is, in many contemporary cases) the bridgehead for conversion, on peaceful terms upon acceptance of the new writ, and otherwise violent. But according to Assmann, this is only one paradigm of the Ancient World. The other is of cultural untranslatability. The typical example of what Assmann calls "secondary religion" (religions that arose as a reaction to other religions) resistant to translation is Judaism. In such religions the divine message is untranslatable to other languages, and thus they are not open to syncretism. Monotheism is a step in the direction of the impossibility of translation, without patron saints like Hermes who play the role of hermeneutical oracle between believers and divinities. Palmisano's paper presents the interesting case of a monotheistic practice with the intervention of an oracle.

The dream of a perfect and universal language was not always the object of a search, but at times was implemented by the prevalence of a dominant language, as is the case of English today in the process of globalization. The Old Testament was in Hebrew, while the New Testament was mostly in Greek. Saint Augustine, who sets out to find the true meaning of the divine word in the Scripture, reads it in a Latin translation. Universal truth and universal language are more often a matter of dominance and of predominance than of origins. The theses of the perfect language and of translation as a spontaneous act between two freely coexisting languages are mythic. History and the experience of the present show that languages are organized along the lines of political hierarchies and that translation seldom is a spontaneous event.

For a long time, Hebrew was thought to have been the language spoken before Babel. Several centuries after Augustine, Isidore of Seville proclaimed that the sacred languages were three: Hebrew, Greek, and Latin (see Eco 1995, 15). Dante speculated about what would have been the language spoken between God and Adam, and concluded that it must have been a highly poetic one. It was the original *forma locutionis,* which he wanted to emulate with his *illustre* vernacular. Thus, in his *De vulgari eloquentia,* Dante tried to approximate that language, creating "a vernacular that might be more illustre ('illustrious,' in the sense of 'shining with light'), *cardinale* (useful as guiding rule or *cardine*), *regale* (worthy of being spoken in the royal palace of the national king . . .), and *curiale* (worthy to be a language of government, of courts of law, and of wisdom)" (ibid., 35). One must remember here Heidegger's celebration of poetry as the beginning of the "new thinking," as well as his own efforts to develop a philosophical language capable of talking about Being without the metaphysical connotations of ordinary German (Maranhão). But, to return to Dante, the divine forma locutionis spoken between God and Adam was adulterated in the language spoken between Adam and Eve and their descendants, and finally completely vulgarized after Babel (ibid., 42–51).

Translation between source and target language needs a point of reference in order to build a bridge. This can be the source language, in which case the translator will strive exhaustively to capture what is said in it. The resolution of translation may be pushed entirely to the target language, as Münzel argues from a metaphorical point of view in his contribution to the anthology. Or there may be the need for a *tertium comparationis,* something like the belief in a universal generative grammar as introduced by Chomsky (as well as several other linguists before him) and foreseen by Descartes, Leibniz, and many other thinkers. The often forgotten medieval practice of translation consisted in the appropriation of a text and its rendition in a new language not as a copy, but as something new and original. The practice of translation makes use of all four options: a focus on the source, or a focus on the target language, resort to a universal linguistic *tertium,* and pure and simple invention inspired by the original text.

With the advent of computer language and electronically processed infor-mation, the dream of a perfect language finally comes together with the practice of translation. Now it is hoped that computers will be capable of bridging all differences, between writing and speaking, hearing and seeing, among different languages, and even among social and economic differences. Whoever learns to "speak" the language of computers would enter a global free market from which social and economic asymmetries would be absent. Computers would be the privileged ground for the tertium comparationis among all languages. However, the dream of a perfect and universal language depends neither on the perfection of the medium nor on its underlying identification with all languages. It depends on the generalized wish to speak such a language. Such a wish would entail a global desire for identification in a univocal direction, and it seems that things work just the other way round—that is, the search for difference overshadows the quest for collective identity, or, to put it succinctly, difference comes first because identity depends on it—provided that they are marked differences with other identities. Any universal language would soon become a diaspora of dialects, as would have happened to Hebrew, or to the language spoken between God and Adam, or, as it happens, to globalized English. As Eco puts it in the Conclusion to his study of the history of the search for a perfect language in Europe:

> *The solution for the future is more likely to be in a community of peoples with an increased ability to receive the spirit, to taste or savor the aroma of different dialects. Polyglot Europe will not be a continent where individuals converse fluently in all the other languages; in the best cases, it could be a continent where differences of language are no longer barriers to communi-cation, where people can meet each other and speak together, each in his or*

her own tongue, understanding, as best they can, the speech of others. In this
way, even those who never learn to speak another language fluently could
still participate in its particular genius, catching a glimpse of the particular
cultural universe that every individual expresses each time he or she speaks
the language of his or her ancestors and his or her own tradition. (Ibid., 351)

It is interesting to observe that there is no reference to translation here; instead, Eco refers to "the possibilities for co-existence on a continent [Europe] with a multilingual vocation" (ibid., 350). Understanding would not result from translation, but from the *"increased ability to receive the spirit, to taste or savour the aroma of different dialects"* (ibid.; emphasis added). Translation domesticates alterity; it denies or attempts to deny alterity by "annihilating difference," as Heeschen puts it noncritically. But in so doing, it also has the capacity to liberate difference, as Münzel suggests, claiming that the primordial role lies with translation and not with the original event—which is, I may add, already a translation of a proto-intended meaning, or of a previously signified meaning. Here the metaphysics of the notion of origin is exposed, while the signification of the original vanishes.

Translation and anthropology, as its intercultural subdiscipline, hide more than reveal, because they provide an account of that which ultimately cannot be comprehended and appropriated, while the natural (if that word can be used here) attitude toward the alterity of that which is supposed to be translated is acknowledgment and responsibility. This amounts not to a stubborn opposition against any translation efforts, nor to a blindness to the benefits of translation. Rather, it aims at taking translation away from its pedestal of a peaceful activity, which promotes common understanding among readers of good will. Translation is more deeply involved with the power hierarchies among languages than with the carefree spontaneity of hosting the encounter between two languages. In addition, as many of the contributions in this volume point out, translation is not all-powerful; it stops short of succeeding in many instances. Following Jan Assmann, Streck talks of the untranslatable "energic dimension of language," while Rottenburg, drawing on Max Weber, refers to the "pneuma," the spirit of the communicative and expressive act, which cannot be conveyed by another act.

Streck captures the ideology of translation with precision, tracing it back to Max Weber's conception of the rationalization process. Streck writes: "[C]reation of meaning occurs through transparency [in the rationalization process], to which also belongs the proposition that any meaningful sentence can be expressed in a foreign language." To this "basic assumption of translatability in general" one must oppose those practices worshiping the mysterious and invisible, which do not have the transparency needed by translation. But since translation is one of those children of Western rationality, it regards opaqueness as a sign of irrationality. The discussion conducted in the articles in this book does not aim at resuscitating old polemics between rational and irrational, universal versus particular, or opaque versus transparent. The totality responsible for keeping such dichotomies alive has been broken at long last. The irrational is another form of the rational, while every rational is replete with irrationalities. The realization of this condition—which is not postmodern, given its resistance to periodization—invites us to recast the problem in ethical terms and to distance ourselves from the ontological line of reasoning, a territory crisscrossed by ways leading to metaphysical notions of origins, originals, and boundaries.

What seems to me to be at the heart of the problem of translation is difference: not ordinary difference, but the injurious and elusive *differance,* with an *a,* as introduced by Derrida (1976), meaning difference coming not out of that which already is, but as something that once manifested is renewed into something else—that is, difference as something that generates difference. The ordinary conception that, given an identity "A" and a "B," there is difference between the two suffers from the metaphysics of the pregivenness of the two entities. Identity and difference come together, as simultaneous and current identifications and differentiations. What is at issue in translation is "a differance that does not posit a supraessential reality beyond existence or beyond essence," as writes Frank Kermode (1996, 75). Most essays included in this collection discuss the issue of translation as difference or as differance, but while some strive to find ways to smooth up difference toward a transition into identity, others—such as those of Okazaki, Mignolo and Schiwy, Münzel, and myself (Maranhão)—argue for the radicalization of difference. The irreducibility of difference to identity proclaims the ethics of the other, who, in his or her autonomy cannot be presented or fairly represented by self's categories of knowledge.

The article by Mignolo and Schiwy places the question of translation within the context of the political hierarchy among languages through the notion of the "modern/colonial world system," or the "colonial difference," with focus on the case of the Zapatista movement in Mexico. Translation is one of the tools in the shaping of the modern colonial world. The historical context is the Age of Discovery, with the ensuing Christian and European colonization of the New World characterized by the expansion and consolidation of mercantile capitalism, slavery, and the missionary Christianization of the conquered domains. Translation plays a decisive role in the conversion and domination of the colonized peoples. The

authors see this process as establishing the colonial difference—that is, the geopolitical strategy that creates metropolis and colonies, and institutes the difference
between the two characterized by a relation of clientelism. There is a translation
innocent of the geopolitics of the colonial difference, for example, from Spanish
to Portuguese. But the translation of interest to Mignolo and Schiwy is the one
involved with the power generated by the colonial difference.

The authors present the Zapatista movement as a reversal of the model of
translation established within the colonial difference by the missionary endeavor
to convert. But there was a contradiction in the heart of the missionary endeavor,
for at the same time that it promoted translation as a form of assimilation, once
it was assimilated and translated, the colonized would disappear as such—that is,
the colonial difference would be erased. Mignolo and Schiwy invoke the concept
of "transculturation" from the late Cuban anthropologist Fernando Ortiz, and
contrast it to Malinowski's "acculturation." Transculturation involves a generalized exchange of cultural traits, something more easily understood if one puts the
idea in the context of Ortiz's effort to explain nation-building in Cuba as based on
mestizaje.

Translation plays an important role in the Zapatista movement, but not as
translation understood in the colonial sense—that is, as a transfer of the "a" of "A"
to the "b" of "B." The colonial difference has rewritten this difference, first identifying it as co-presence with metropolitan moral values, and then quickly transforming it into a subaltern value—that is to say, an "a" that cannot fully exist until it
is converted into the "b" of "B." Zapatista translation is then a rediscovery of the
displaced and incomplete "a" and an attempt not to restore its original belonging
to "A," but to understand it and express it in its subaltern betwixt, extricated from
"A" and on its way but never to arrive at "B." This approach to translation is part
of a philosophy of border thinking, of thinking at the margins, without fighting
historical marginalization from the outset. It is no longer Mexican thinking, but
Chicano thinking, not anticolonialist thinking, but a thinking that sprouts at the
margins of the colonized, of that which has been transformed by the colonial
differential from a co-present difference to a subaltern difference. Mignolo and
Schiwy characterize border thinking as "a double consciousness from a subaltern
perspective in confrontation with hegemony." What seems to be unique in the
Zapatista struggle is the refusal to be seduced by black and white situations of the
type "We are good, they are evil," characteristic of so many struggles for emancipa-
tion.

One of the interesting elements concerning translation with respect to the

Zapatistas is that the movement itself depends on internal translation among four indigenous languages (Tojolabal, Tzeltal, Tzotzil, and Chol) plus Spanish in order to achieve unity. How might one arrive at a common language without repeating the translation strategies embedded in the colonial difference? How might one speak Spanish without emulating the colonial voice? Or speak from Chol to Tzeltal without falling into clientelistic relations of dominant versus subaltern? It is here that the notion of translation as transculturation, that is, a give-and-take among ethnic, cultural, and linguistic backgrounds comes to the fore.

Most anticolonial political movements take the form of nationalist crusades. In Latin America, the struggle for nationhood was identified with the struggle against European colonial domination. It was in this spirit that the independence of the United States and of most Latin American countries severed the political links of colonialism and inaugurated nation-states in the New World. In Europe, the nation-state emerged from the struggle against the monarchy. The sense that nationalism is a form of anticolonialism runs so deep in Latin American consciousness that it is on nationalism that the political elites generally draw in order to fight capitalist imperialism and to promote state socialism of Marxist inspiration or fascism, although most Latin American countries have been nation-states for a century.

The Zapatistas' is a multicultural movement, it cannot be co-opted by nationalist ideologies, but it has to begin always from the mestizaje of its indigenous multicultural base. This is in stark contrast with other indigenous movements in the Americas, where, for example, in North America, the different Indian groups have lost their group identity insofar as their political struggle for recognition is concerned, and have become merely "Indian." One sees the same process taking place in Brazil, in Peru, in Colombia, and other countries. The category "Indian," like the category "black" is a colonial invention implanted in the wake of the destruction of collectivities that had nothing to do with the mechanics of nationalist identifications in the process of establishing the nation-state. It is difficult to apply that reduction to the Zapatistas, for their struggle begins from a mosaic of indigenous groups speaking different languages.

One of the issues with which the articles in the anthology deal extensively is the question of straightforward versus interpretive or metaphorical translation. In his contribution, Rottenburg calls these "scientistic" and "mimetic" regimes of translation. The former is based on objective methodologies whose steps can be traced back, while the latter cannot be reconstructed for objective discussion and evaluation. Rottenburg argues that translation is a copy of an original and that anthropology is a science of translation. He sees many of the epistemological discussions within anthropology as resulting from a poor integration between the scientistic and mimetic regimes of translation. Anthropology operates with mimetic approaches, argues Rottenburg, but claims to be proceeding scientifically. In general, anthropologists tend to regard all frames (originals and copies) as symmetrical, but they resort to metadiscourses in order to accommodate differences and asymmetries. Cultural relativism is the quintessential example of the epistemological paradox in anthropology. Rottenburg argues that scientistic translation cannot conceal its interpretive component, while mimetic translation, unable to be persuasive about its objective methods, glamorizes its approach as an interpretive art, thereby mystifying it. The author's solution consists in having scientistic and mimetic translation operate as partners, with the former acknowledging the presence of the interpretive component in its procedures, and the latter recognizing the impossibility of making its interpretations commensurable.

Dealing with a very similar issue, but in American Constitutional law, Crapanzano argues that the interpretation of the meaning of the law as a translation of intentions plays alternatively the game of translation as a strict textualist exercise and as an exercise in metaphorical contextualization. He examines the positions of two currents of interpretation of Constitutional law. The conservatives, who could also be dubbed "originalists," are divided into textualists and intentionalists; they have in common the advocacy of the unchanging meaning of the written law. On the opposite side, the liberals, also called "aspirationalists," maintain that the meaning of the text needs the contexts of production, interpretation, and application of the law. A paragon of the liberals, law professor Lawrence Lessig proposes a translation theory of law; according to him, as quoted by Crapanzano, the task of translation "is always to determine how to change one text into another while preserving the original text's meaning." Crapanzano takes to task the jurist's theory of translation, acknowledging at the same time that one needs to take into consideration metaphorical uses of the notion of translation in order to arrive at a theory of what that practice means.

In my own contribution (Maranhão), I discuss a series of words that have the status of technical lexicon commonly used in the ethnography of South America—such as "war," "kinship," "marriage," "myth," "cannibalism," "hunting," and "society"—but miss by and large the signification of those Amerindian beliefs, practices, and passions that they intend to describe. Like Okazaki, I contend that the ethnographic mistranslation has deep roots in the political history of the nation-state introduced in Western Europe and in the Americas in the eighteenth and nineteenth centuries as the political, economic, and cultural correlate of society. The persistence of European languages in shaping fundamental concepts and in claiming their universality is no mere accident, but is inscribed in the political processes of colonialism and of imperialism (those processes are discussed in Mignolo and Schiwy's essay about the Zapatista movement in Mexico). I briefly review outstanding events in the history of translation, such as the Buber-Rosenzweig translation of the Hebrew Bible into German, Paul Celan's memorial Holocaust poetry written in German, and Heidegger's philosophical efforts to create a language (the dream of a perfect language) with which to talk about the forgotten question of Being in the Western heritage. In the recent history of philosophy, the opposite of Heidegger's focus on the question of the existence of *Dasein* is Levinas' philosophy of the Other, or as one of his foremost interpreters puts it, "to the Other" (see Peperzak 1993).

I conclude with a few thoughts on the relevance of Heidegger's ideas for the science of translation. The Heideggerian ideas that language calls things, that words and things interpenetrate each other, that the space and time between words and things is the site of difference, and that the saying reveals at the same time that it conceals—all point in the direction of a deep revision of the taken-for-granted understanding of translation. While Streck argues in his essay that translators and humanists are the much needed bridge–builders of civilization, I conclude that anthropology should abandon the translating strategy and try to be a forum for the discussion, the debate, and even the clash between radically different epistemologies and cosmologies, such as the cosmopolitan and the sylvan.

The topic of Basso's article is the notion of self-cultivation present in the Japanese and Chinese cultural heritages, which she tries to translate in order to characterize everyday practices of the Kalapalo Indians of Central Brazil. She defines self-cultivation as a continuous effort by each individual in these cultures to articulate his or her humanness, embodied and ever-changing, surfacing in everyday practices. In the Asian context, the notion of self-cultivation is designated by a name in each language. It relates to performance and enactment, explains Basso, and not to an essentialist self with an identity. The performer of such practices of self-cultivation is perceived as cause and effect of the performance. The notion brings to my mind the German *Bildung,* but in its Asian and Amerindian contexts, Basso reminds us, it does not refer to either refinement or education, but to strengthening and enhancing personality with a focus on the body. The translation effort undertaken by Basso is mirrored among the Kalapalo themselves, as they try to share with one another their daily experiences of self-cultivation. Shamans and bow masters are two examples of models of self-cultivation deeply engendered in both traditional and innovating practices. Basso notes about these two models "their distinctive ways of participating in relations with others; the particular forms and content of their memories; their discursive and nondiscursive use of esoteric knowledge; physical appearance, gestures, and body-acts (e.g., the detach-ability and reattachment of body parts in the case of shamans, the ability to fly in the case of some bow masters); and their particular habits of speech." The Kala-palo explanations of self-cultivation do not come across as conclusive, but invite the listener to supply his or her own articulation of the experience. Basso remarks that self-cultivation plays an important role in postnational contexts (the case of the Zapatistas, discussed by Mignolo and Schiwy, immediately comes to mind) in which what is at stake is not the expression of identity but the practice of tentative identifications.

If Basso writes a translation of a concept, Münzel writes a parable on trans-lation based on a myth that a Kamayura Indian (of Central Brazil) called Snake told him some thirty years earlier. The story plays with phonetic variations among the Kamayura words for moon, sun, and wood, contrapuntal to the Indians' reflec-tion about light and dark, knowledge and ignorance, mortality and immortality. Münzel shows how his partial understanding of Snake's story evolved over the years, and argues from the end of the interpretive process, with Paul de Man and Walter Benjamin, that translation between source and target languages should not be regarded as a natural process; rather, the original should be understood from the perspective of the translation. But, he adds, the mediating process between original and translation perhaps is not elucidation but forgetting. Münzel dis-cusses the notion of a "pedagogy of hope" as an alternative to the contemporary emphasis on a "pedagogy of fun" in which children are taught with childish ap-peal. Arguing along the lines of a Koranic hermeneutics, Münzel writes that the Muslim interpreter of the Koran "learns" things he does not yet understand, with the hope that one day they will be understood. In this pedagogy, translation is im-possible and can be subversive. Münzel calls attention to the resemblance between the Koranic hermeneutics of hope in a future understanding and the ethnographic deferral of meaning in the fieldwork story he tells.

In Heeschen's contribution, he argues that in multilingual areas there is a process of natural translation, but that there is also an antitranslation reac-tion, establishing boundaries among languages. What create the boundaries of resistance against translation, he says, are collective processes of social identifi-cation at the levels of clans, genders, communities, and so on. In the translation of popular biblical sayings in West Papua, for example, the moral value of the statement in the source language may be unacceptable to the speakers of the target language. Thus, "Turn the left cheek" becomes "Don't turn the left cheek." One of the defenses against the possibility of translation, proceeds Heeschen, consists of couching statements in the source language in highly stylized forms of particular-ization of meaning.

The main thesis of Heeschen's article is that there are great similarities between the work of the ethnographer and of the philologist. The separation of linguistics from philology left the latter discipline freer to develop its work as a form of translation. The philologist is a "contingent" reader of a text freed up from any momentary communicative situations. The ethnographer proceeds similarly, for after fieldwork, like the philologist, she has to pierce through stacks of notes now transformed into a context-free text. Heeschen writes that philology is "the art and the science of annihilating the difference between a text and its reader, or between speaker and hearer," as does ethnography.

There is a certain hermeneutic circle within the interpretive analytics of both philologist and ethnographer. The work of interpretation consists in a jour-ney of the communicative interventions culminating with the text. The worldview and the perception and representation of the world are not plotted one to one, and they largely vary from one cultural and linguistic system to the next. Translation is a metadiscourse about a text, which is part of *parole* as opposed to *langue;* it opens and destroys linguistic specificity, which can only survive "in comments and meta-discourse and in carefully displaced postnative competence," writes the author. Indeed, he insists, translation brings language out of the domain and control of native competence. Following in the footsteps of Quine's reflections on the prob-lems of translation, Heeschen writes that "sentences and texts are incomplete," and that "understanding and translation are means of continually re-establishing com-pleteness." He invokes the Quinean "fundamental vagueness between original and translation," arguing that a relationship of exteriority is established between the native's incomplete language—incomplete in the sense of failing to fulfill a total-ity, which in turn is sought by the philologist and by the ethnographer alike—and the language of the metadiscourse of translation. The parallel between the work of the philologist and the ethnographer is summed up in one of his statements, in which he writes that "both are involved in understanding life-moments and in translating ephemeral speech acts." Therefore the task of both ethnographer and fieldworker, argues Heeschen, is to build the totality absent from the ephemeral moments of speech situations and from the native competence. This process, he contends, can be called "annihilation of difference" or " dealienation."

The next paper, by Palmisano, deals with a highly metaphorical application of translation. Palmisano studies trance as translation in the *zar* cult of Ethiopia. The master of the zar is possessed by the divinity known as Wofa ("ridden as a horse") and is hidden by Wofa, who speaks through his mouth in an esoteric language. The *aggafari* ("guardian of the doors," an oracle figure), in trance, translates the esoteric language to Oromo and to Amharic, mediating conflicts among the believers and answering their questions concerning existential and physical pains, discomforts, and grievances. The pronounced sentences are divine and, as such, indisputable, but the aggafari's translations are open-ended and subject to a more or less free interpretation on the part of believers. Palmisano discusses extensively the structure and organization of the *gennet* (cult center), a paradisiacal space like the Garden of Eden at the center of which lies the sanctuary, the *gelma,* where the seances take place.

Okazaki discusses how and why central notions in the cultural heritage of the Gamk of Sudan are mistranslated as the concepts denoted by the words "dream," "body," and "self." For the Gamk, dreams come from outside; they say: "A dream ate me"—different from the Western idea of dreams as generated by intrapsychic forces. Gamk dreams contain information about causes and consequences of everyday life events, and they are widely and frequently discussed. Connected with the difficulty of translating the Gamk *caalk namsa* ("dreams ate me") to an Indo-European language is the fact that there is no sense of self as a substantive entity in that Sudanese culture. In the same way that dreams are always the subject of the sentence, or the agent in the passive voice ("I was eaten by dreams last night"), the notion of self appears only in verbal reflexivity. Okazaki reminds us that Godfrey Lienhardt was chastised as someone who would have denied that the Dinka had "mind," a universal concept and fundamental trait of humanness. Okazaki quotes Needham in defense of Lienhardt, arguing that "the prejudice . . . is that human nature is essentially the same everywhere, and that inner states, dispositions and capacities have already been adequately discriminated by the psychological vocabularies of Western languages." But Okazaki goes further, showing that the problem can be traced back to the cosmopolitan dilemma between body and mind.

The Gamk also do not have a word for what in Indo-European languages is called "body." Like the notion of "self," "body" is expressed through reflexive pronouns and overlaps with the sense of "self." The Western substantialization of the self as something self-shaping has the effect of controlling not only the agent of selfhood but also the other's mode of being, by assuming the universality of a given concept of self. Consequently, argues Okazaki, ethnographic or intercultural translation ought to be an exercise in self-defamiliarization, questioning the presuppositions and assumptions of the observer rather than exoticising the observed, as he concludes with Rimbaud's famous phrase: *Je est un autre* ("I is an other").

Approaching an issue apparently removed from the immediate concerns of translation, the verbalization of pain, Jackson touches on a fundamental problem of translation—namely, the proto-intended translation of meaning into the source language before its translation to a target language. The expression of the pain experience, or the attempt to express pain, shows one of the limits of translation—that is, of conveying the "a" of an "A" as the "b" of a "B." In the case of pain, while "B" is a language and "b" a word or phrase in its lexicon, the "a"—that is, the concrete pain experience in its complexity of the physical and the emotional, the subjective and the objective, the internal and the external, the visible (a lacerated tissue) and the invisible (a chemical process)—is a reference mediated by a subjective practice and belongs to an "A" split among different discourses, chiefly the medical-etiological and the sufferer's subjective-objective report. The extreme case of the attempt to translate the feeling of pain into a verbal description underscores the perhaps most pervasive and obdurate problem hindering the practice of translation—namely, that every "a" of an "A" always already denotes or betrays a lack of adequacy between the signifier and the endless possibilities of signification of the signified. The signified is a problematic instance of that which is. The problem is no less pronounced in the "b" of "B," into which translation is being made. The problematic has run the gauntlet of the Western philosophical tradition, from Plato to Kant, and has remained unresolved as formulated.

The patients in the clinic where Jackson conducted her study were encouraged to objectify the pain experience, but they reacted against it; the attempt, in their view, distorted and betrayed the experience of pain. The author writes: "If a text is aversive in both form and content, and if it is inscribed on a would-be translator's body, he will be ambivalent about producing a 'faithful' translation." The problem is that a felicitous expression of pain does not rid the patient of the pain. Is there not a resemblance between the dissatisfaction with the verbal translation of pain and the linguistic translation of the world? And does not the translation of the translation of the world by one language into another compound the problem?

The volume closes with Streck's contribution, in which he defends the art of translation as the paradigmatic metier of humanists and social scientists. He contends that perhaps there is some irony in the fact that it is in the age of technical globalization, when one would presumably be under the pressure of claims for universalization, that understanding alien cultures has come closer than ever. Drawing on the architectural model of Babel as a complex of arches, pillars, and floors linked by bridges, Streck uses the image of the bridge-builder—that is, the pontifex—as a symbol of the translator and, more broadly, of humanist scholars. Streck argues that twentieth-century art searched for untranslatable objects and texts, as poststructuralism and postmodernism would have also done. He sees this as an attack on the past and cessation of the *pontificium.* Only the humanists would have held fast to the tradition of bridge-building.

Streck agrees that there are dimensions of language and of the saying that are untranslatable, and that translation colonizes with violence—but he feels that the result of such endeavor constitutes culture. In the historical controversy about the possibility and the impossibility of translation—the latter represented by thinkers such as Benedetto Croce, Ortega y Gasset, and Nietzsche—he takes the side of Hölderlin, Novalis, and Rosenzweig, who defended translation as a pursuit of freedom. Streck takes his basic point of reference from the history of religions. If ancient religion was translatable, there was no need for conversion. With its untranslatable god, monotheism closed the door to the possibility of translation. In contemporary religion, translation seems to mean dissolution. The religions, sects, and cults branching off from the trunks of the great religious traditions tend to replace translatability with fundamentalism, and ecumenical faith with belief in the true faith. These are religions of the chosen ones, but the choice now is not God's but that of the individual. Streck writes: "In postmodernism, it is not the heathen multiplicity of Babylon that is returning, but the multivocality of Jerusalem. [And the multivocality of Jerusalem does not require] translation in the Babylonian sense because, although [composed of] many tongues, [it proclaims] only one spirit. For the same reason, the postmodern ethic does not require any translation either. [That is something] it has in common with modern art." In spite of the closure Streck finds in postmodernism and in contemporary art, the search for freedom continues beyond universalism and beyond untranslatable particularism. At the same time that there is a refusal of translatability, there is also dissemination of translations and of the endeavor of translating. Even the spread of sectarianism can be regarded as a feverish copying, parodying, mimicking, and reinventing. In a certain way, concludes Streck, dissemination reopens or rebuilds old bridges crossed by newcomers and remote villagers, aborigines, autochthonous dwellers, and indigenous and native peoples.

References Cited

Assmann, Jan. 1996. "Translating Gods: Religion as a Factor of Cultural UnTranslatability." Pp. 25–36 in *The Translatability of Cultures*, ed. S. Budick and W. Iser. Stanford, CA: Stanford University Press.

Derrida, Jacques. 1976. *Of Grammatology*, trans. G. Spivak. Baltimore, MD: Johns Hopkins University Press.

Eco, Umberto. 1995. *The Search for the Perfect Language*. Oxford: Blackwell.

Kermode, Frank. 1996. "Endings, Continued." Pp. 71–94 in *Languages of the Unsayable*, ed. S. Budick and W. Iser. Stanford, CA: Stanford University Press.

Peperzak, Adriaan. 1993. *To the Other: An Introduction to the Philosophy of Emmanuel Levinas*. West Lafayette, IN: Purdue University Press.

Translation and Ethnography

Transculturation and the Colonial Difference

Double Translation

Walter D. Mignolo and Freya Schiwy

 1

"Translation" is indeed a large issue, and the accumulated bibliography is not easy to summarize. Our interest in it is limited to the geohistorical frame of the modern/colonial world-system,[1] in its double relation with modernity and coloniality and their related but differing perspectives. We would interrogate translation beyond the domain of the "word," oral or written, and beyond the literary model that has pervaded thinking about translation in the recent past. Framed by the modern/colonial world-system, translation is theorized here as one element in a larger set of processes we call "transculturation," following Cuban anthropologist Fernando Ortiz (1995).[2] In our argument, translation and transculturation are conceptualized as fundamental processes in building the very idea of modernity and its constitutive companion, coloniality. The process of translation and transculturation, as we will show, is also crucial to current efforts at reshaping modernity/coloniality. However, now it will be an enactment and theory of "double translation" that reverses the translation and transculturation that has followed in the global scenario.

The initial scene of the modern/colonial world is the Atlantic as an emergent commercial circuit linking communities and civilizations of the "Old World" (Asia, Africa, and Europe) to the "New World" (America). In this scene, the violent contact of Christian ideals with the great civilizations of Mesoamerica (Aztecs and Mayan) and the Andes (Incas and Aymaras) brought translation/transculturation into contact situations and established them as part of the consolidation of mercantile capitalism, slavery, and conversion to Christianity. The Christian mission, projected from Rome and implemented by Spain and Portugal in the New World and elsewhere, found in translation/transculturation a useful and necessary tool. "Conversion" necessarily relied on and was inseparable from translation and transculturation. Further, translation and transculturation in the service of conversion were marked by a value system and a structure of power—the coloniality of power implemented by the bearers and metaphorical soldiers of modernity—of the right religion and of the true word. Structured by the coloniality of power, translation and transculturation became unidirectional and hierarchical and, therefore, one pillar for the foundation and reproduction of the colonial difference,[3] from the sixteenth century to the Cold War and beyond.[4]

Territorial Thinking and Translation/ Transculturation in the Modern/Colonial World-System

Critical reflections on translation in the last fifty years have shown how the realm of linguistics—literature, philosophy of language, and anthropology—presupposes the macronarrative of Western civilization from the Greeks to the invention of the alphabet through modern/colonial and European languages (Robinson 1997). Not all translation involves Europe or the United States. Certainly there have been translations from Chinese to Taiwanese or from Argentinean Spanish to Brazilian Portuguese. Our interest, however, lies in theorizing translation across the colonial difference and as shaped by the coloniality of power. Anthropology, for instance, presupposes cross-cultural understanding brought about by coloniality and modernity, such that the expansion of the Western world in the name of modernity justifies coloniality. Anthropology often remains caught up within Eurocentric notions of progress and civilization, thereby dooming to disappearance any alternatives to Western cultural models (Alexandrov 1998).

Missionaries and men of letters faced a similar problem in the sixteenth century. They set the stage for what later would be codified into the emerging social science of anthropology. Between the ninth and the twelfth centuries, the intense traffic of ideas and linguistic interactions among Arabic, Greek, and Latin implied constant effort at translation and transculturation. However, the underlying structure of power differed from the one that would operate after 1500 upon the emergence of the modern/colonial world. Since then translation contributed to the construction of hierarchical dichotomies that have imposed certain rules and directionalities of transculturation. Translation helped build the colonial difference between Western European languages (languages of the sciences, knowledge and the locus of enunciation) and the rest of the languages on the planet (languages of culture and religion and the locus of the enunciated).

Translation was indeed the process wherein the coloniality of power articulated the colonial difference. Franciscans and Dominicans in Mesoamerica, in the first half of the sixteenth century, and Jesuits in China, toward the end of the sixteenth century, planted, so to speak, the banner of the modern/colonial world imaginary in terms of translating knowledge and establishing the principles of epistemic colonial power (Quijano 2000). This is illustrated by the imbalance in translation efforts aimed at assimilation and by the imposition of urban and a European gender imaginary. Christian missionaries initiated a massive project of writing grammars and vocabularies of Amerindian languages. The approximately fifty years (from 1528 to 1578) that the Franciscan Bernardino de Sahagun devoted to translating Nahuatl into Latin and Spanish and the time that many religious orders devoted to translating Spanish and Latin into Nahuatl for the purpose of conversion are dramatic and exemplary cases of translation for assimilation. They are dramatic and exemplary because these became models that later were reconverted and adapted by subsequent religious orders in Africa and Asia.

This translation machine entailed an enormous effort to write grammars of non-European languages and to adapt them to the Latin grammar, or to translate the concepts and ideas of other cosmologies to the Christian one that emerged in the New World (Mignolo 1995, ch. 1). And here the question was not simply the incommensurability of different worldviews but of different worldviews tied up by the coloniality of power in the making of the colonial difference. Translation and interpretation designated one particular epistemic/theological perspective as correct, conceiving as deviant and insufficient other forms of knowledge, be it Confucianism or Buddhism in China (Jones 1999; Hart 1999), or unnamed forms of knowledge among the Aztecs and the Incas (Mignolo 1995, chs. 2 and 3).

During the Renaissance, translation in service of conversion intersected with debates over the body that established the idea of fixed, dichotomous, and unchangeable gender identities, no longer subject to medieval conceptions that explained gender as a result of body heat and thus capable of sudden change.[5] These medical debates were linked to the issue of colonialism, as the New World continued for some time to function as a space wherein undecided gender identities could continue in their ambiguity. The life of Catalina de Erauso may be an example in point. The anxiety about Amazons may be another (Mott 1992; Montrose 1991).

At the time of conquest, land was conceptualized as feminine, a territory to be penetrated and governed by masculine rule. Communicating with or representing to the self and to the authorities in the Spanish homeland an unknown reality created problems of translation that were resolved by containing the unknown in European metaphors. The indigenous populations were thus translated as innocent children, fierce barbarians, or Amazons. In the case of the Amazons, indigenous social roles that clashed with European expectations symbolized a gender-bending threat that needed to submit and be contained at home as well as in the colonies (Mott 1992; Montrose 1991). Each of these subject-images lacked the civilized masculinity that was under construction in early modernity and that would come into its full after the European Enlightenment. By the end of the Renaissance, these ambiguities were translated and fixed into the dichotomies that differentiated civilized from uncivilized men and women, self from other.

In the nineteenth century, Eurocentric definitions of colonial relations again employed gender imagery to construct progress, development, science (knowledge), and Europe (or in Latin America, the European-oriented city) itself as masculine. The rural space of barbarianism, often populated by Amerindian people, was landscaped as the city's/Europe's binary other, identified as static and again fitted with the lack of a particular masculinity. Until recently, the rural/urban divide that allocates knowledge within an urban and public geographic sphere continued to firmly associate the private and rural with femininity (Massey 1994). The gendering of the colonial difference thus operates on a one-way notion of translation that resists contamination by the "other" despite the insufficiency of language to represent the "other" within the dominant order.

Translation was indeed unbalanced. In the sixteenth century, conversion to Christianity offered the general frame for establishing the directionality of translation and transculturation. Although neoliberal economics is not the same as Christianity, neoliberalism's logic contains a hidden principle of "conversion" even as the strategies and discourses have changed. Today it amounts to nothing less than a total conversion to global market relations and consumerism that leaves no space for alternatives. We locate translation and transculturation as processes within the overall frame of the colonial difference and the context of the modern/colonial world-system, grounded in an ethnoracial, gendered, and epistemological foundation.

Cosmologies, Cultural Practices, and Translation/Transculturation

⌒ If chroniclers and missionaries fixed an enduring model of translation in the sixteenth century, the Zapatistas drastically changed this model at the end of the twentieth and contributed to a theory of translation/transculturation that is undoing the principles under which colonial differences were established all over the world. The missionaries' project consisted of translating Amerindian languages into Spanish for the twin purposes of assimilation and conversion. Like the chroniclers, the missionaries' translations were conducted from the hegemonic perspective of local Christian histories projecting and enacting global designs (e.g., to Christianize the world).

On the contrary, the Zapatistas' theory of translation and the project attached to it underscore how the missionaries' translation constructed the colonial difference at the same time the missionaries intended to erase this difference by assimilation through conversion. The Zapatistas brought the colonial difference to the foreground as a place of epistemic and political intervention (Mignolo 2002). The dictum "Because we are all equal we have the right to be different" is the most concise and clear formula of the colonial difference as a place of translation/transculturation from a perspective of subalternity. The Zapatistas' enactment and theory of translation (see the example from Subcomandante Marcos below) was performed from the subaltern perspective of local Marxist and Amerindian histories in resistance against and transformation of global designs. Their performance and theory of translation is not merely from one language to another, but also a complex and double movement. First, there is the double translation/transculturation of Marxism and also of feminism into Amerindian cosmology and vice versa. Second, this double translation is not isolated, but rather it occurs in response and accommodation to the hegemonic discourse of the Mexican state that, in 1994, was identified as neoliberal. Let us explore this scheme and explain our perspective on translation/transculturation and the colonial difference by focusing on Major Ana Maria's opening address to the Intercontinental Encounter in the Lacandon Forest in August 1996:

> *For power, the one that today is globally dressed with the name of neoliberalism, we neither counted nor produced. Did not buy or sell. We were an idle number in the accounts of Big Capital. Here in the highlands of the Mexican Southeast, our dead ones are alive. Our deads who live in the mountains know many things. Their death talked to us and we listened. The mountain talked to us, the macehualo, we the common and ordinary people, we the simple people as we are called by the powerful.*
>
> *We were born war [sic] with the white year, and we began to trace the path that took us to the heart of yours, the same that today took you to our heart. That's who we are. The EZLN [Ejército Zapatista de Liberación Nacional/Zapatista National Liberation Army]. The voice which arms itself so that it can make itself heard. The face which hides itself so it can be shown. The name that keeps quiet in order to be named. The red star which calls to humanity and the world, so that they will listen, so that they will see, so that*

they will nominate. The tomorrow that is harvested in the yesterday. Behind our black face. Behind our armed voice. Behind our unspeakable name. Behind the we that you see. Behind us we are (at) you [Detras de nosotros estamos ustedes]. (Major Ana Maria 1997)

The last sentence, *Detras de nosotros estamos ustedes,* deserves careful attention. First, there is the word order between "we" and "you." The sentence could have been translated as "We are behind you." Second, there is the ungrammatical use of *estamos* ("are") instead of *somos* ("are") that dislocates a simple rendering as "we are you." Instead, estamos creates a fracture in Spanish that has to be rendered by the "non-sense" (in Spanish and English!): "We are at you." The important point is not whether Ana Maria should gloss and explain for nonspeakers of Tojolabal what she "means" in Spanish or English, but that the fracture in the sentence is produced by the intervention of the "other" grammar, the grammar of an Amerindian language. More than this, two interrelated elements deserve attention. One concerns the grammar and the other, the cosmology that grammar mirrors. In the fracture produced by translation from Tojolabal to Spanish to English, the cosmologies of grammar highlight the dimensions of colonial difference.

Carlos Lenkersdorf (1996) describes Tojolabal as an intersubjective language, by which he means that, unlike Spanish or English, it lacks direct and indirect objects. In languages like Spanish, the grammar places some portion of the world, including persons, outside a speaker's realm of interactions. Amerindian languages such as Tojolabal are based on a cosmology in which persons, living systems, and nature are not objects but subjects. This interaction between grammar and cosmology has been noticed in other Amerindian cosmologies. As long as grammar, cosmology, and knowledge remain interrelated, translation/transculturation cannot be controlled by one type of correlation between language, worldviews, knowledge, and wisdom.[6]

If we think of the modern/colonial world-system and consider the fact that, since the sixteenth century, God and Reason (a Christian reason, to be sure) became the anchor of the overarching imaginary of the modern/colonial world and the West (or Occident), then the question of translation/transculturation is no longer one of dualism. We are no longer facing the question of "the West and the Rest" but "the Rest in the West" as well as "The West in the Rest." This is the reinscription of the colonial difference from the perspective of subalternity that the Zapatistas have been teaching us and that impinges on the ways translation/transculturation can be theorized and enacted in the future.

Major Ana Maria's discourse and Lenkersdorf's observation on Tojolabal language unlock a four-hundred-year history of repressive translation. With apologies for jumping from Tojolabal in southern Mexico to Aymara in Bolivia, let us offer one example from Aymara. The Aymara word *Pachakuti* caused missionaries and anthropologists in the twentieth century a lot of headaches. The problem was to find the "right" translation and interpretation for Pachakuti: what kind of "god" was he, after all? Ethnographic information was very complex, and the full understanding of Pachakuti very elusive. Recently, however, a different understanding about Pachakuti has come from French, British, and Bolivian anthropologists Therese Bouysse-Cassagne, Denise Arnold, Tristan Platt, Olivia Harris, and Veronica Cereceda (Bouysse-Cassagne et al. 1987; Arnold et al. 1992).

A simple but accurate description of *Pacha* is to say that it condenses Western notions of space and time. *Kuti,* on the other hand, means a shift of opposites when contrary terms are irreducible to one another. (Contrary terms are collapsed in another term, *Tinku,* which means the encounter of contrary terms.) If Kuti is the shifting of contrary terms, then Pachakuti is a turn or revolt, a violent turnaround of events. Naturally the situation created by the arrival of the Spaniards was referred to as Pachakuti. So, after all, Pachakuti did not name a "god" but instead described intersubjective relations. Languaging,[7] for Aymara speakers, was slightly different than for a Spanish speaker: the Aymara speaker was not naming, but rather establishing relations with the world. That world was not divided between human beings, objects, and gods (as objects), but rather it was conceived as a network of living interactions, including those with nature, gods, and—to the Occidental eye—seemingly lifeless objects. *Pacha,* hence, is not the object of space but the relation of space and time.

Perhaps we should understand Major Ana Maria in this sense when she stated that "our dead ones are alive. Our deads who live in the mountains know many things. Their death talked to us and we listened. The mountain talked to us." Perhaps it also refers to the way that space is a visual archive of knowledge that contains memory—that is, time (Rappaport 1998, 161–73; Salomon and Urioste 1991). In any case, the discourse of Ana Maria and Zapatismo conflates space and time, trans-lates *(tras-ladar)* the past into the present. Amerindian memories of the past are transformed by the perspective of today. They conflate, in a specific manner, the past into the necessities of the present.

The translating subject, Ana Maria, also trans-lates the Amerindians into the present of global time. She claims coevalness with the West, as has Rigoberta Menchú. In so doing she unravels metaphorical attachments between nature, femininity, stasis, and indigenous people that have held them at bay in Western conceptualizations of development and modernity.[8] Amerindians are not primitives located on a temporal axis of development and occupying a position of premodernity. Amerindians and Amerindian memories are present, and there is no primeval authenticity. They are present in and through the colonial difference as the place where transculturation and the coloniality of power are constantly at work. This transculturation takes place on Amerindian terms; there is no integration to the nation on national terms. Instead, there is a particular kind of translation/transculturation going on in which a dense history of oppression and subalternization of language and knowledge is being unlocked.

There is a fundamental difference between what goes on in the case of the Zapatistas and recent academic approaches to translation, even when the latter are grounded on postcolonial principles.[9] Liu (1999), for instance, situates the problem of translation in the context of coloniality. She combines linguistics (de Saussure) and semiotic theory (Baudrillard) with Marxist notions of exchange value to signal broader contexts of power difference that inform the relations between China and the West. She argues that a theory of translation must consider circumstantial meetings of languages and people that are based on interactive and conflictual processes in colonial contexts, rather than on fixed identities.

Unlike our explorations of Zapatismo in Mexico, however, Liu capitalizes on the violence accompanying colonization and colonial relations as well as the cooperation of colonial intellectuals in translating from English to Chinese—the focus of much recent postcolonial work. The difference is that Liu does not question the geopolitical directionality of translation—that is, the relations between language, knowledge, and power. While the Zapatistas' political visions stem from the translation of Western thought into Maya cosmovision and vice versa, all the while confronted with the hegemony of the state, postcolonial approaches to translation (e.g., Liu 1999; Niranjana 1992) seem to want to prove that an original, multiple way of thinking is legitimized in its existence by the European master's deconstructions. However, this need for legitimation only reinstates the colonial directionality of translation/transculturation.

Still, the centrality of the concept of exchange value in Liu´s argument allows her to recognize contexts of translation as exchange not only of verbal and symbolic concepts but also of material objects or "tokens," as she calls them. The terms seem useful in order to think translation/transculturation as a situated practice that includes various forms of engagement.

Perhaps the concept of transculturation, introduced in 1940 by Fernando Ortiz (see Ortiz 1995), can help clarify what is at stake in the issues raised by the Zapatista revolution. Ortiz sought to correct the unidirectional process of translation and acculturation in British anthropology (in this case, as articulated by Bronislaw Malinowski; see Asad 1986). For Ortiz, "transculturation" was a tool for thinking about nation-building in a society wherein homogeneity had to account for mestizaje. But important for our argument, it also indirectly underscored how cultural transformations do not go only from East to West but also from West to East or North–South and South–North. The fact remains that transculturation was a process perceived from a postcolonial society, while Malinowski saw acculturation only from the vantage point of a colonizing nation (Coronil 1995).

When Ortiz wrote about transculturation in human communities, he thought of what we would call cultural diversity within Cuba. But Ortiz also talked about the transculturation of commodities—that is, of the social life of things (see Appadurai and others in Appadurai 1986). In doing so, he extended beyond the boundaries of the nation to consider what would be conceptualized later as the modern world-system, or what we call the modern/colonial world-system (see Mignolo 2000). Following Ortiz, transculturation works bidirectionally in the social life of things. It trans-lates objects that transform modes of being and thinking while also transforming the "original" uses and life of the object. Ortiz provided the example of African drums in Cuba. He thought about transculturation as a world process that made Cuba what Cuba was, as a nation, in the first half of the twentieth century—namely, a part of a new commercial circuit that formed in the sixteenth century and that linked Cuba to the Mediterranean across the Atlantic. This circuit created the conditions for the slave trade from Africa and the basis for Cuba's demographic profile.

Ortiz advocated rationality and objectivity, free of interests and emotions like "enthusiasm," but he also wrote *Cuban Counterpoint* from the perspective of culture and literature—a genre lacking the rationality, objectivity, and (masculine) subjectivity of science. In the *Counterpoint* he launched a contribution to knowledge that entailed a different engagement by a new subject of knowledge. To gain admittance, however, he would have to successfully question the location of knowledge production and his own claim to a universal scientific objectivity. This was not possible in the absence of a global context that would support such a translation. Ortiz could not begin a mutual cross-fertilization with Afro-Cuban intellectuals that would bring the results we find with the Zapatistas. In contrast, the Zapatistas' theoretical revolution in the domain of translation/transculturation offers a change in directionality: it is a process of double translation, a historical condition for political intervention by subaltern languages. Let us explain.

As noted above, sixteenth-century missionaries translated in both directions between Amerindian languages and Spanish. Amerindians initially assisted in those projects; translations, however, were controlled and manipulated by the dominant group. The missionaries and their translations did not transform the imperial design but instead were absorbed into its logic.

In contrast, syncretism as practice may indicate a long-standing strategy of translation/transculturation that has worked against imperial translations. A tradition of syncretic practices may supply a foundation that allows the Tojolabales to perceive the Marxist/Leninist guerrillas as a revolutionary potential adequate to their needs. In the case of the Zapatistas, the subaltern group manipulates translation but now in multiple directions. First, translation occurs among the four Amerindian languages of the Zapatista movement: Tojolabal, Tzeltal, Tzotzil, and Chol. Second, and most important, translation from Amerindian languages to Spanish no longer implies a unidirectional translation of Amerindian languages into Spanish concepts and systems of understanding. Rather, an Amerindian understanding is rendered in and even in violation of Spanish syntax, becoming transformed in the process but not entirely losing its difference from Western understanding. In the other direction, from Spanish and Western languages to Amerindian languages, Spanish/Western thinking is transformed and its words inserted and interpreted according to Amerindian cosmologies.

Subcomandante Marcos (Marcos 1997) has talked about these various levels of translations. For Marcos, translation was not just interlinguistic but also intercosmological. He uses the term "translator" *(traductor)* to refer to the "indigenist element" that made possible communication between the Marxist-Leninist guerrilla forces and the indigenous communities in the Chiapan highlands. Crucial to this translation was the transportation of concepts, thoughts, and, ultimately, of revolutionary needs and goals from one cultural context to another. This transport did not go primarily in the direction it has traditionally taken when revolutionary actors equipped with Occidentalist (Western) knowledge have confronted "the masses." Marcos explains that the Marxist-Leninist revolutionary organization encountered a reality that could not be explained by Western concepts. The organization therefore realized that it needed to "listen": "The [new] EZLN was born from the very moment that it realized that there is a new reality for which it has no answer and to which it subordinates itself to be able to survive" (ibid., 149).

Marcos calls the moment when these two cultures come together a *choque,* a "clash." But rather than a moment in time, this clash produces a space of contact and conflict wherein translation takes place. The EZLN notices that it needs to learn rather than teach. A space opens up where knowledge flows from the Mayan indigenous communities into the thinking of Marxist-Leninist revolutionaries. The pressure for this flow is created because the Amerindian components become a majority in the political organization. Marcos calls this process "translation." It is facilitated and encouraged by "translators," principally Old Antonio and the leaders of the communities.

Marcos's encounter with Old Antonio *(el viejo Antonio)* goes back to 1984. Old Man Antonio is the first translator or, at least, the one who makes Marcos aware of the need for translation. Now, from the perspective of urban intellectuals, the process of translation turns into a process of re-education. "And that is where Old Antonio and the leaders of the communities and the indigenous *guerrilleros* became the teachers of this military-political organization [the EZLN]" (ibid., 148): "We went through a process of re-education, of re-modeling. It was like they unarmed us. As if they had dismantled all the tools we had—Marxism, Leninism, socialism, urban culture, poetry, literature—every thing that was a part of ourselves, and also that we did not know we had. They dismantled us and put us together again, but in a different configuration. And that was for us [urban intellectuals] the only way to survive" (ibid., 151).

Marcos asserts that this process of translation "indianized" the urban part of the EZLN. Crucial once again is the existence of subjects connected to Amerindian knowledges and traditions who were simultaneously taking part in the Occidental urban culture of the cities. In other words, this is how "the indianization of the EZLN tactically displaced itself [*se traslado*—that is, shifted place and translated itself], contaminated the urban part and indianized it as well" (ibid., 150). Old Antonio emerged in the Zapatistas' horizon in the first Amerindian town the EZLN encountered, in 1985. He explained to the urban intellectuals "who we were and what we shall be doing" (ibid., 154). It was Old Antonio "who gave us the indigenous elements that you find in Zapatistas' languages when we address ourselves to the Mexican or the world audience" (ibid., 155).

But Marcos himself also is a translator. More than that, since the moment of encounter with Old Antonio, he transformed himself into something else. Precisely as Rafael Guillen began to be erased, Marcos transformed himself into what they (the Amerindians) want him to be—a paradigmatic case, indeed, of translation/transculturation transacting the colonial difference and the coloniality of power from a subaltern perspective. Marcos became a transculturated/translated new persona. "What happened," explains Marcos, "is that the glass of that window is dirty, and people began to see themselves in it and it is at that moment that Marcos becomes a symbol, that persona that is being constructed since 1994" (ibid.). He converted himself into someone who could be used by the Amerindians. Marcos, as translator, is the window through which to look both inside and outside (ibid.). However, the temptation to underscore Guillen's vita instead of the significance of the transformation of Guillen into Marcos would take us away from the major point of the argument.[10] That is, translation and transculturation (not just "cultural translation") lead to a theoretical revolution in political as well as ethical terms.

If the window is dusty, as Marcos emphasized, it also reflects what is left of Rafael Guillen and perhaps even a struggle over whose Amerindian perspective engages in the translating process among the men and women actively figuring in the EZLN. In our previous example, Major Ana Maria's address, the subject speaking is a female indigenous guerrillera. Her gender alerts us to the subjectivities that are created and organized through the colonial difference and its translation processes. With the protagonism of Old Antonio, Marcos establishes a masculine genealogy wherein Old Antonio is the primeval translator, now transformed into the voice of Marcos who prolongs the process, publishing the EZLN perspective for national and international audiences. If this procedure seems to affirm the requirement of masculinity, asserting that Indian males are also men, the simultaneous protagonism of Mayan women in the EZLN resists this logic as they themselves engage in a process of double translation next to, not through, Marcos. Translations by the female majors and comandantes are not restricted to gender relations; instead, they insist on questioning and reshaping Mayan traditions in order to construct more equal Tojolabal, Tzeltal, Tzotzil, or Chol societies. In the process guerrilla experiences are translated/ transculturated through a critical, but not antagonistic, attitude toward both Mayan tradition and feminist theories.

Marcos emphasizes that the first communities with which the guerrilla entered in contact in the second half of the 1980s were "the most isolated" (ibid., 151). He implies that traditional knowledges were well preserved. However, the Lacandon forest constitutes a heterogeneous place of migration (Leyva Solano et al. 1996). It may be understood as a "borderlands" (Anzaldúa 1987) that precisely enables the processes of translation and the elaboration of a new, transculturated cosmovision. This contradiction points to a tension in which Marcos is still partially caught. The terrain on which indigenous voices are heard and understood is still informed by a need for authenticity on the part of the West, a need to which indigenous people cater as they simultaneously undo it.

Still, border thinking seems to be an able concept for grasping the theoretical potential of the Zapatista revolution. We can now emphasize that the translators emerge out of border spaces where contact has already been taking place and without subsuming the actors in the tale of integration and acculturation. Whether this contact be the quincentennial relations between Spaniards, Mexican Creoles, and Mestizos in the modern world order or the national conflict between Mexico and the United States that was formalized in 1848 by the Guadalupe-Hidalgo treaty and the drastic relocations of the national frontiers, or whether it be the Zapatistas or the emergence of a Chicana/o consciousness, we face the emergence of a border-space that rearticulates the colonial difference from a subaltern position and that makes the new kind of translation/transculturation possible. It creates experiences that open up new ways of thinking, not as inescapably or necessarily so, but as a possibility (Moya 1997).

Our notion of border thinking is related to Gloria Anzaldúa's (1987) exploration of consciousness and borderlands. She begins this task by retelling or "translating" Chicano history against the dominant Mexican nation-making version, made famous by Octavio Paz's *Labyrinth of Solitude*, by inserting both Chicano and feminist perspectives. She does not discard any of the "identifications" that are only partially available to her, but uses them with and against each other to construct a concept of identity that seeks to go beyond biological fixation, constructivist disembodiment, and harmonious homogeneity. It is a space for ambiguity in constant transition that "translates" (in order to make sense in a new value system) the cultural baggage that seeks to define and fix her. Feminist rewriting is crucial to this translation, but its knowledge is not rooted in Western discourse alone.

For the Zapatistas, the translation of Amerindian knowledge becomes a matter of urgency, both for physical survival and for the survival of revolutionary potential. In this process, it transforms some of the blind spots in Marxist-Leninist revolutionary ideals and brings to light their limitations. Similarly, Ana Maria and Comandante Ramona are reworking Maya "identity" by translating "feminism." Dominant feminist theory—as it has been elaborated in France or by white, middle-class women in the United States—has been called "white" feminism because it abstracts from class difference and racism in an effort to identify a universal concept of "woman" and the causes for her oppression. This strand of feminist theory, widely criticized by what could be called "postcolonial feminism," has found itself translated into Spanish and into the cultural context of national Mexican society. Mexican middle-class feminists have found it difficult to address feminism in relation to domestic service and Latin American racism. Some have criticized the participation of women in the military ranks of the EZLN and in battle as a betrayal of feminine culture and as adverse to feminism. As the EZLN becomes "feminist"—both in person and in discourse—the protagonism of in-digenous women in the leading positions of command again points the process of translation in a different direction.[11] Feminist demands for a transformation of indigenous societies goes hand in hand with the search for solutions to economic and racial discrimination. Feminism being translated back from Mayan cosmol-ogy becomes inseparable from issues of race and clan. The essentialized notion of woman as the bearer of a pacifist feminine culture is unmasked as a myth that serves to cover up the complicity of women in perpetuating a modern/colonial world order.[12] Border thinking emerges here not as representation of anything or as a happy hybrid surrounded by repressive purity, but as a place of epistemic and political confrontation with the neoliberal thinking of the state. At the same time, border thinking undoes the dichotomies that sustained the modern/colonial world-system and its hegemonic epistemology. It is precisely here that the Zap-atistas' theoretical revolution is located, where the colonial difference emerges as the locus for the epistemic potential of border thinking and where translation/transculturation has to be remapped. Border thinking, as a new perspective to think translation/transculturation, is precisely this double consciousness of subal-terns in confrontation with hegemony.

An "Indigenous" uprising, with a new language, was and is a social move-ment yet difficult to process within either the neoliberal frame of mind of the Mexican government or that of intellectuals (like the early Octavio Paz), as well as from orthodox Marxist, leftist, and even feminist positions. It is an epistemo-logical revolution that impacts on how to talk about and think about translation/transculturation. Zapatism, indeed, began to be defined by the indigenous intel-lectuals with previous political experience, like Tacho, David, Zevedeo, and Mari-bel. They are, according to Marcos, the true creators of Zapatism and the leading theorists for new conceptions and enactments of translation/transculturation: "The true creators of Zapatism are the translators, translators such as Mayor Mario, Mayor Moises, Mayor Ana Maria, all of those who also had to be translated from dialects [Marcos is referring here to indigenous languages] such as Tacho, David, Zevedeo. They are indeed the Zapatistas' theoreticians; they built, they are building a new way for looking at the world" (Marcos 1997, 338–39).

Translation/Transculturation from the Borders

There are a series of issues that the Zapatistas' theoretical revolution helps us in framing and arguing. First, the links among language, nation, and writing can no longer be sustained. Second, the ties of language, location, and subjectivity to epistemology are coming unglued. Third, a new potential for intercultural communication in border spaces requires reflection, not least of all, on academic practice.

The Zapatistas call for redefining the concepts of translation and transculturation. Both terms have a close link with imperial and national beliefs and assumptions, as we have outlined in this article. Translation, in terms of translating texts and literature, was redefined in the modern world (from the Renaissance) under the presupposition of the unity and uniqueness of certain languages based solely on their grammar. In the modern world, the proliferation of grammatical treatises based on alphabetic literacy and the expansion of Western Christianity (generally referred to as "Western expansion") are interpreted to mean the unity and distinctiveness of certain (other) languages. As self-contained entities they are placed into dichotomous relations that are not equal with or even complementary to each other, but rather defined hierarchically by the geopolitical location of the language as nation. Talal Asad insisted on keeping in mind the inequality of languages that were involved in the production of anthropological knowledge. The Zapatistas opened up a new possibility, the possibility of speaking and writing Amerindian languages through Spanish, or using and appropriating Spanish as the official language of the nation. Such a possibility also has important consequences for indigenous movements in Latin America, from Bolivia and Ecuador to Guatemala and Mexico as well as for international and interlingual relations in the production of knowledge and its political consequences.

For three centuries, 1500 to 1800, Amerindians were targeted for conversion to Christianity and to learn Spanish. Translation was part of a project of transculturation, equated with "conversion" or "assimilation." After 1800, Amerindians were marginalized as the target of bilingual education in emerging nation-states. That is, Amerindians had to learn Spanish, but the Creole elite in power did not have to learn Amerindian languages. Today, Amerindian debates within nation-states across the Latin American continent take place in Spanish, while English, as in the case of the Zapatistas, connects indigenous peoples at a global level. "Transculturation" is here best described as a social conflict between languages and cosmologies in hegemonic and subaltern positions, respectively.

Thinking translation/transculturation from the perspective of the Zapatistas makes clear that the war of interpretation being waged at the national level
in Mexico can no longer be contained by the boundaries of a nation-state. If the
government and its media seek to codify the indigenous people as primitive or
infantile, they rely on a traditional/colonial translation that anachronistically
reiterates masculinity as a requirement for citizenship, along with an obvious Enlightenment framing that gathers children, women, the insane, and (Europe's)
racial Others into the group lacking this masculinity. But the Zapatista discourse
reverberates with developments at a supranational level that cannot be isolated
from thinking in Mexico itself. This is what makes the Zapatista discourse forceful
in the "war of interpretation." The global situation at the end of the twentieth century witnessed a certain preparation of terrain that is significantly different from
the conditions of possibility in the sixteenth and nineteenth centuries. Today we
are witnessing a desubalternization or a decolonization of knowledge that places
translation/transculturation into a new epistemological context and structure
of power. Western Christian rationality, an imaginary that is also identified as
"Occidentalism" (Deloria 1978), confronts "multiple others" that have been elabo-
rating alternative engagements with Reason, on both its interior and its exterior
borders.

The rethinking of gender dichotomies, for instance, challenges binaries
on the inside by proposing that gender is a socially assigned category and ultimately a performance of identity (Butler 1990). Critics like the Brazilian Mott
(1992) have explored the way these gender constructions have shaped Western
(mis)understandings of their colonial objects. Postcolonial feminist critics like
Mohanty (1988) challenge the category "women" across the external borders of
the modern/colonial world-system by pointing to the different economic and
epistemological positions this system has assigned to women because of their
ethnicity or geopolitical location. With the 1992 award of the Nobel Peace Prize to
Rigoberta Menchú, Amerindian thinking has been valorized to some extent—and
with it, the *testimonio* as a narrative genre (as a means of transporting/translating
subaltern voices) emancipates itself from ethnography and becomes a challenge
to the disciplines of literature and history, since we shall be reading more than a
"peace manifesto." Testimonio may still be allocated within the poetic realm, but
on its borders; it is now breaking open the dichotomies of fiction and science, of
Self and Other, toward a continuity of knowledge and memory, opening up not
only the directionalities of translation but also writing as its genre.

Marcos's writings exploit precisely this tension as he disguises a political discourse as magical realism. Nevertheless, his writing consistently escapes this frame:
fictional writing mixes with Amerindian knowledge and political declarations
that are backed by a mortal war between indigenous peoples, landowners, and
the Mexican army in Chiapas and thus construct new terms for public discourse.
The Zapatistas are translating/transculturating Western languages into Amerindian knowledge and enunciating it back in Spanish (and English and German
translations) at a global audience. They are profoundly undoing the binaries at the
basis of their subalternity, creating border spaces for translation/transculturation
from the epistemic potential of the colonial difference—at the other end of the
spectrum, so to speak, from early missionaries in the New World. The thesis of
incommensurable cosmologies begins to be rethought in terms of an intervention
in the colonial difference from a subaltern perspective. The concurrency of these
interventions provides the link that creates the basis for their impact. Dichotomies
are dissolved because these multiple others challenge the center and critically
engage with each other, on its interior and exterior borders.

The colonial difference in the modern/colonial world is the location of
cosmologies in conflict articulated by the coloniality of power. Thus, the concept
of translation/transculturation we are developing here is related to borders established by the colonial difference. Our conceptualization runs contrary to the concept of translation/transculturation generally known and defined in the territorial
internal domain of empires (translations, say, between English and Spanish), as
well as contrary to the one direction/translation on the external borders of the
modern/colonial world-system where the colonial difference operates (translations, say, between English and Hindi, English and Arabic, English and Chinese,
or, if you prefer, Spanish and Aymara or Nahuatl).

Translation/Transculturation and
Disciplinary Knowledge

There is, therefore, another dimension to the inequality of languages, and
not just between English and Swahili or Aymara, as Talal Asad implies, or between
Tojolabal and Spanish. The various imperial languages are themselves unequal,
as with Spanish vis-à-vis English. Among the imperial languages of the modern
world (Spanish, Portuguese, French, English, and German), Spanish is itself a subaltern language, a part of a complex spectrum of unequal languages of business

in the modern world-system. There is, on the one hand, a hierarchy among imperial languages and, on the other hand, the hierarchy of languages on the borders
of the world-system. Arabic, for instance, is not the same as Aymara or Nahuatl,
although both of them are marginal to the system. The result is that translation
from English or French into Arabic is very common, although not into Aymara.
For the same reason that links language to knowledge, Arabic translations into
English or French are less common than are translations in the opposite direction. The same happens with Spanish or Portuguese. Translations from German,
French, and English into Spanish abound; there are not many translations in the
opposite direction (Heilbron 1999).

What gets translated is literature, but literature, we know, has its place
within the intellectual distribution of labor in the system: Third World, or Third
World–like countries seem to produce culture, not knowledge. With this frame in
mind, Talal Asad's final recommendation makes sense: "I have proposed that the
anthropological enterprise of cultural translation may be vitiated by the fact that
there are asymmetrical tendencies and pressures in the languages of dominated
and dominant societies. And I have suggested that anthropologists need to explore
these processes in order to determine how far they go in defining the possibilities
and the limits of effective translation" (1986, 164). This conclusion and recommendation is made with the scenario in mind of an anthropologist from the
United States going around the world and coming back to translate knowledge
for the academic community. As we have shown, language translation concerns
the hierarchies of power between nations and, above all, has been and is shaped
by the coloniality of power and the colonial difference. We can revamp the notion
of "internal colonialism" here to understand how the coloniality of power and the
colonial difference worked in the nation-building process. Modern nation-states
reproduced, within the territorial frontiers, the structure of power put in place by
the colonial model. That is why the coloniality of power is not a question related
only to colonial "periods," here and there, but also to the entire modern/colonial
world-system from its inception to its current form of global and transnational
coloniality.

The epistemological dimensions opened up by the Zapatistas cannot be
divorced from the geopolitics of knowledge and the colonial difference: the new
scenario for translation/transculturation. It is within the Cold War and area studies frame that such observations make sense. The question for us is, What about
anthropologists in Bolivia or Argentina, working and living in the Andes? Are

their translation efforts similar to paradigmatic examples governed by area studies where Third World culture is translated into First World anthropology? Do they experience the ideological underpinnings of area studies for anthropological knowledge in the same way?[13]

The anthropological work that consists of "studying" Aymara or Quechua communities—that is, of translating from Aymara and Quechua into Spanish—is an interesting case because the three languages coexist as languages of the nation, although only Spanish is recognized as the official national language. But not only that, the emergence of an Amerindian intellectual community in academia complicates issues further. And it is here where, at least as a projection toward the future, the Zapatistas' theoretical revolution begins to make sense, since it becomes a model for academic-institutional work and a theoretical model for theoretical production. It is communication not only between peasants and scientists but also between different versions of intellectual knowledge, each translating and transculturating the other. The "disadvantage" of epistemic subaltern languages—languages, that is to say, that are not seen as "sustainable" from the perspective of the Western production of knowledge—begins to offer an epistemological potential unfamiliar and strange to the epistemic/hegemonic languages. In all these cases, including the emergence of Amerindian intellectuals (for which the Workshop for Oral History in Bolivia has been a very important institutional site), translation and transculturation as epistemic and political practice are moving beyond area studies and beyond the modern/imperial versions of translation/transculturation. There is thus a geohistorical sequence that will be displaced, and this geohistorical sequence is the following:

1. Translation of Amerindian languages into Spanish in building "Occidentalism";

2. The translation of Arabic, Hindi, or Chinese into English and French as the second phase of the modern world-system, building "Orientalism"; and finally,

3. Area studies and the rise of the social sciences and the reconversion of anthropology, in which discipline "became" a crucial issue and re-elaborated epistemic sites in the polar distinction of subject and object of knowledge.

There is still another aspect of translation/transculturation and subaltern languages and knowledge that we would like to consider in the colonial horizon of the modern world-system. The problem arises with the use of Spanish, an imperial language of the modern world-system (but a minority language in the United States) from the perspectives of Aymara intellectuals in the Andes and from the perspective of hegemonic knowledge production.

The area studies anthropologist and Andean specialist has a specific issue to solve with Spanish and the "Hispanic" component in the United States and within the U.S. academic community. If the anthropologist studying the Andes deals with Aymara or Quechua, the question is again Spanish because of the way in which it mediates between the language and culture "studied" (Aymara or Quechua) and the language and culture from which the former is "studied" (English and the U.S. anthropologist). On the other hand, writing in Spanish for Andean speakers of Aymara and Quechua is an ethical responsibility and a political imperative if anthropologists are interested in more than appropriating knowledge and information from the culture that is the object of study. Thus Spanish, in this case, is part of the object of study but also part of the language of scholarship. These strategies are balanced by another move: the recuperation of indigenous languages through bilingual education efforts of indigenous movements.

"Language" no longer equals "nation" as multiple languages and knowledges transculturate, breaking down the dichotomy of nation and Other. On the other hand, although language is linked to memory and shapes understanding, this link is not ontologically necessary. As the appropriation of Spanish by Tojolabal shows us, language in translation can also become the means of transport for other knowledges and memories. The same may be said for English. English language does not necessarily go with English memory. This presupposition, based on national ideology, is no longer sustainable in a transnational world. Rosario Ferré, writing in English in Puerto Rico (*The House on the Lagoon*, 1995) and filling and transforming English with Spanish memories, is a case in point. So are the claims to indigenous identity by people who no longer speak indigenous languages, like many of the Nasa (Paez) in Colombia. If English is the hegemonic language in a transnational world, English can also be the transnational language in which positions of subalternity are rearticulated.

However, Spanish continues on a regional level as the means of transnational communication, while indigenous languages are being recuperated through the bilingual educational efforts of indigenous social movements. If networking, information systems, and technoglobalism are shaping the world today, the same are also being appropriated by those who seek social transformation as subalterns,[14] relocating neoliberal global coloniality from the perspective of subalternity. This is not to say that Rosario Ferré is offering the "right answer," but rather that she is contributing to asking new questions and offering a critique of national language assumptions upon which modern approaches to translation have been operating.

The theories of translation/transculturation we foresee are coming from a critical reflection on the colonial difference and from seeking to overcome the national-language ideology frame in which translation was conceived, practiced, and theorized in the modern/colonial world. Translation can no longer be understood as a simple question of moving from object language A to subject language B, with all the implications of the inequality of languages. Rather, translation becomes a "translanguaging," a way of speaking, talking, and thinking in between languages, as the Zapatistas have taught us. This translanguaging is a form of border thinking, opening new epistemic avenues beyond the complicity between national languages and cultures of scholarship established in the modern/colonial world-system and in which the "modern" concept of translation was articulated (Mignolo 2000, ch. 6). We surmise that this direction will keep on gaining ground in the future, as intellectual production is being recognized beyond the academe and theories are . . . where you can find them.

~

Notes

1. We refer here to the notion of "modern world-system" as proposed and elaborated by Immanuel Wallerstein (1974, 1999), and as modified by Walter Mignolo to account for the double perspective of modernity/coloniality (Mignolo 2000).

2. "Transculturation" as a concept emerged, precisely, from the perspective of coloniality. See Ortiz (1995) and Fernando Coronil's analysis of the colonial differential between Malinowski's concept of "acculturation" and Ortiz's "transculturation" (Coronil 1995).

3. "Colonial difference" is a concept introduced by Indian historian Partha Chatterjee to account for the differential relations between India and the subsequent legacies of British colonialism (Chatterjee 1993, 16–18). It was extended by Mignolo to account for the formation and transformation of the modern/colonial world-system (Mignolo 2000, 49–90).

4. There is a history of translation theory in the Western world with which we cannot engage here. Of importance is that our argument develops in relation and in epistemic, ethical, and political conflict with that tradition. We refer to a concept of translation founded, on the one hand, in a philosophy of language from Plato to contemporary analytical philosophy (Quine, Davidson) and, on the other, in

a philosophy of language linked to the hermeneutical tradition that goes from Greek philosophy to Heidegger and Derrida. Both philosophical traditions have been blind to the colonial difference, and, although critical of modernity itself, neither moved beyond modernity toward recognizing coloniality and the colonial difference. Beyond this history of translation theory, there is now emerging a sociological theory of translation "within" the concept of world-system (Heilbron 1999) that, although closer to our own conception, still remains blind to coloniality of power and the colonial difference. On the contrary, we feel that our position is very compatible with the one developed in the volume edited by Liu (1999). In this book, Chinese scholars as well as Chinoists take on the theory of translation from the very foundation of the colonial differential since the arrival of the Jesuits in China, at the end of the sixteenth century.

5. The medical tradition conceived of four different genders, depending on the degree of body heat and amount of body fluid (Huarte de San Juan 1989 [1594]). Sudden changes in body heat were understood to produce hermaphrodites by causing the vagina to reverse to the outside (Daston and Park 1985). For a general idea of the status of sexuality and the body in the Renaissance, see Goldberg (1994).

6. See also Vine Deloria, Jr., (1978) and Roger Hart (1999). Deloria has devoted many essays to redrawing the map of translation/transculturation that has been dominated since the sixteenth century by a hegemonic view of Spanish and English cosmology, language, and epistemology. He uses the word "relatedness" to describe Native Americans' experience of the world, instead of "isolation," the word used to describe Spanish or English patterns of experience. Deloria's formulation, as with the one offered by Lenkersdorf, may sound like a reinscription of Western dualism. Hart (1999) correctly criticizes the reproduction of the "incommensurability" in translating worlds or cosmologies in J. Gernet's "incommensurability" thesis on the confrontation of two cosmologies (assuming, of course, that Taoism, Buddhism, and Confucianism are part of the same cosmology or episteme). Our point of engagement, in any case, is not with incommensurability, but with negotiations across the colonial difference.

7. See Mignolo (2000) for a detailed account of "languaging."

8. See Massey (1994) for the production of gendered space; see Schiwy (2000) for the link between gendered spaces, temporalities, and indigenous peoples. See Escobar (1994) for a critique of the underlying assumptions of developmentalism.

9. See again Robinson (1997) and Alexandrov (1998). See also Flotow-Evans (1997)

for a feminist critique of translation. See Niranjana (1992) and Liu (1999) for postcolonial approaches to translation.

10. For example, the misguided biography written by two journalists, one from Spain and the other from France (La Grange and Rico 1998). Mexican sociologist Pablo González Casanova has pointed out the same blindness among the European left: the Italian former director of Il Manifesto, Rosana Rossanda, described Marcos as Leninist and Castrist and added that Latin American revolutionaries are "Leninist" by definition (González Casanova 1996a, 33). The colonial difference cuts across and reveals the silence occupied by universal theories, (neo)liberal or (neo)Marxist. Obviously, these theories were aware of the colonial difference, although they did not recognize it as an epistemic location but merely as a space for expansion of capital and of the proletarian revolution. Translation/transculturation were caught in the same limitations.

11. For an account (elaborated from extensive interviews) of the often difficult process of women's organizing and integration into the EZLN, see Guiomar Rovira (1997).

12. For critical evaluations of the engagement of women in violent military actions from preconceived feminist positions, see several essays in Rosa Rojas (1994–95).

13. There has already been an interesting discussion in Current Anthropology (35, no. 1 [1994]) about these issues, provoked by Orin Starn's article "Rethinking the Politics of Anthropology: The Case of the Andes" (Starn 1994). We cannot summarize it here, but we take it as a reference point to draw on our own knowledge and experiences of the issue.

14. The use of the Internet by the Zapatistas is of course a case in point, as is the use of video and television by indigenous peoples from Australia to Latin America (Ginsburg 1994; Aufderheide 2000; Schiwy 2003).

References Cited

Alexandrov, Vladimir A. 1998. "Lotman's 'Semiosphere' and Varieties of the Self." *Working Papers and Pre-Publications, Centro Internazionale di Semiotica e di Linguistica,* serie C 270, Università di Urbino, Italia.

Anzaldúa, Gloria. 1987. *Borderlands/La frontera: The New Mestiza.* San Francisco: Aunt Lute.

Appadurai, Arjun, ed. 1986. *The Social Life of Things: Commodities in Cultural Perspective.* Cambridge: Cambridge University Press.

Arnold, Denise, Domingo Jiménez Aruquipa, and Juan de Dios Yapita, comp. 1992. *Hacia un orden Andino de las cosas: Tres pistas de los Andes meridionales.* La Paz: Hisbol, ILCA.

Asad, Talal. 1986. "The Concept of Translation in British Social Anthropology." Pp. 141–64 in *Writing Cultures: The Poetics and Politics of Ethnography,* ed. J. Clifford and G. E. Marcus. Berkeley: University of California Press.

Aufderheide, Patricia. 2000. "Grassrootsvideo in Latin America." Pp. 219–38 in *Visible Nations: Latin American Cinema and Video,* ed. Chon A. Noriega. Minneapolis: University of Minnesota Press.

Bouysse-Cassagne, T., O. Harris, T. Platt, and V. Cereceda. 1987. *Tres reflexiones sobre el pensamiento Andino.* La Paz: Hisbol.

Butler, Judith. 1990. *Gender Trouble: Feminism and the Subversion of Identity.* New York: Routledge.

Chatterjee, Partha. 1993. *The Nation and Its Fragments: Colonial and Postcolonial Histories.* Princeton, NJ: Princeton University Press.

Coronil, Fernando. 1995. "Transculturation and the Politics of Theory: Countering the Center, Cuban Counterpoint." Pp. ix–lvi in Introduction to *Cuban Counterpoint,* F. Ortiz. Durham, NC: Duke University Press.

Daston, Lorraine, and Katherine Park. 1985. "Hermaphrodites in Renaissance France." *Critical Matrix* 1: 5.

Deloria, Vine, Jr. 1978. "Civilization and Isolation." *North American Review* 263(1): 11–14.

Escobar, Arturo. 1994. *Encountering Development: The Making and Unmaking of the Third World.* Princeton, NJ: Princeton University Press.

Ferré, Rosario. 1995. *The House on the Lagoon.* New York: Farrar, Straus and Giroux.

Flotow-Evans, Louise. 1997. *Translation and Gender: Translating in the "Era of Feminism."* Ottawa: University of Ottawa Press.

Ginsburg, Faye. 1994. "Embedded Aesthetics: Creating a Discursive Space for Indigenous Media." *Cultural Anthropology* 9(3): 365–82.

Goldberg, Jonathan, ed. 1994. *Queering the Renaissance.* Durham, NC: Duke University Press.

González Casanova, Pablo. 1996a. "Globalidad, neoliberalismo y democracia." Pp. 45–55 in *El mundo actual: Situación y alternativas,* ed. P. G. Casanova and J. Saxe-Fernández. Mexico City: Siglo XXI.

———. 1996b. "Las etnias coloniales y el estado multiétnico." Pp. 37–62 in *Democracia y estado multiétnico en América Latina,* coord. P. G. Casanova and M. Roitman Rosenmann. Mexico City: UNAM.

Harrison, Regina. 1989. *Signs, Songs and Memory in the Andes: Translating Quechua Language and Culture.* Austin: University of Texas Press.

Hart, Roger. 1999. "Translating the Untranslatable: From Copula to Incommensurable Worlds." Pp. 45–73 in *Tokens of Exchange,* ed. L. Liu. Durham, NC: Duke University Press.

Heilbron, Johan. 1999. "Towards a Sociology of Translation: Book Translation as a Cultural World-System." *European Journal of Social Theory* 2(4): 429–44.

Hill Boone, Elizabeth, and Walter Mignolo, eds. 1994. *Writing without Words: Alternative Literacies in Mesoamerica and the Andes.* Durham, NC: Duke University Press.

Huarte de San Juan, Juan. 1989 [1594]. *Examen de ingenios para las ciencias.* Letras hispánicas 311. Madrid: Cátedra.

Jones, Andrew. 1999. "The Gramophone in China." Pp. 214–38 in *Tokens of Exchange,* ed. Lydia Liu. Durham, NC: Duke University Press.

La Grange, Bertrand, and Maite Rico. 1998. *Subcomandante Marcos: La genial impostura.* Madrid: El Pais/Aguilar.

Lenkersdorf, Carlos. 1996. *Los hombres verdaderos: Voces y testimonios tojolabales.* México City: Siglo XXI, UNAM.

Leyva Solano, Xochitl, Gabriel Ascencio Franco, and Luis Aboites. 1996. *Colonización, cultura y sociedad.* Chiapas: Universidad de Ciencias y Artes del Estado de Chiapas.

Liu, Lydia, ed. 1999. *Tokens of Exchange: The Problem of Translation in Global Circulations.* Durham, NC: Duke University Press.

Major Ana Maria. 1997. "Discurso inaugural de Ana Maria al Primer Encuentro Intercontinental (Julio 1996)." *Chiapas* 3: 101–5.

Marcos, Subcomandante. 1997. *El sueño zapatista: Conversaciones con Yvon LeBot.* Mexico City: Plaza y Janes.

Massey, Doreen. 1994. *Space, Place, Gender.* Minneapolis: University of Minnesota Press.

Mignolo, Walter D. 1995. *The Darker Side of the Renaissance: Literacy, Territoriality and Colonization.* Ann Arbor: University of Michigan Press.

———. 2002. "The Zapatistas' Theoretical Revolution: Its Historical, Ethical and Political Consequences." *Review Fernand Braudel Center* 25(3): 245–75.

———. 2000. *Local Histories/Global Designs: Coloniality, Subaltern Knowledges and Borderthinking.* Princeton, NJ: Princeton University Press.

Mohanty, Chandra Talpade. 1988. "Under Western Eyes: Feminist Scholarship and Colonial Discourse." *Feminist Review* 30: 65–78.

Montrose, Luis. 1991. "The Work of Gender in the Discourse of Discovery." *Representations* 33(winter): 1–42.

Mott, Luiz. 1992. "As Amazonas: Um mito e algumas hipótesis." Pp. 33–57 in *America em tempo de conquista*, ed. R. Vainfas. Rio de Janeiro: Jorge Zahar.

Moya, Pat. 1997. "Postmodernism, 'Realism,' and the Politics of Identity: Cherrie Moraga and Chicana Feminism." Pp. 125–50 in *Feminist Genealogies, Colonial Legacies, Democratic Futures*, ed. C. T. Mohanty and M. J. Alexander. New York: Routledge.

Niranjana, Tejaswini. 1992. *Siting Translation: History, Post-Structuralism, and the Colonial Context*. Berkeley: University of California Press.

Ortiz, Fernando. 1995. *Cuban Counterpoint: Tobacco and Sugar*, trans. H. de Onís. Durham, NC: Duke University Press.

Quijano, Aníbal. 1998. "The Colonial Nature of Power and Latin America's Cultural Experience." Pp. 27–38 in *Sociology in Latin America (Social Knowledge: Heritage, Challenges, Perspectives)*, ed. R. Briceño-Leon and H. R. Sonntag. Proceedings of the Regional Conference of the International Association of Sociology, Venezuela.

————. 2000. "Coloniality of Power, Eurocentrism, and Latin America." *Nepantla: Views from South* 1: 533–80.

Quijano, Aníbal, and Immanuel Wallerstein. 1992. "Americanicity as a Concept, or the Americas in the Modern World-System." *ISSA* 1: 549–57.

Rappaport, Joanne. 1998 [1990]. *The Politics of Memory: Native Historical Interpretation in the Colombian Andes*. Series Latin America Otherwise, rev. ed. Durham, NC: Duke University Press.

Robinson, Douglas. 1997. *What Is Translation? Centrifugal Theories, Critical Interventions*. Kent, OH: Kent State University Press.

Rojas, Rosa, ed. 1994–95. *Chiapas, y las mujeres qué?* 2 vols. Mexico City: La Correa Feminista.

Rovira, Guiomar. 1997. *Mujeres de maiz*. Mexico City: Ediciones Era.

Salomon, Frank, and George L. Urioste. 1991. *The Huarochiri Manuscript: A Testament of Ancient and Colonial Andean Religion*, trans. F. Salomon and G. L. Urioste. Austin: University of Texas Press.

Schiwy, Freya. 2000. "Camerógrafos indígenas, ecoturistas y la naturaleza: El papel del género sexual en las geopolíticas del conocimiento." In *La reestructuración de las ciencias sociales en Latinoamérica*, ed. S. Castro-Gómez. Bogotá: Pensar, Instituto de Estudios Sociales y Culturales.

————. 2003. "Decolonizing the Frame: Indigenous Video in the Andes." *Framework* 44(1): 116–32.

Starn, Orin. 1994. "Rethinking the Politics of Anthropology: The Case of the Andes." *Current Anthropology* 35(1): 13–38.

Wallerstein, Immanuel. 1974. *The Modern World-System: Capitalist Agriculture and the Origins of the European World-Economy in the Sixteenth Century.* New York: Academic.

————. 1999. *The End of the World as We Know It: Social Science for the Twenty First Century.* Minneapolis: University of Minnesota Press.

Some Theoretical Remarks

Crossing Gaps of Indeterminacy

Richard Rottenburg

 2

From Representation to Translation

The business of ethnography can be considered to be about the translatability of narratives on the meaning of life and the world from one cultural frame of reference to another. As a practice of representation, ethnography is forced to have, or at least to assume, a universal yardstick that can be used as a third and independent token. Various forms of realism (naive, ironic, polyphonic) suggesting an independent referent are the usual (and unavoidable) rhetorical forms applied for this purpose. As a practice of representing difference, ethnography is forced to treat all frames of reference symmetrically. The distinction between right and wrong beliefs would undermine the very business of ethnography as a genre of difference. Various forms of relativism denying the availability of an independent referent are the common rhetorical forms utilized to this end.

However, without at least a preliminary distinction between valid and invalid statements, the attempt to produce representations plausible in two or more frames of reference, representations of otherness would remain futile. Ethnography is born out of the paradoxical relation between, on the one hand, treating all frames of reference symmetrically, and on the other hand, requiring a metacode to cross over the differences (Crapanzano 1992).

The classical solution to this paradox was offered by cultural relativism. It was simple, elegant, and for quite some time convincing, as long as it could rely on four basic assumptions: Firstly, it was presupposed, any human statement only makes sense within a given frame of reference or culture. Secondly, all cultural frames were taken to be equal in terms of their potentials to legitimize statements. Thirdly and consequently, some statements that appeared reasonable within one, sounded unreasonable within the other cultural frame. Some cultural differences hence reached the level of incompatibility. As the main task of ethnography related to this challenge, a fourth assumption was offered as solution to the dead end of incompatibility: ethnography itself was excluded from this paradoxical condition.

Ethnographic representations were thus assumed to be independent of any cultural frame of reference. As scientific statements they were considered to have universal validity. During most of the last century, anthropology worked with serenity and success on the basis of these four assumptions by restricting cultural relativism to semantic, normative, and aesthetic relativism.

Sometime around the beginning of the 1980s this tranquillity seemed lost—at least for some notable anthropologists. While this is not the place to debate the actual beginning and the intricate history of this turn toward epistemic and ontological relativism (it can, for instance, be dated back to Protagoras), I must revisit its core assumption. Once the difference between science and culture became problematized and blurred (for instance, after Thomas Kuhn 1976 [1962]), ethnographic representations found themselves uncomfortably situated in one line with those sociocultural representations re-represented by ethnography (Geertz 2000 on Kuhn). Ethnographers subsequently ran into enormous difficulties by representing other people as sitting within their caves watching their shadows while they—the ethnographers—sovereignly pretended to move up and down in bright daylight outside all caves, including the cave they originally must have come from.

It is a common misunderstanding—or strategic distortion, particularly widespread in hermeneutic Germany—to subsume the loss of tranquillity mentioned above and the subsequent "crises of representation" of the 1980s under the older quarrel about the relation between empiricism and interpretivism. Working under the assumption that social reality is constructed by those one studies is simply something other than working under the assumption that the (social) sciences are a major force in this construction work.

Ever since anthropological analysis was applied to anthropology itself, we have had a new, virulent, and sometimes acrimonious debate on the consequences to be drawn out of the reflexive turn. The various and diverse positions taken up in this controversy can be arranged in three camps, or rather voices (if only for the purpose of clarifying my argument): a first position rejects the assumption that science is culture and continues along the established paths of epistemic universalism. Interpretive anthropology of the hermeneutic tradition sometimes speaks in this voice, together with less reflexive empiricist orientations. The bolder empiricist protagonists of this position are called "naive objectivists," "positivists," "realists," and so forth by their opponents, who look down at them as somewhat simple.

On the other hand, these opponents maintain that no representations whatsoever are possible without being dependent on a particular frame of reference. They shift the attention from the issues of external reference to issues of internal reference and their performative effects. Their move is thus to abandon the difference between political representation (which always constitutes power and those represented) and ideational representation, including their own scientific representations (Callon 1986). Protagonists of this position are known under various labels, of which "antiobjectivist" is perhaps the most neutral and encompassing. Their opponents look down at them as "literati" who suffer from some kind of "philosophical angst" that is considered to be grounded in their cultural frame of reference and less in the nature of representation. Postmodernism is exposed as the ideology that is finally responsible for this deplorable state of mind (Gellner 1995).

Like any conflict, however, this one too is based on an assumption common to both positions: both assume that only one of them can possibly be right. Either ethnography is a scientific practice that represents social realities and that can be subjected to tests of verification and falsification, or ethnography is, inescapably, a genre of fiction that creates rather than represents foreign worlds. In this version, the value and validity of ethnographic stories comes from their power of cultural critique and from the defamiliarization of their own frame of reference (Marcus and Fischer 1986).

The first voice maintains that everything is decided by facts that can be collected out there in reality. The second voice counters that everything is decided by the frames of reference and methods that are necessary in the first place in order to create the facts that otherwise have no existence. The obvious response to this is: How can you know that this is the case if not by referring to some facts? Even though these facts might be situated on a different level, you still need to take them as facts! Or even worse: How do you expect anybody to listen to your story if it proclaims little else than self-referentiality?

A third position, developed over the past several years, becomes discernible here. Its main justification can be interpreted as a pragmatic escape from the aporia caused by the confrontation of the first two camps. The third voice proposes to bypass the trouble by refuting the underlying assumption about the elementary distinction between reality and representation, between world and words. Instead of struggling for a perfect correspondence between representation and reality, and instead of assuming that in the end representations can be held against reality in order to verify their correspondence, it suggests starting in the middle. The middle, as the space-in-between, is considered as the realm of representational practices that aim at the production of the two poles: the world and its representations, the original and the copy. In this perspective, reality as represented reality is not the beginning but the result of these practices (Latour 1995 [1991]; Pinch 1985).

In order to emphasize this shift from reality as starting point to reality as outcome, the practices of re-presentation are understood as acts of mediation or translation arranged in chains and nets. Conceiving representational practices as acts of translation draws attention to the unavoidable gaps that exist between each two consecutive representations in a chain of re- re- . . . representation. These gaps are crossed over by translations, the point being that the strength and durability of translations is not entirely grounded in the source or target representation, nor in any external referent. Translation is thus considered a practice sui generis that cannot be reduced completely to what is translated. The responsibility for the act of translation cannot be delegated entirely to what is translated. To some degree it remains an act of creation—creating the right links—and it is precisely because of this that correspondence theories of representation have to render invisible their own translations (Robinson 1996).

The paradox of translation can be constituted to be analogous to the paradox of decision-making. If a situation would be entirely clear and under control and if the effects of an intervention into this situation would be fully predictable, one would not speak of making decisions. One would rather say that the obvious and unavoidable was done. The precondition for making a decision at all is in fact a certain amount of indeterminacy and thus of unpredictability. However, public self-representation of decision-making pretends that no risks were implied. The gap of indeterminacy is carefully glossed over (Luhmann 1991). Our decisions are good because they are based on an objective analysis—that is all one ever hears about decisions of public interest.

Perhaps the most famous paradox of the same type is the pure gift. The oxymoron "gift exchange" contains this paradox in a beautifully clear form. Exchanging gifts means that the issues of indebtedness and reciprocity are realized and hence the gift is no longer a pure gift, since it asks for a countergift. In fact it is sufficient to name something or even to think of something as a gift for abolishing its gift character (Derrida 1993 [1991]). In analogy, to think of something as a translation usually means to shift it to the level of a different practice—namely, of copying an original with the aim of maximum fidelity. Again, the gap of indeterminacy is glossed over.

The business of ethnography—to translate complex semantic narratives from one cultural frame to another—appears in a different light if viewed against this background of a general theory of translation. According to the argument I am putting forward in this paper, the characteristics and peculiarities of ethnographic translation have been misconceived so often because they were not interpreted against this background (Gellner 1974; Asad 1993 [1986]). In order to pursue this argument further, I will now distinguish between two regimes of translation: scientistic and mimetic.

Scientistic Translation

⌒ The scientistic translation regime of ethnography follows the model of the natural sciences. While Radcliffe-Brown was probably the last anthropologist who explicitly and emphatically propagated this position in a strong version, it is nowadays implicit and self-evident in all ethnographic writing, at least in a soft version.

Original experiences and observations in the field are mentally divided in parts that are supposed to be elementary enough to be acceptable as facts that carry their own evidence independent of sociocultural frames. These elementary parts are treated as originals of which one tries to make exact copies in the form of statements and perhaps photographs. A great deal of taking field notes is just about this analytical work: producing a thin and exact—that is, a decontextualized and consequently meaningless—description of what actually goes on.

In the next steps of ethnographic work, the mobile field notes—being copies in lieu of the immobile originals, which cannot be transferred to the ethnographer's desk—are reassembled in a way to make sense for readers who do not have firsthand experience. The idea is that the first thin or flat description can be produced before it is made thick or deep by recontextualization—that is, by adding cultural meaning in the following steps of ethnographic work.

The question now is this: from where does this cultural meaning come, during the later stages of ethnographic work, when it was eliminated during the early stages in order to produce the thin description?

The scientistic translation regime offers the following answer: at the lowest end of a chain of several acts of translation, one has reality out there as it exists independent of being observed or not observed, represented or not represented. In the case of ethnography this reality can be acts of behavior, objects and artifacts of all kinds, and speech acts. At the highest end of the translation chain one has a statement objectively representing the reality at the other end. The many links of the chain consist of distinct acts of translation that are methodologically guided.

Anybody interested in verifying the validity of the final description could follow the whole chain back to its lowest end and thus—in principle—grasp reality out there.

Borrowing from Latour (1996a, b), one can visualize the movement of a message from its initial context "out there" on the periphery of the scientistic and anthropological world through a succession of transfers as it moves through a sequence of contexts. At last, the message, or some translation of it, "arrives" in a recognizably final form, with its original meaning presumably intact, despite its successive translations and recontextualizations.

According to the scientistic translation regime, the cultural meaning of a hermeneutic unit (a pattern of cooperation, a ritual act, an artistic expression, etc.) has to emanate from the elementary parts collected during fieldwork, transferred as immutable mobiles through the translation chain, as through a telephone line, and reassembled at the ethnographer's desk. Relying on this understanding of the translation process is nothing less than glossing over the gaps of indeterminacy given within each joint of the chain (visualized by the question marks in diagram 1). The glossing device is methodology, which pretends that the crossover is safe in the sense that the message is not trans*formed* but simply trans*ferred*. The impression is created that facts can travel without being distorted. While this in itself is a problem (Latour 1996a), what happens when this approach is applied to meaning (Czarniawska and Joerges 1996)?

The ethnographer at her desk is privileged over those who live with the cultural meaning that she tries to reconstruct because she is in the singular position to command an overview. From her distant point of view she can discern patterns

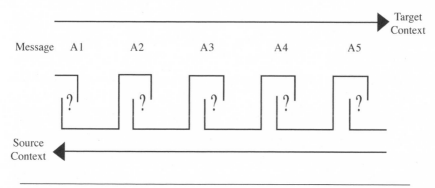

Diagram 1

that remain unobserved for those at the grass roots who are entangled in those patterns and never manage to see much more than unconnected bits and pieces.

To some degree the scientistic translation regime seems to be stating the obvious. Institutionalized cultural patterns operate behind the backs of those who adhere to these patterns. And nobody can seriously pretend that ethnographic work could do without this basic assumption. Or, as Marx put it in his "18th Brumaire": "People make their own history, but not under circumstances of their own choosing." The major ambition of all social sciences is directed toward deciphering some order within these circumstances. It is within this endeavor that the scientistic translation regime of ethnography encounters two problems. The first problem is related to the issue of rationality raised when people make their own history. The second problem is related to the connection of part and whole or figure and ground in the realm of cultural meaning.

The unresolved rationality problem becomes apparent when the scientistic translation regime is confronted with statements and patterns of thought that do not make sense within the frame of reference at the upper end of the chain. Statements like "twins are birds," "this cucumber is an ox," "he is a witch," "she was hit by an ancestral spirit," "this stone makes rain," and so forth become denunciated when processed by the scientistic translation regime. While the regime pretends to keep or even to rehabilitate the rationality of these statements, it can do so only by shifting it onto a different level—namely, the level of "society," which is not the level at which the believers argue. Society, as those circumstances mentioned by Marx, is, so to speak, always behind their backs and never at their disposition.

The most famous example is of course Evans-Pritchard's witchcraft analysis (Evans-Pritchard 1972 [1937]). While the Azande believe in witches because there are witches, the readers of Evans-Pritchard's analysis are made to believe that the larger sociocultural frame of the Azande produces those witches. If the readers are prepared to step into the Azande frame—and the book invites them to do so—they also begin to see witches as Evans-Pritchard began seeing witches while among the Azande.

According to David Bloor's persuasive observation (1991 [1976]), the price for this rehabilitation is a new denunciation that turns out to be more severe than the first one contesting Azande logic. The readers and the ethnographic author "understand" the Azande thought style only by assuming that their own mental operation is a form of pure rationality free of institutional interferences. The basis for this deconstructive criticism of the scientistic translation regime is the opposite assumption. According to this postulate all operations, including operations by the scientistic regime, are dependent on cultural frames of reference—or, in other words, on institutional setups, exactly as the Azande witchcraft belief was. That is to say: Evans-Pritchard's ethnography does not describe but creates Azande witchcraft beliefs in exactly the same way in which the Azande frame of reference creates witches that are then taken to be real.

Now the problem with this symmetrical approach is that, in the end, it too confirms what it pretends to challenge. In order to give an account of some state of affairs one has to make the claim that one's own account is valid. Otherwise it would be pointless to give the account in the first place. The only difference between Evans-Pritchard's account of Azande witchcraft and any deconstructive account of Evans-Pritchard's ethnography is the level at which the external referent of the account is situated. In the first case the external referent is given by instances of witchcraft practices and emic comments on those practices. In the second case the external referent is given by statements within a text written by Evans-Pritchard. Obviously, this is no difference in principle. Both accounts pretend to relate to something outside themselves and thus operate on the basis of external reference.

This observation, in fact, should come as no surprise. Any account given of any state of affairs lives from making invisible its own internal reference (Ashmore 1989). One cannot present a narrative that claims validity and at the same time invalidates the narrative itself by drawing attention to the fact that this very validity depends on a series of assumptions that all could as well be different—if one would only choose another frame of reference (Pinch 1988). This basic rule thus also applies to all those accounts deconstructing ethnographic narratives by focusing on the problems of internal reference within these ethnographic narratives. In the vocabulary of this paper, acts of translation have to be turned rhetorically into acts of or representations of external referents in order to appear acceptable.

If that is the case, the deconstructive approach does not seem to solve the initial problem of how to account for something as being culturally different without denunciating it at the same time. If ethnographic representations are inevitably enunciative and denunciative at the same time, so the deconstructive argument goes, one should better "write against culture" (Abu-Lughod 1991). Avoiding the above-mentioned aporia caused by the illusionary dichotomy between reality and representation and focusing instead on the realm in the middle—where both sides of the dichotomy are produced by acts of translation—seems to boil down to some sort of iconoclasm.

It goes without saying that this is no real solution to the initial problem.

Deconstruction is not there to replace construction but only to improve it or to cut down its pretensions to size by reflexivity. The oscillating move between belief and skepticism is a kind of code-switching one has to live with since there is no metacode available. In order to work out the eventual gain to be achieved by operating beyond correspondence theory with the translation approach, one has to come back to those gaps between each two consecutive joints in a translation chain (pointed out by question marks—see diagram 1). These gaps are due to the degree of artifice needed to join each successive translation of a message to the next context. That, at the same time, means to come back to the problem of part and whole, of figure and ground.

Mimetic Translation

⟳ The analytical procedure of the scientistic translation regime has, as mentioned above, a problem: to explain from where it takes the cultural meaning of the ethnographic end product. The thin descriptions fabricated at the beginning of the ethnographic work deliberately exclude cultural meaning by decontextualization. The elementary parts in which the fieldwork experience is split in order to have immutable mobiles do not contain in themselves their meanings. And reassembling the elementary parts on the ethnographers' desks to form a complete picture necessarily generates meanings different from the local ones—as just explained with the help of Azande witchcraft. It would, nevertheless, be unrealistic if not ridiculous to stand up here and deny ethnography as it is practiced, written, and read any competence to convey emic meanings. It rather seems that on the backstage of ethnographic work something additional to scientistic translation is going on.

According to my argument, this additional and mostly hidden work operates by what I would like to call the mimetic translation regime. The basic figure of this regime is not to analyze (i.e., to divide wholes into constitutive elementary parts) but, to the contrary, to convey the emic meaning in one go, so to speak. One might imagine that the meaning/message, rather than translating relatively unscathed across contexts, transforms into a series of messages in each new context (see diagram 2), each connected to the prior one and capturing the initial meaning in a Gestalt-like fashion, but without subjugation to a reductionist, analytic translation process (again, see Latour 1996a, b).

An expression from context 1 is remade, reconstructed, or refigured in context 2, and so forth from one context to the next. The success of mimetic

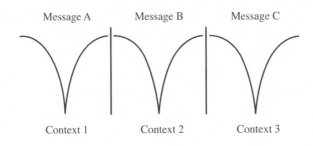

Diagram 2

translation as a philological and aesthetic operation is based on finding analogies: expressions, mental pictures, or narratives that convey meanings in context 2 similar to those encountered in context 1.

Once again: Dividing—as under the scientistic translation regime—an original expression of context 1 into its elementary parts till one gets to denotative statements that can be transferred as immutable mobiles within the chain does not result in a statement that would make sense in context 2. Just as linguistic word-to-word translations of single sentences regularly miss the meaning, also part-to-part or sense-to-sense translations of hermeneutic units usually do not make sense without a translation of the whole (the ground or the context), which is something else than the addition of the parts (or the figures).

Juridical hermeneutics is one locus classicus for this argument: the "spirit of a law" can never be found in any of the paragraphs of that law, and not even in the assemblage of all its paragraphs. It always has to be read between the lines of the law and is thus always disputable. Religious hermeneutics is the other locus classicus. Any attempt to account for the meaning of a revelation at the upper end of the translation chain by splitting it into constituent parts and tracing those parts back to the historical moment and event of revelation at the lower end of the chain results in harsh disappointment. The historical documents on Jesus cannot possibly stand for what his mediators made him to become during the centuries.

According to the argument I am presenting here, ethnography unavoidably operates with both regimes of translation. Ethnographic translators who pretend to be full-hearted mimetic translators cannot avoid the scientistic regime, since they would otherwise have no ground at all on which to present their ethnography. Ethnographic translators who pretend to be hard-core scientistic translators cannot avoid using mimetic translation, since otherwise their texts would simply be incomprehensible or void of meaning. Yet most of them are not aware of the amount of mimetic translation they have just accomplished. As a result, their translations are not fully accountable to validation.

This is because they replace the question marks within the joints of the translation (see diagram 1) chain with "methodology," while in fact they are at the same time guided by something else that evades the type of methodology appealed to. This "something else" is the Weberian *pneuma* ("spirit") of the other context (ground) they have experienced during fieldwork. Scientistic translation tries to exclude this dimension as occultism and thereby produces its own form of obscurantism.

The act of stating this under postcolonial circumstances might seem to raise irritation and resistance among the readers who would otherwise follow my criticism of the scientistic translation regime. However, I argue, this holds only at first sight. The point is rather the other way round. The official high aspiration by the scientistic translation regime to entirely exclude the pneumatic dimension from its procedures unavoidably generates a "hidden transcript." Ethnographers are guided by what they experienced as pneuma—or, more mundanely, as way of life—but they believe they have to deny this illegal influence on their translation work in order to defend its objectivity. The end result of this is a picture of alterity that claims objectivity in the sense of scientific methodology. According to my argument, this is the point that deserves criticism, and not the assumption about pneumatic differences between ways of life. The issues of heteronomy, heterogeneity, and polyphony can be accommodated easily within an approach that allows for pneuma and hence for *influence* on the ethnographic observer.

Allowing influence—or, to use a stronger term, allowing to be captured and to surrender to alterity—is the point where mimetic translation comes in. Evidently, thus, the problem with mimetic translation is its accountability. A mimetic relation is always in between two sides, its point being exactly to transgress a subject-object relation by allowing heteronomous subjectivities. If the act of translation can be fully justified neither by those parts of the ethnographic transfer that are verifiable nor in fact by the source context as a whole, since mimesis is in between, how can one be sure to do the right thing without ending up in fiction—that is, in a construction dependent exclusively on the target context?

A full-scale methodology of mimetic translation subscribing to the standards of empiricism seems impossible, and would contradict my own definition of translation as a crossing over of the unavoidable gaps between the joints of

	Fidelity	Infidelity
Identity	(1) original expression	(2) exact copy of (1)
Difference	(3) translation of (1)	(4) forgery of (1)

Diagram 3

the chain without the usual safety devices. However, the option to make invisible this gap of indeterminacy, as more positivist representationists do, appears more treacherous than to admit this weakness. The best one can do under this condition is to be as specific as possible about how the gap is actually crossed over.

For this purpose diagram 3 will be helpful. It visualizes the relation between mimetic and scientistic translation. We start with line one and move horizontally from field 1 to field 2. This means, for instance, to record a conversation somewhere in the remote world at some point in time on a tape and to play the tape now in this room. By this exact repetition one achieves high fidelity between original and copy. In most cases the understanding will be lost to a greater part, though. At worst, what we receive is unstructured noise. Hence the overall result is infidelity.

The move from field 1 to field 2 stands for the scientistic translation regime in ethnography. A hermeneutic unit from field 1 is reduced to an assembly of elementary denotative statements that can be transferred to field 2 and later verified by going back to field 1 to check their correspondence. In most cases of complex semantic narratives the overall result is infidelity, since the meanings the narratives had in field 1 are lost in field 2. One thus easily falls down in field 4.

Moving vertically within column 1 from field 1 to field 3 means compromising with the ideal of correspondence. The identity of an expression of field 1 is preserved by *making a difference* in field 3. The basic operation of this move I propose to call mimetic translation. Pursuing this line—as stressed above—does not offer a guarantee for not ending up in field 4 and producing a forgery of what was meant in field 1. The hardest test of falsification to which this move can be submitted is an inversion of the usual procedure of testing correspondence as in the move from 1 to 2. Here, in the move from 1 to 3, the crucial question is: does the result have a defamiliarizing effect on the implicit presuppositions of the target context of translation? If this effect is achieved the ethnographic translation is very likely to have made a valid point and thus not to have landed in field 4.

If it would be generally acceded and accepted that ethnographic translation is always and unavoidably an exercise of balancing between scientistic and mimetic translation (or, in diagram 3, between the two steps from 1 to 2, and from 1 to 3), then both could be performed on the front stage. As a result of this, both steps could be made more accountable. The rhetoric of scientistic ethnographic translation would lose its chance to offer itself as objective representation, and the rhetoric of mimetic translation would be liberated from its aura of an occult art and perhaps also from the charge of "othering" (Taussig 1993).

                                              ⟿

References Cited

Abu-Lughod, Lila. 1991. "Writing against Culture." Pp. 137–62 in *Recapturing Anthropology*, ed. R. Fox. Santa Fe, NM: School of American Research Press.

Asad, Talal. 1993 [1986]. "Übersetzen zwischen den Kulturen: Ein Konzept der britischen Sozialanthropologie." Pp. 300–334 in *Kultur, soziale Praxis, Text: Die Krise der ethnographischen Repräsentation*, ed. E. Berg and M. Fuchs. Frankfurt am Main: Suhrkamp.

Ashmore, Malcolm. 1989. *The Reflexive Thesis: Writing Sociology of Scientific Knowledge*. Chicago: Chicago University Press.

Bloor, David. 1991 [1976]. *Knowledge and Social Imagery*. Chicago and London: University of Chicago Press.

Callon, Michel. 1986. "Some Elements of a Sociology of Translation: Domestication of the Scallops and the Fishermen of St. Brieuc Bay." Pp. 196–233 in *Power, Action and Belief*, ed. J. Law. London: Routledge and Kegan Paul.

Crapanzano, Vincent. 1992. "Hermes' Dilemma." Pp. 43–69 in *Hermes' Dilemma and Hamlet's Desire: On the Epistemology of Interpretation*. Cambridge, MA: Harvard University.

Czarniawska, Barbara, and Bernward Joerges. 1996. "Travels of Ideas." Pp. 13–48 in *Translating Organizational Change*, ed. B. Czarniawska and G. Sevón. Berlin and New York: de Gruyter.

Derrida, Jacques. 1993 [1991]. *Falschgeld*. Munich: Wilhelm Fink.

Evans-Pritchard, Edward E. 1972 [1937]. *Witchcraft, Oracles and Magic among the Azande*. Oxford: Clarendon.

Geertz, Clifford. 2000. *Available Light: Anthropological Reflections on Philosophical Topics*. Princeton, NJ: Princeton University Press.

Gellner, Ernest. 1974. "Concepts and Society." Pp. 18–49 in *Rationality*, ed. B. R. Wilson. Oxford: Blackwell.

————. 1995. "Anything Goes: The Carnival of Cheap Relativism which Threatens to Swamp the Coming *fin de millénaire.*" *TLS* 16: 6–8.

Kuhn, Thomas S. 1962 [1976]. *Die Struktur wissenschaftlicher Revolutionen.* Frankfurt am Main: Suhrkamp.

Latour, Bruno. 1991 [1995]. *Wir sind nie modern gewesen: Versuch einer symmetrischen Anthropologie.* Berlin: Akademie Verlag.

————. 1996a. "Der 'Pedologen-Faden' von Boa Vista: Eine photo-philosophische Montage." Pp. 191–248 in *Der Berliner Schlüssel: Erkundungen eines Liebhabers der Wissenschaften.* Berlin: Akademie Verlag.

————. 1996b. "Engel eignen sich nicht als wissenschaftliche Instrumente." Pp. 249–76 in *Der Berliner Schlüssel: Erkundungen eines Liebhabers der Wissenschaften.* Berlin: Akademie Verlag.

Luhmann, Niklas. 1991. "Sthenographie und Euryalistik." Pp. 58–82 in *Paradoxien, Dissonanzen, Zusammenbrüche: Situationen offener Epistemologien,* ed. H. U. Gumbrecht and K. L. Pfeiffer. Frankfurt am Main: Suhrkamp.

Marx, Karl. 1996 [1852]. "Der achtzehnte Brumaire des Louis Bonaparte." Pp. 34–121 in *Marx-Engels IV. Studienausgabe. Geschichte und Politik,* ed. Iring Fetscher. Frankfurt am Main: Fischer.

Marcus, George E., and Michael M. J. Fischer. 1986. *Anthropology as Cultural Critique: An Experimental Moment in the Human Sciences.* Chicago and London: University of Chicago Press.

Pinch, Trevor. 1985. "Towards an Analysis of Scientific Observation: The Externality and Evidential Significance of Observation Reports in Physics." *Social Studies of Science* 15: 3–36.

————. 1988. "Reservations about Reflexivity and New Literary Forms, or Why Let the Devil Have All the Good Tunes?" Pp. 178–97 in *Knowledge and Reflexivity: New Frontiers in the Sociology of Knowledge,* ed. S. Woolgar. London: Sage.

Robinson, Douglas. 1996. *Translation and Taboo.* Illinois: Northern Illinois University Press.

Taussig, Michael. 1993. *Mimesis and Alterity: A Particular History of the Senses.* New York and London: Routledge.

The Metaphoricity of Translation

Vincent Crapanzano

The pretension of my title betrays its superficiality. It does not, I hope, deny its provocation. I am most broadly concerned with the metaphorizing potential of translation/"translation" and the way that metaphorization feeds back on translation/"translation." As an anthropologist I cannot avoid this observation, since translation has often been used as a metaphor—or model—for describing, and indeed theorizing, the representational practices of anthropology. What is striking about this usage is the slippage between the practice of translation—put most simply, the reconstruing, or refiguring, of an utterance or text in one language into another—and the theorizing of that practice. It is this confusion that has led me to the awkward phrasing: translation/"translation."[1]

I will look at the way in which the translation metaphor has been used recently in American legal thinking, but before doing so, I want to make several observations about translation generally. "Translation" connotes etymologically "a carrying across": the French and Italian equivalents, *traduction* and *traduzione,* suggest "a leading across."[2] The German, *Übersetzung,* connotes "a setting across," though, as I have noted elsewhere, *über* also means "over" and suggests a palimpsestic relationship between the original and its translation (Crapanzano 1997). The etymological connotation of "translation" is the same as for "metaphor" (Greek, *metaphorein,* "moving over," "moving across").[3] Hence, to speak of the metaphoricity of translation is to speak of the metaphorical capacity of metaphor. There is, I believe, in the law—and anthropology—a curious twist in using translation metaphorically, for its metaphorized use, as a "substantive" vehicle for a practice of judicial argument or the representation of another culture, ends up denying its etymologically rooted connotation as metaphor. "Translation" serves, thereby, as a concrete prop for (the denial of) a metaphorical process that bears all the negative baggage of figuration in certain literalist-prone practices such as practicing law or anthropology.[4] In both these instances, and others too, a border is declared, the need for bridging assumed, and a subterfuge employed to deny the inevitable figuration required for bridging (itself, incidentally, a metaphor) in a practice that "requires" literal certainty.

In another language, the translation can only partially capture the meaning of the original. It is always tentative, always subject to improvement in a way in which the original is not (except in authorial revisions). Few translations last; few are integrated into a literary tradition. The St. James Bible and Schlegel's German translations of Shakespeare are noteworthy exceptions. It is possible to view translation as an opening up of the original, as mirroring changes in the interpretation and evaluation of the original as it ages, but, given the value we place on fidelity to the original, its canonization, we do not normally view translation this way. Translation does subject the original to contemporary linguistic understanding, communicative etiquette, and hermeneutical conventions. It arises in different circumstances—those that have been shaped, at some level, by the existence of the original, if only by the acknowledgement of its existence and the need to translate it. These new circumstances influence the translation in complex ways. They affect the reading of the original, the value we give it, the significance we find in it, and how we circulate it and its translations. These, in turn, affect the translation—its interpretation, evaluation, significance, and circulation. We must not ignore the pragmatic—the contextualizing—force of the original and its translations.

It is possible that the metaphorical model of translation masks its pragmatic force, paradoxically, by exploiting the pragmatic force of the metaphor itself. Put simply, no doubt too simply: we understand metaphor in terms of the meaning that arises from the juxtaposition of two semantically understood terms or entities. The metaphorizing term, the vehicle, affects the way we understand the topic—the metaphorized term. We speak of the relationship between topic and vehicle as the tenor of the metaphor, which we take as the meaning of the metaphor.[5] In other words, through metonymy, the vehicle recontextualizes the topic, giving it, if not a new meaning, then new significance. We tend to give determining priority to the vehicle. But, the topic is not without effect. It influences the way the vehicle is taken. The tenor of the metaphor has, therefore, to be seen as the product of the tension between topic and vehicle. Do we give determining power to the one or the other? Is the tenor the effect of mutual engagement? Does the pragmatic force of the juxtaposition of topic and vehicle determine the metapragmatic weighing of the one or the other in the constitution of the tenor of the metaphor? Does the "shock" of the metonymy that underlies all metaphors demand immediate hermeneutical resolution, most often by discovering a "similarity" between the two terms? However derived, the weighing of the two terms of the metaphor can be figured as a palimpsest. One term covers the other; it dominates. But insofar as the now "weighted" metaphorical relationship evokes an etymologically supported understanding of the metaphor as a "crossing-over" of (semantic) meaning, that understanding masks the role of power in determining our take on metaphor. It integrates that take with broader cultural understandings that perpetuate the masking—the mystification. We speak of metaphors in terms of an opening up of horizons, illumination, magic, and creativity. But, we can also, and sometimes do, speak of them in terms of violence and rupture. These too can cover the power plays that delimit the metaphor's meaning and significance.

Given our stress on the semantico-referential function of language, we tend to ignore the pragmatic effect of translation—what Michael Silverstein calls transduction.[6] We might argue, as I have, that the priority we give the semantico-referential function of language masks its pragmatic function, which constitutes relevant context and appropriate interpretation (Crapanzano 1992 [esp. the Introduction], 2000a). The metaphorization of translation-as-metaphor, understood as a carrying across of (semantic) meaning, facilitates this mystification. It leads us to ignore the violence done to the original through the complex recontextualizations and recodings that occur with translation (repetition in another register). Although we evaluate a translation in terms of its relationship to the original, we do not usually derive meaning from the juxtaposition of the two texts, as we do in metaphor when we speak of its tenor.[7] We might better regard translation as a palimpsest—a more or less respectful imposition on the original. I suggested this in an earlier paper, which I cited above. I would now like to modify that suggestion by stressing, as I have for metaphor, the contestatory nature of translation. Does the original dominate? Or the translation? There is no easy answer to these questions. Whatever answer we give, however, finally has to account for the practice and not the proclaimed etiquette of translation. True, etiquette has normative value, but, as we know, it can be transgressed. In the case of literary translation, as in any literary work that resists the cliche, there is virtue (within conventional limits) of transgression, which we tend to understand in terms of personal style. (There are, of course, societies that value literary conformity over stylistic diversion.) It is in the often tedious discussions of how to capture the style of the original that the contestatory nature of translation is given fullest recognition.

The etiquette of translation reflects the weight we give the original or the translation. That we normally value the original over the translation, the author over the translator, leads us to demand subservience and humility in the translator. We evaluate translation in terms of fidelity. The translator must be faithful to the original. Of course the object of fidelity is rarely, if ever, specified as more than the original. When we speak of being faithful to a text, however, we cast the text in a particular way: among other things, we are led to ignore its instability, the way it—and its interpretation, evaluation, and significance—change with time. How can we be faithful to that which changes? Our understanding of fidelity demands constancy. In the case of translation, it fixes the text to be translated as an original. We attach to it all that we comprehend by the "original," including, as Walter Benjamin would have it, its aura (Benjamin 1968, 217–51). We must not forget, however, authenticity, purity, invention, and origination. I am, of course, discussing the original in its contemporary Euro-American setting. Originals need not be so valued; translations need not be faithful.

Fidelity provides its own cover. Not only does it proclaim a text to which it is to be faithful, but it also presumes the possibility that one can—or ought to—be faithful to a text. It situates the text—its reading—in the ethical realm, relating it, thereby, to other ethical considerations, including fidelity itself. "Fidelity"—"faith"—has enormous rhetorical potency, particularly in a society like the American in which one's (religious) faith ought neither be questioned nor criticized. Fidelity and faith invoke the horror of their abuse—faithlessness, deception, betrayal, and treachery—which is their constant, rhetorically potent undersong. We speak of the lie—the betrayal—of a translation. *Traduttore, traditore,* the Italians say: "translator, traitor." Indeed, translation is one of the most morally charged of our literary endeavors. It is rivaled perhaps only by pornography, which has itself been used to characterize deceptive translations. Now, I do not want to deny the ethical dimension of interpretation and translation—of any communication.[8] I want rather to point to the way in which their moralization figures in their metaphorical usage. It too facilitates the masking of the role of power in translation and can have enormous, mystifying consequences, as we shall see, when translation serves as a metaphor for other practices, such as the law.

~ American law differs dramatically from the codified law of Continental Europe. Its roots lie in English common law. Today, it has three principal interacting domains: Constitutional, statutory, and common law. Although all laws have ultimately to conform to the U.S. Constitution, they are not centralized and often differ in even contradictory ways at federal, state, and municipal levels.[9] (Jurisdiction can have, as a result, enormous consequences.) Until the constitutionality of a law is contested, there is no guarantee that it conforms to the Constitution, for

there is no agency that decides on the constitutionality of a law when it is written. In effect, the "legal field" in America is characterized by a tension between
formal and informal, centralizing and decentralizing forces. Given the hierarchical
structure of the law—lower-level laws have to confirm to higher-level constitu-
tions—there is an institutional push toward coordination at the state level, and
insofar as all laws have to conform to the Constitution at the national level. Feder-
alism and an often stubborn, self-interested localism impede, however, coordination and centralization. States, counties, and municipalities are jealous of their
rights and the benefits that accrue from them. Under these circumstances, it is not
at all surprising that the Constitution is treated with an awe and reverence that
verges on the sacred (Levinson 1988). Unlike its counterparts around the world,
it has been minimally amended: only twenty-seven times in its more than two-
hundred-year history. That, as a text, it has been hardly altered does not mean that
its interpretation has not changed in often dramatic, and still contestable, ways
in court decisions, which serve as precedent for future decisions.[10] The Supreme
Court is the final arbiter, and its decisions become governing precedent (insofar as
they are deemed relevant) at all levels of the court system.

Aside from the Constitution (which is treated in many respects like a super-
statute), American law is, as I have said, either statutory or common law. Common
law is based on previous decisions, which become precedents for future ones, and
is, therefore, cumulative and—by the standards of codified law—contingent,
unsystematic, and poorly rationalized. Insofar as the decisions of individual cases
become precedent, common law is particularistic and depends, to an even greater
degree than statutory law, on analogical argument. It is true that, in most cases,
a final "holding" is announced or at least extractable from the opinion, but other
elements of the opinion, known as dicta, along with dissenting opinions when
they occur in multijudge tribunals like the Supreme Court, have argumentative
weight and may be used to clarify the meaning of the holding. (I should note that
many opinions at the Constitutional level run to scores of pages.) Statutes are, of
course, less particularistic in application. Their interpretation depends far more
on precedent than in European law, where, at least in France, court decisions simply state the determining statute. Arguments are not published and decisions do
not have formal precedental value. Thus they guarantee a concept of pure, timeless
Law, removed from political considerations, which the more pragmatic and less
philosophical American lawyer finds mystifying if not downright delusional. The
gap between the two legal traditions is enormous (Lasser 1998).

Constitutional law is the source of the richest judicial thinking in America.

Given the near-sacred and quasi-unalterable status of the Constitution, the question of how to apply this "unchanging" normative document to a changing world becomes paramount. To admit change is, at least in conservative eyes, to diminish the Constitution's authority, risk legal—if not social—chaos, and betray the intentions of the document's framers, who are given, in argument at least, near superhuman perspicacity and foresight. Most conservatives assert the primacy of the original meaning of the text, while liberals—often referred to as aspirationalists—take a more flexible approach. The former—let us call them the originalists—fall into two basic, though overlapping schools: the textualists, who focus on "semantic meaning," and the intentionalists, who stress original intention. The textualists assume that meaning is in the text, quite independent of any context, or at least any but the context in which the text was written. The intentionalists argue that the only way one can discover the meaning of the text is to uncover the intention of its author(s), through historical research or through one or another intention-oriented textual reading.[11] They ask how the framers would have responded to the legal question at stake. We should note a possible contradiction in intentionalist arguments. Although, in the determination of authorial intention, they acknowledge implicitly the role of external circumstances in the production of the text, they tend to argue in terms of the contextual independence of the text once produced.

The aspirationalists give greater importance to the relationship between text and context, both in textual production and in subsequent interpretation and application. They assume, if only implicitly, that interpretation cannot be separated from explication and application, that the meaning of a text will change with the context in which it is read and applied. They are far more likely than the originalists to argue in terms of moral philosophy, social policy, and what they take to be the basic values of American democracy. They ask the judge to take account of current needs, attitudes, and values. Their position is anathema to the conservatives, who see it, if not as destructive of the law, then as unleashing legal judgments unconstrained by the law. Conservatives refer to the latter "baneful" practice as "judge-made law," which, they argue, threatens the delicate balance among executive, legislative, and judicial functions and institutions.

There is a good deal of hype in these arguments. Law is in essence an argumentative discipline in which meaning is always in question. Whatever hermeneutical sophistication a lawyer may have, however cynical he may be, he cannot, at least in court, in the heat of argument, acknowledge the weakness of his interpretive position. Such arguments are for the law journals. (There are almost a thousand of them published each year in the United States.) In the argument, a particular interpretive stance, whatever its strengths, whatever demand for purity it makes, is always used, if it is used at all, rhetorically. Of course, in practice, lawyers are never purists. Even the most diehard conservative has to recognize that over the years there have been acceptable changes in the "meaning" of the Constitution—say, over the meaning of "cruel and unusual punishment"—and even the most insistent aspirationalists recognize that for the law to exist, for courts to function, for equitable judgments to be made, and for the minimal assurances of social continuity, there has to be some permanence to textual meaning.[12]

It is within this context that the model of translation as a mediator between the changeless norms embodied in the Constitution (and other laws) and ever-changing circumstances and values has to be seen. Reconciliation is, of course, immensely difficult, if not impossible. Decisions have, however, to be made; the courts cannot rest suspended in epistemologically generated indecisiveness. This was well put by Justice Robert A. Jackson in 1943 in *West Virginia State Board of Education v. Barnette*, in which the court ruled that a state cannot force children in a public school to salute the flag by expelling them if they refuse. Jackson was one of the first justices to refer to reconciliation as translation. He wrote:

> *True, the task of translating the majestic generalities of the Bill of Rights, conceived as part of the pattern of liberal government in the eighteenth century, into concrete restraints on officials dealing with the problems of the twentieth century, is one to disturb self-confidence. These principles grew in soil which also produced a philosophy that the individual was the center of society, that his liberty was attainable through mere absence of government restraints, and that government should be entrusted with few controls and only the mildest supervision over men's affairs. We must transplant these rights to a soil in which the laissez-faire concept or principle of non-interference has withered at least as to economic affairs, and social advancements are increasingly sought through closer integration of society and through expanded and strengthened governmental controls. These changed conditions often deprive precedents of reliability, and cast us more than we would choose upon our own judgment. But we act on these matters not by authority of our competence but by the force of our commission. (319 U.S. 624, 639–40 [1943], quoted in Lessig 1993, 1267, and 1999, 261–62, n. 15)*

We should note that Justice Jackson's notion of translation rests on a particular understanding of his contemporary world, one that was challenged by the opponents of the New Deal and is again under fire today. (His observations concerning the role of the government in economic affairs seems digressive, however, in a case that is concerned specifically with the role of states in enforcing the salute to the flag and generally with their ability "to coerce uniformity of sentiment in support of some end thought essential to their time and country.") Although the court may aspire to be nonpolitical (even when it is dealing, as in *Barnette*, with a manifestly political issue), it cannot, in fact, bracket off fully the political from its decisions. Translation, in the law at least, is not between two unambiguous, agreed-upon entities—a text and prevailing circumstances—but on two interpretations: the text as originally understood and an always amorphous and somewhat ad hoc representation of prevailing conditions. These interpretations and their reconciliations are made in a political environment and cannot be divorced from that environment. Translation figures inevitably in that politically saturated environment. The reading of the law it produces is, I would argue, a palimpsest—an imposition that not only determines the case at hand but also becomes an authoritative precedent for future authoritative decisions. Precedents have enormous pragmatic force, for they frame cases in such a way that arguments and decisions come to be taken as inevitable and just continuations of a valued, if not sacred, legal tradition, which has itself been and continues to be constituted by the "precedentiality" of precedent.

〜 Although Paul Brest was one of the first judicial scholars, if not the first, to use the translation model in the law, its principal advocate today is Lawrence Lessig (Brest 1980; see Lessig 1991, 1993, 1995, and 1999).[13] Lessig argues that the central task of translation "is always to determine how to change one text into another, while preserving the original text's meaning" (Lessig 1993, 1173). He is particularly concerned with the problem of maintaining fidelity to the law in a changing world. "Can an interpretive change be interpretive fidelity, and, if so, how can we know when?" (ibid., 1170). He notes that when circumstances change, fidelity to "original meaning" can, in fact, lead to a distortion of that meaning. Without discussing any particular philosophy of meaning, though obviously influenced by behavioral linguistics, Lessig stresses meaning's dependency on context. "If meaning is what these [any words in context] *do*, then it is as if these words pull certain levers, press certain buttons, or (for boomer children) tap certain keys on a keyboard; these levers or buttons or keys are structured. If they are structured in one way, they have one meaning; another way, another meaning. Any author choosing her meaning relies upon how these contexts are structured" (ibid., 1174–75). "Meet me in

⌒ 3

Cambridge" will mean one thing in Massachusetts and quite another in England. He notes the interpretive gap between the contexts of writing and reading. Where the gap is great, the reader cannot ignore the context and remain true to the text's original meaning; for it is possible that in ignoring a change of context, one does not remain true to the text's original meaning.[14] A jurisprudence of fidelity "needs a way to *neutralize* or *accommodate* the effect that changing context may have on meaning" (ibid., 1177) It also needs a way of determining contextual relevance.[15] How do we determine when changes in context change meaning? Lessig answers: "We can say that the most significant elements [Lessig calls them presuppositions] are not just relevant to an author's use, but are indeed relied upon by the author when using the text—relied upon in just the sense that *had they been other than they were when the author first used these words, then the author would have used words other than she did*" (ibid., 1179–80). Where presuppositions change, so meaning changes and the problem of fidelity arises.

Lessig's test is not without merit, but it does rely on at least putative authorial intent and assumes a clarity and freedom of intention, indeed of rational intention, that is altogether questionable. The framers of a law are no more possessed of omniscience than "omniscient" narrators in literary works. The assumption of omniscience is, in both cases, a fiction, an artifice. It is a generally accepted one, however, in most intentionalist arguments in the law. We cannot say that the framer(s) of a law did not mean to use the words they did or that they meant something altogether different by those words than was commonly accepted at the time they wrote the law. But we have also to recognize that most laws are the result of compromise. They are rarely the products of a single lawmaker but of a group of lawmakers with singular interests. It is never clear that all of the lawmakers understood the words in the same way. Who then is the author of a law? Are we not dependent on another fiction: singular authorship—the reduction of multiple intentions to a single one? Words—not to mention more complex locutions—are rarely if ever unambiguous. They are always subject to interpretation, and, as we know, interpretation is itself the result of complex interlocutory dynamics that may be limited (but only limited) by dictionary definitions and literalist understanding. The law operates on the basis of these fictions, which, though questionable on epistemological grounds, are of necessity unquestioned (or questioned in conventionally limited ways) in legal argument.

Lessig distinguishes between "one-step" and "two-step" fidelity. In the former, as soon as the contextually sensitive original meaning is determined, one simply applies that meaning. "[O]nce we find meaning in the originating context (the context of writing) we simply apply that meaning in the context of application (the context of reading)" (ibid., 1183). This is the standard originalist position. It fails, according to Lessig, to preserve meaning across interpretive contexts because it fails to take account of "the effects of context upon the *application* meaning in the *application* context" (ibid., 1189). The latter—two-step fidelity—recognizes that there are, in effect, two original texts: the law and its application. If the context between a normative text—the law—and the application changes, then the meaning of the application may become inconsistent with the normative text's original meaning. "[T]he two-step asks how to apply the text now and here so as to preserve the meaning of an application then and there—how, that is, to make the meaning of the current application equivalent to the meaning of an original application, or alternatively, how to *translate* the original application into the current context" (ibid., 1185).

Translation provides the "device" for neutralizing the effect of changed context on application's meaning; for, according to Lessig, "translation is a practice that neutralizes the effect of *changed language* on a text's meaning" (ibid., 1189). (Language is part of context, for Lessig.) His understanding of translation is stubbornly commonsensical and practical; it is an extension of what happens in any communication.[16] The translator is always confronted with "translative gaps." "[I]deas well or simply expressed or constituted in one language will be invisible or distorted or mangled in another" (ibid., 1201). Lessig finds three sources of translative gaps:

1. underdetermined source: translating "I hired a worker" into Russian requires knowledge of the worker's sex.
2. overdetermined source: translating the above from Russian into English.
3. transformed significance: translating the German *Wald* into English— woods or forest—where there is still a physical and perhaps significant difference between their respective referents.

As Lessig sees it, translation involves two distinct processes: familiarity and equivalence. Familiarity refers to the translator's need to master the text and context of the original; equivalence to finding a way to convey the same meaning in another language. Although Lessig does not consider the role of "creativity"—and the constraints on that creativity—in the establishment of context, he does worry about it in the process of finding equivalencies. He recognizes that norms of translation have changed over time and vary according to genre and institution, but he neither develops the relationship between norms and styles of translation and

～ 3

theories of translation nor does he relate norms, genres, institutions, and theories to plays of power and desire. He argues simply that equivalence in translation depends on purpose, which is defined by the institution in which translation occurs. "The translator must select—or a practice of translation must select—the nature of the equivalence that it [*sic*] will demand before translation can proceed" (ibid., 1197). "The differences in institutions suggest how 'equivalence' is endogenous to a practice of translation, and that the practices themselves determine what will be considered equivalent. Practices will differ, and if practices differ, 'equivalence' will differ. Nothing in the notion of translation could arbitrate among these different conceptions of equivalent translation; all that can resolve such a dispute is something about the practice of which it is part" (ibid., 1201). Lessig never asks what this "something" is. He attributes "immense power" to the translator and stresses the importance of humility in re-creating "a text that preserves meaning," without fully appreciating the structural constraints of a sociopolitical nature on the translator—indeed, on the construction of "humility" (ibid., 1193). He opts rather for an agency model in which the translator operates as an agent for the author and is constrained by the "trust" and "institutional respect" required for him to proceed (ibid., 1208–11).

In developing his model of translation for the law, Lessig compares interlanguage and legal translators (ibid., 1212–14). The former constructs a text equivalent to an original in another language. It is the meaning of the two texts that has to be preserved. The latter constructs "an application of a text in different context." Its source is the text's first or hypothetical application. It is the meaning of the two applications that must be equivalent. A change in presuppositions signals the need for translation. Having identified the changed presuppositions, the legal translator constructs "an accommodation to account for that change." Often there will be more than one possible accommodation, Lessig has to admit—that is, more than one way "to restructure the application to preserve meaning." The choice in the final analysis lies with the translator who is, however, constrained by humility and by a general legal principle (a sort of deus ex machina that Lessig suddenly evokes): the translator has to select the most conservative—the smallest possible—change in the legal material and still achieve fidelity.

Toward the end of his essay, Lessig risks undermining the interpretive value of his theory of translation by suggesting that the principle of humility may require the translator to ignore changes in presupposition, if (a) the changes are of a political nature, and/or (b) the accounting for change would be beyond his institutional capacity (ibid., 1251–61). Let me treat the second of these limitations first, because it is less problematic than the first. By institutional incapacity, Lessig means "the inability of a court as it is currently structured to account for certain kinds of changes in presuppositions, either because the material at issue is itself too complex, or because the resources necessary to track them are too strong" (ibid., 1261). As he does not offer any criteria for determining incapacity, it is difficult to decide whether a court is using its "incapacity" to make a decision—to preserve the status quo—without appearing to do so.

As for the first limitation—Lessig offers an intuitive definition of political presuppositions: they are political if accommodation to changes in them is best decided by the legislature. Recognizing that such an intuitive definition cannot serve as a principle for determining when translation is or is not required in the law, he suggests that the translator should consider only changes in those propositions that were thought true at the time the law under consideration was written. Political presuppositions would be those that were thought best. As Lessig himself recognizes, he has opened a can of philosophical worms (ibid., 1255): "This distinction, between propositions that are acknowledged because they are viewed as best and those that are acknowledged because they are viewed as true, is no doubt hard to maintain. For of course what is viewed as best is a function of what is viewed as true, and what is viewed as true is a function of what is viewed as best." Lessig eschews any philosophical way to make the distinction by claiming that "the distinction rests not on some philosophical claim about the nature of the presuppositions themselves, but rather on the rhetoric about those presuppositions contingently available to speakers within a particular legal culture." It might well be the case that the distinction between truth and value is in the final analysis rhetorical, as indeed the deconstructionists maintain, but such a position countermines the thrust of his argument about fidelity in translation. Its admission in any legal argument would, in any case, undermine that argument. Lessig claims, however, "that at a particular time, there will be some propositions that will be considered truth propositions, and some that will be considered value propositions, and that the more a proposition seems to be a value proposition rather than a truth proposition, the less the translator constrained by structural humility may account for it" (ibid.). Lessig opts here, as elsewhere when he finds himself in conceptual difficulty, for the practical and the particular. He offers no criteria for distinguishing between truth and value propositions and, therefore, between political and nonpolitical presuppositions. Are we left to intuit the distinction?

⌒ 3

⌒ Where has Lessig's model of translation led us? Are we not exactly where we started—confronted with the problem of how to preserve the law in changing circumstances? We are left finally with individual choice, constrained to be sure by a legal principle, that of conservation, and an ill-defined (however pragmatically justified) ethical stance: humility. This is not the place to pursue Lessig's specific application of "translation" to the law. His illustrations, which constitute an important segment of his essay, are more sophisticated than his discussion of translation and fidelity, which are questionable on a number of grounds. I will mention several of them, less to criticize Lessig than to call attention to aspects of the theory and practice of translation that are of metatheoretical significance and to point to the way in which the metaphorization of translation conceals the role of power (and desire) in the practice it metaphorizes.

The first is the confusion of practice and theory, which I mentioned at the outset of this paper. I will only observe that practice serves a rhetorical role in theory and theory in practice (its rationalization). Practices do not occur in a vacuum but in a structure—call it social, political, economic, or cultural—that defines and delimits them as they confirm and at times even modify that structure. Obviously, as in the law, particularly in argument, they cannot call witting attention to their determinants. They require the illusion of a certain autonomy. For the practitioner, except perhaps in his most critically reflective moments (when of course he is not practicing), theory serves, among other things, to bolster his practice, the illusion of its autonomy. The model of translation in the law as developed by lawyers has to be understood from this perspective. For the outsider—the ethnographer, for example—it is symptomatic of the particular social arrangements that frame, among other things, the practice and theorizing of the law.

The second is the confusion of context and medium or, in Jakobson's terms, context and code (Jakobson 1960). I am not sure that a change of language can be taken as a change in context—certainly not in any way that resembles the changes of context that Lessig discusses in the law. Were there perfect equivalence between the original and the translation, there would, I suppose, be no change of context with change of language, but, of course, there is no perfect equivalence—not only because languages articulate reality differently and have different connotative implications but also because they call contexts, including the linguistic, differently. In any case, translation always declares the antecedence of the original and therefore reframes it.

The third concerns the postulation of context, its relationship to text, and its textualization. Lessig understands context as affecting the (meaning of) the text it "contains" but not as being significantly affected by the text. His understanding reflects the rhetorically stabilizing function of the "container" metaphor even if it is implicit. It also reflects a (coordinate) semantico-referential linguistic ideology that ignores the pragmatic function of referential and propositional locutions (Silverstein 1979, 1998; Crapanzano 1992). Contextualization is, as Silverstein notes, a radial concept (Silverstein 1998).[17] Contexts are never immune to the texts, which may be thought of as (partially) constituting or precipitating them—at least "confronting their resistance." Acknowledging that texts "highlight" or "call attention to" features of context, which is no doubt true, serves often enough to mask the constitutive, or creative, force of (segments of) the texts themselves. Put differently, as a result, perhaps, of what the French call *déformation professionnelle,* Lessig is unable to acknowledge the rhetorical use of context.

I should note that on epistemological, linguistic, and sociological grounds this position does not necessarily lead to the chaos its opponents claim.[18] Here I can only stress that recognition of the pragmatic force, or function, of a locution calls attention, less to the instability and artifice of meaning, than to its institutionalization—to the role of power (or desire) in its constitution and in the mystification of that constitution, that institutionalization. Lessig does call attention to the institutionalization of the norms of translation, though he does not discuss how these are manifested at either a communicative level (in genre, for example) or a sociological one (in reading practice, pedagogy, or the law). He certainly does not consider the relationship between the institutionalization of norms and the textualization of application he advocates. He ignores the way different texts are conceived in any one society, not to mention across cultures, even legal cultures, and how these understandings affect the rhetorical—argumentative—potential of a textualized context—indeed, how they affect translation.

My fourth observation concerns application and its textualization. Whether one refers to the application at the time a law was written or at the time it is read, it is an amorphous state of affairs. Its delimitation and textualization are dependent upon a number of factors, the implications of which Lessig, as a lawyer writing from within the law with even the "freedom" afforded the law-review author, seems unable to consider. These include the way context, text, and application are understood, including, notably, their analytic separation from one another and their mutual engagement; descriptive genres and conventions; rules of relevance and irrelevance; and the way that all of the above relate to social arrangements and arrangements of power. Put simply: on what basis is application textualized? The construction and textualization of one application context is not immune to the construction and textualization of the other. This is especially true when one is engaged in argument. Nor, finally, can we separate application from legal text, since the interpretation of the legal text itself affects and is affected by application. Texts are, as I have insisted, never without pragmatic force. We may strive to free textual interpretation from contextual factors, as, say, Christian Fundamentalists do, but in the end we are defeated by both the "pressure" of context on text and the pressure of the text on context. Texts, like language, like any communication, however self-referential they may be (as, say, in the poetry of Mallarmé) are always referential—always outer-directed even if that outer-direction is aimed at themselves: their exteriorization.

Presuppositions, as Lessig understands them, may well provide the law with a relatively neutral way of determining relevant contextual change. It assumes, however, precisely the formative interaction between law and application, text and context, that threatens the constancy of the law that both conservatives and liberals recognize as essential not only to the law but also to social stability and predictability. It depends finally, as I have suggested, on the construction of the lawmaker's intention in determining meaning, which, though dominant in American law, need not be so in other legal systems or indeed theories of meaning.

Intention has been one of the principal subjects of debate in American law, particularly during the Reagan years, when political conservatives, such as the then attorney general Edwin Meese III, opted for interpreting the law principally in terms of (what they presumed to be) the original intention of lawmakers (Meese 1988, 1990). If we were to take an intentionalist position, we would have to ask what constitutes evidence for intention? Is it derived from the text of the law itself? Is it derived from debates about the law in the legislature? Is it based on what we know about the legislature at the time? About the personalities of the legislators? Debates about intention tend to conflate two levels of intention: what I have called the communicative and the constructive (see Crapanzano 2000b, 287–89). Communicative intention refers to the underlying assumption of intention in any communication. Empty of content, it is yet a prerequisite for interpretation. Constructive intention refers to the particular way in which that intention is substantively constructed—psychologically, for example, psychoanalytically, sociologically. It depends on prevailing norms of construction—ultimately on ideological factors. The construction of intention involves a certain (imaginative) creativity on the part of judges and lawyers, which, like creativity in translation, requires interpretive constraint. Whether "neutral" rules of constraint can be developed remains an open question. Given the argumentative nature of the law, it would seem that such rules of constraint would have to be understood from within the practice of legal argument. However convincing, they will always play a rhetorical role in the immediate and mediate power plays that characterize not only legal argument but also legal decision. Power is always at play in the law—and that fact has to be given recognition, as it has to be denied in the name of justice. That is the ultimate paradox of the law—the source of its authoritative artifice.

My fifth observation concerns the role of humility, or, as Lessig sometimes calls it, structural humility, in translating in the law. It constrains the translator by insisting that he "translate" only when there is a significant change in presuppositions—to repeat, when changes in context are so great that they would have resulted in a different law in the originating context—and that he make the smallest possible change in the established law. Putting aside the two occasions in which humility, according to Lessig, would preclude translation, which I discussed above, we still have to ask whether Lessig's constraints on translation lead to the humility he deems necessary for fidelity. Although we may see them as encouraging a limited practice of humility, we have to recognize that neither lawyers nor judges are ever so fully immune to extralegal values and interests, including the political, that they can bracket off those values and interests. As it does with respect to the constraints on the construction of intention, the argumentative nature of the law facilitates the rhetorical manipulation of even the most mechanical of legal and interpretive principles. Have we finally to rely on the translator's moral commitment to uphold fidelity, however conceived?

In the end, we have to ask whether Lessig's model of translation can resolve, or even help to resolve, the inevitable conflict between law that demands constancy and changing circumstances. Given the several and often contradictory theories and practices of translation, it seems unlikely that it could serve as a useful model for resolving interpretive conflict. Indeed, I would argue that it obfuscates the practice of legal interpretation. As I have said, translation in the law is not between two unambiguous and generally accepted entities, but between two highly ambiguous and contested entities: the law, and its several contexts of application. As I read Lessig, I find myself asking whether his model of translation is necessary for what I take to be his most important contribution to legal interpretation: the elaboration of two-step fidelity. Would it not have been more profitable to look at the way in which application contexts are textualized and how this textualization relates to the legal text that is being interpreted? Would it not have been more useful to recognize the pragmatic force of the law in casting contexts of relevance and irrelevance—in determining (however partially) the contexts of application?

Or to recognize the pragmatic force of context in the reading of the law? Or to admit that the relationship between text and context, text and multiple contexts, is always unstable—always contestatory? It is power that resolves this contest—the power of the judge, yes, but perhaps even more important, a more diffuse power that governs the articulation of the law and application, and in consequence argument and decision. To avoid considering the role of power is to perpetuate a perhaps socially and legally necessary mystification, but a mystification all the same.

It would seem that any theory of translation would have to take into account the role of power in its practice and in its various metaphorizations, as in the law or in ethnography. As mentioned earlier in this essay, there is an important difference between metaphor and translation that has often been ignored by those theorists who want to relate them. In the case of metaphor, it is the juxtaposition of two terms, topic and vehicle, that produce the tenor, or meaning, of the metaphor. In the case of translation, meaning is said simply to transfer from the original to the translation. It does not arise from their juxtaposition. Legal translation, at least as Lessig understands it, has, like metaphor, a triadic structure. The two textualized contexts of application are always engaged with a third, the law in question, which, though implicated in its application, has a certain (ideologically proclaimed) authority over those applications. Although clearer in the law, the tenor of the metaphor is also authoritative. It fixes the relation between topic and vehicle. We have to ask whether translation also has an embedded triadic structure, in which the third term, one of governance, is hidden. If so, one immediately perceives the mystifying role of translation as a metaphor for other practices.

~

Notes

1.   I will, for the sake of readability, use translation without quotation marks throughout this paper to refer indifferently to both the practice and theorizing of translation.

2.   The situation in the Romance languages is, in fact, more complicated, because the Medieval *translatio* meant both "translation" and "displacement." In the Renaissance, these two meanings were separated in the Romance languages (French, *translation* and traduction; Italian, *translazion*, traduzione) but not in English. See Stierle 1996, 56ff.

3.   See de Man 1986, 83. Strictly speaking, *meta* in Greek does not correspond exactly to "trans" or *über*. See Crapanzano 1997.

4. I am referring here primarily to American law and anthropology, which are perhaps more "literalist" than they are in other societies. Locke's philosophy of language played an important role in the jurisprudence that lay behind the framing of the U.S. Constitution.

5. I am making use of the terminology developed by I. A. Richards (1936), though my understanding of the metaphor differs from his.

6. See Silverstein (1979) for a discussion of the priority we give to semantico-referentiality.

7. This point is ignored, as we shall see, in arguing for a translation model in the law.

8. See Crapanzano (2000b, 10–24) for a discussion of the moralization of the signification.

9. "Constitution" with a capital C refers hereafter to the U.S. Constitution.

10. The literature on Constitutional change is enormous. In his two-volume, magisterial though controversial *We the People,* Bruce Ackerman (1991, 1998) argues that, though the Constitution has been amended only a few times, it has undergone amendment-equivalent changes through decisions like those surrounding the New Deal.

11. See Crapanzano (2000b, 279–303) for a discussion of intention and bibliography.

12. See Scalia (1989) for a discussion of the cruel and unusual punishment clause of the Eighth Amendment. See Crapanzano (2000b) for additional discussion and bibliography.

13. Lessig (1993, 1171, n. 32) lists other legal scholars who have used the translation model. As my concern is not with the law here but with the metaphorization of translation, I have restricted my discussion to Lessig's work.

14. Lessig cites as an example *Walters v. National Association of Radiation Survivors* (473 U.S. 305 [1985]), in which the Supreme Court upheld the 1864 statutory limit of ten dollars that a veteran could pay an attorney for services related to his benefits, even though that fee was no longer realistic and would essentially preclude any attorney's services. The Court argued that the purpose of the statute was to keep proceedings simple and cheap and, were it changed, it would allow attorneys "to muck up the process." In fact, the purpose of the statute, when it was written, was simply to limit lawyers' fees. In 1988, Congress amended the provision. A lawyer could charge no more than 20 percent of any benefits awarded.

15. Lessig (1993, 1178) defines context as "just that range of facts, or values, or as-

sumptions, or structures, or patterns of thought that are relevant to an author's use of words to convey meaning."

16. As with meaning, Lessig cites in his bibliography all sorts of often contradictory theories of translation, from the behavioral to the phenomenological, without attempting in any way to reconcile them.

17. Indexicals, of which any text contains a "temporal-serial multitude," "point from an original that is established in their occurring as the here-and-now 'center' or beginning point of finding what they index. And in whatever modality, and along whatever perceptually or conceptually understandable dimensions, the 'space' that surrounds the indexical sign-vehicle is unboundedly large (or small), characterizable in unboundedly many different ways, and almost limitlessly defeasible." Silverstein does not discuss the way the text as a whole can serve as a summary and detemporalizing indexical, though he does speak of the indexical role of the propositional texts that are derived, if I understand him correctly, from interactional discourse as mediated by interactional texts.

18. See Silverstein 1998 for a discussion of contextual indeterminacy from a linguistic perspective.

References Cited

Ackerman, Bruce. 1991. *We the People: Foundations.* Cambridge: Harvard University Press.

———. 1998. *We the People: Transformations.* Cambridge: Harvard University Press.

Benjamin, Walter. 1968. *Illuminations.* New York: Schocken.

Brest, Paul. 1980. "The Misconceived Quest for the Original Understanding." *Boston University Law Review* 60: 204–38.

Crapanzano, Vincent. 1997. "Translation: Truth or Metaphor." *RES* 32: 45–51.

———. 1992. *Hermes' Dilemma and Hamlet's Desire: On the Epistemology of Interpretation.* Cambridge, MA: Harvard University Press.

———. 2000a. "Directed Reflections: Pragmatic and Metapragmatic Corralling." *Ethos* 27: 536–49.

———. 2000b. *Serving the Word: Literalism in America from the Pulpit to the Bench.* New York: New Press.

de Man, Paul. 1986. *The Resistance to Theory.* Minneapolis: University of Minnesota Press.

Gadamer, Hans-Georg. 1961. *Wahrheit und Methode.* Tübingen: J. C. B. Mohr.

Jakobson, Roman. 1960. "Closing Statement: Linguistics and Poetics." Pp. 350–77 in *Style in Language,* ed. T. Sebeok. Cambridge: MIT Press.

Lasser, Michel de S.-O.-l'E. 1998. "'Lit. Theory' Put to the Test: A Comparative Literary Analysis of American Judicial Tests and French Judicial Discourse." *Harvard Law Review* 111: 689–770.

Lessig, Lawrence. 1991. "Fidelity and Constraint." *Fordham Law Review* 65: 1365-1433.

———. 1993. "Fidelity in Translation." *Texas Law Review* 71: 1165–1268.

———. 1995. "Understanding Changed Readings." *Stanford Law Review* 47: 395–472.

———. 1999. *Code and Other Laws of Cyberspace.* New York: Basic.

Levinson, Sanford. 1988. *Constitutional Faith.* Princeton, NJ: Princeton University Press.

Meese, Edwin III. 1988. "The Law of the Constitution." *Tulane Law Review* 61: 979–90.

———. 1990. "Interpreting the Constitution." Pp. 13–21 in *Interpreting the Constitution: The Debate over Original Intention,* ed. J. Rakove. Boston: Northeastern University Press.

Richards, I. A. 1936. *The Philosophy of Rhetoric.* Oxford: Oxford University Press.

Scalia, Antonin. 1989. "Originalism: The Lesser Evil." *Cincinnati Law Review* 57: 849–65.

Silverstein, Michael. 1979. "Language Structure and Linguistic Ideology." Pp. 193–247 in *The Elements: A Parasession on Linguistic Units and Levels,* ed. P. Cline, W. Hanks, and C. Hofbauser. Chicago: Chicago Linguistic Society.

———. 1998. "The Indeterminacy of Contextualization: When Enough Is Enough?" Pp. 55–76 in *The Contextualization of Language,* ed. P. Auer and A. di Luzio. Amsterdam/Philadelphia: John Benjamin.

Stierle, Karlheinz. 1996. "Translatio Studii and Renaissance: From Vertical to Horizontal Translation." Pp. 55–67 in *The Translatability of Cultures: Figuration of the Space Between,* ed. S. Burdick and W. Iser. Stanford, CA: Stanford University Press.

The Politics of Translation and the Anthropological Nation of the Ethnography of South America

Tullio Maranhão

The "politics of translation" refers to the fact that languages in any given historical time are organized into a hierarchy of power established by the relations among political units such as nation-states, monarchies, tribes, religious states, churches, and so on. The pure and simple notion of translation as a transportation of meaning from one semiotic system to another is always embedded in a history defining the political relations between the two systems. Thus, translation does not begin with an accidental and spontaneous choice of rendering in one language something from another. There always are power-related reasons justifying why something "needs" to be spoken or written in another language. In the jargon of translation, the languages into which something is translated are called "target languages," while those from which something is translated, "source languages." The initiative to translate does not always arise within the community of the source language, nor does the target language always have the upper hand in the sense of being the language spoken by the hegemonic political unit. The missionary translation of the Bible to aborigine tongues obviously illustrates the dominance of the Christian language, playing the role of a source language, while the translation of science, technology, or literature from hegemonic (e.g., English) to nonhegemonic languages (e.g., Romanian) does not bestow on the latter inter-linguistic one-upmanship. Interlinguistic translation is not an immediate reflection of global power hierarchies. However, the languages of hegemonic powers do make a claim to the universality of their sayings, to the cosmopolitanism of their culture, and to the supplementary character of their reason, which replaces that which it supplements.

Cosmopolitan languages have a long history of expressing colonialist and imperialist interests and are deeply entwined with the interests of production and of political domination of the nation-state. What is more important is the fact that they are spoken with imperium by the people of a political unit whose social identification belongs to that sense of imperium. Here the notion of nation must be extended beyond the political unit. The social sciences, for example—an intellectual development of Western Europe and North America—are special languages for talking about a certain reality organized and represented from the point of view of the languages of those nations. Anthropology is a language of German, English, and French (and also, to a certain extent, Portuguese, Spanish, and Italian), and only surfaced in Bantu or Korean, Brazilian, Portuguese, or Hindi already as translation. For example, the anthropological reflection about cultural identity and difference in Brazil in the first half of the twentieth century emerged in literature, not in ethnography. After anthropology was established as an academic discipline in Brazil, in India, or Nigeria, it did not develop a cultural map of the world like its mother anthropological nations, but focused on the national problematics of those countries with a critical perspective. In this sense, one can talk about "anthropological nations" as specific discourse formations of the discipline of anthropology linked to the intellectual interests and inclinations of a nation-state and its national language.

Translation generates the comfortable expectation of stating a relative truth lighter than absolute truth: the claim of being truthful at least to the truth propounded in the source language. Whether the original statement was true does not matter as long as the target language was faithful and transparent to the proposition in the source language. Emboldened by such presupposition, translation cannot help but assume that the communicative felicity entailed by the happy match between two languages is the paragon of multiculturalism, cultural relativism, and an unflinching respect for the exteriority of alterity—the other's word conveyed in my own language with crystal clarity and free from any value judgments. Multiculturalism, however, is not the juxtaposition of different forms of identification in the same space and time of a geopolitical unit. Multiculturalism is associated with the history of the nation-state; it comes in as cultural ideology in the political space where nationalism wanes; like nationalism, it consists in a specific attribution of values to difference amid certain forms of social identification.

I would like to review a few words and concepts frequently used in the technical lexicon of the ethnography of South America in Amerindian studies. The vocabulary consists of terms often correlated to native words and expressions as their translation into anthropological language. However, the writing of ethnography consists in the endless task of defining and redefining the technical lexicon, of agreeing with and extending previous uses, or disagreeing with and opposing such uses. Sometimes the effort leads the ethnography writer to propose a new term to be introduced in the lexicon, such as the Lévi-Straussian "mythème," for example, but such daring efforts are rare.

Let me begin with the word "hunting." In the anthropological vocabulary of Indo-European languages it refers to the activity of killing an animal to eat it or for sport. The Amerindian hunter, however, although killing the prey to feed his group, does so in a broader and more complex range of meanings. Many groups of Amerindians regard hunting as an act of seduction between the hunter and the prey. The man adorns himself as if he were going to a sexual encounter with a woman, wearing festive body painting, feathers, and aromatic essences. The activities involved in the act of hunting are equated with copulation and with killing an enemy, and thus, in the moment of hunting, the hunter is doing something identical to what he does as a warrior—another controversial word to be discussed later—and as inseminator of women. Before the hunter leaves on a hunting expedition, the shaman must consult the invisible guardian entity responsible for the species of the animal to be felled. The shaman engages in negotiations and pleas, and allows the hunter to go only after striking some sort of agreement with the animal guardian. The parts of the prey are often preassigned among commensals—for example, wives and children eat the legs, the elderly eat entrails, the brother-in-law eats the hump, and so on—while the hunter himself abstains from eating. What is at stake in the complex and delicate operation called "hunting" is a transference of metaphysical substances such as flesh and blood from an animal to a human. It is an act of appropriation with consent, a consent negotiated beforehand by the shaman, surrounded by strict rules of etiquette that can be discussed not only as forms of politeness but also and especially as a religious liturgy and as a philosophical speculation about the nature of the human being vis-à-vis animals and immortal entities (see discussion of "soul" and of "myth" later). Animals eat each other and so do humans, but in order to assert their humanity, the latter must master their need to eat in ways that differ radically from those of animals. Eating like an animal is a sign of a life crisis, perhaps even the consequence of witchcraft, dangerously placing the eater on the ontological border between human and animal. Hunting belongs to the chain of actions culminating with eating, and hence it is an important aspect of being in the world as human, of living, of existing and of living toward the great transformation of life from mortality to immortality (to be discussed below).

Thinking about hunting as a subsistence activity leads to another concept in the linguistic genealogy of the anthropological nation, production. Indeed, along these lines of thinking, in order to physically survive in the forest, the Amerindians must hunt productively. Hunting becomes an economic activity linked to the production project of a society managed by a nation-state. This chain of thoughts has a long tradition in anthropology and includes efforts to outline a stone age economics, or to equate Amerindian practices with work, work destined to subsistence and suffused by Marxist analytical categories such as surplus value. The metaphysical communication among groups becomes intersocietal exchange in the middle of the struggle between trade and use value, scarcity and abundance, monopolism, dominance, and so on. Some anthropologists even find in this so-called stone age economics[1] signs of what would be an ecologically minded Amerindian attitude toward the flora and fauna of the forest absent in the white colonist. It is as inadequate to dub Amerindian hunting "productive work" as it would be to use the same concept to characterize liturgical actions in the great religions of the world and discuss the productivity of a particular priest in baking wafers and consecrating them in the Eucharist. Since I am making this comparison between Amerindian hunting and religious liturgy, let me state that I am not proposing that certain Amerindian practices are liturgical. In point of fact, what I am trying to show is how equivocal is the habit of using taxonomies of cosmopolitan beliefs and practices—economics, religion, politics, and so on—to understand Amerindian beliefs and practices. Obviously, I hope to do more than just criticize the vices of the anthropological nation and propose an alternative way in the politics of translation.

Another area of studies in the ethnography of Amerindian South America that is steeped in a conceptual muddle is kinship and marriage. Perhaps in the history of anthropology no other field reveals a more tormented hermeneutical endeavor than what *Notes and Queries,* already in 1851, christened "kinship and social organization." In the history of this anthropological subfield the hairsplitting was carried beyond limits in the zeal to describe with precision that which seemed to be the foremost candidate to pitch the tent of anthropology in the camp of the sciences of nature. This is precisely the role that *The Elementary Structures of Kinship* played for decades, in the wake of the debacle of previous identifications of kinship with the sociality and with the juridical order of cosmopolitan societies. Kinship would be the sylvan equivalent of cosmopolitan bureaucracy, politics, and the juridical system. But the effort did not stop with Lévi-Strauss's alliance theory of marriage in savage societies. It proceeded in the fields of linguistic and mathematical sophistication, and went so far as to seek an explanation for the complex aboriginal Australian systems of marriage in the language of computer science. After the agony of many debates among proponents of different theories—I mention a few names to evoke the memory of those debates: Leach, Lounsbury, Schafer, Schneider, Needham, Maybury-Lewis—the field died abruptly, vanishing from conferences, publications, dissertations, and curricula.

Without resuscitating the field of kinship studies back into life in the anthropological nation, the ethnography of Amerindian South America has shown since the 1970s that the cornerstone notions used in the subfield were seriously inadequate. The domestic groups of Amerindians, originally regarded as stable political units of a larger social order, gained autonomy in and of themselves. These groups passed from being regarded as states in a federation to being understood as houses sheltering cohunters/fighters, codisseminators of semen, coreceivers and takers of gifts, and so on. Such groups can include different languages and do include actual allies and potential enemies along the lines of affinal relations. Ethnographic facts previously ignored and relegated to the corners of the house of the anthropological nation came to the foreground in the attempt to rethink kinship studies. Thus, marriage by kidnap and rape had to be understood at least as a modality of marriage; but then the word loses any descriptive usefulness. The term "kinship" itself and the search for basic principles sustaining it—blood, warfare, political and commercial exchange, group identity, and so forth—were radically revised and perhaps should be given up altogether.

A group of coresident Amerindians on the bank of an Amazonian river is not a social and political unit, but a metaphysical community that is not a social or political being; nor is it living on the way to become one. As anthropologist Roberto da Matta puts it, it is a community of substance (1982). However, I would contend, it is not yet a community in the sense coined by Tönnies of *Gesellschaft* and *Gemeinschaft*. It is rather a being reminding me of Heidegger's *Dasein*, or, if you prefer, of Buber's and Rosenzweig's Dasein, to be discussed below.[2] It is a being toward something the most outstanding characteristic of which resides in the fact that itself is a question about the relation and difference between itself and the Being of beings, or between itself and that which is other than itself. The Amerindians do not articulate philosophical questions verbally. Their metaphysical quest unfolds along the lines of a metaphysical experimentation with substances such as blood, flesh, semen, and bones. It is not clear how much of it a community of substance, a community-to-be, should have or give up. As a matter of fact, this line of political economic thinking is inadequate in the search for the meaning of the Amerindian domestic group as a Dasein community of substance-to-be.

Unlike the Dasein of Heidegger, or of Buber and Rosenzweig, the main concern of Amerindian Dasein is not with self-presentation but with the Other. At the level of residential life, the relations are between semen disseminators and sexually active mothers, brothers and fathers-in-law, allies and enemies, mortal and immortal beings, human, animal, and divinity, the dead and the living, man, jaguar, and anaconda, and so on and so on. What stands out in this panoply and congeries of beings is the care, the concern, and the anxiety with alterity, with the faces of otherness showing up to selfsameness, and so radically marking the difference and irreducibility of one to the other. Basically, what we are beginning to understand following the groundbreaking work of ethnographers such as Bruce Albert (1985), Joanna Overing (1975), and Eduardo Viveiros de Castro (1992) is that the we-group of coresidents is not a political, or social, or ontological whole with an identity or in search of one like subjects under a nation-state. Coresidence is a process, and in its heart one already finds the mechanisms of difference operating between selfsameness and alterity.

One such mechanism has been most inappropriately called "war," or "ritual warfare." War is a category of the imperium of the nation-state in a continuum with politics characteristic of the struggle for dominance. Amerindian fights and killings are something entirely different. The avenging raids against enemies aim to restore a metaphysical balance in the domestic group, which has just suffered the loss of one of its own. The characterization I have just advanced does not fit all ethnographic cases, but the common theme of killing enemies is always a settling of scores, not with a group of enemies but through them, with the community or the world of the dead. In killing an enemy or an animal, the killer spills blood, may lose some of his own, concretely or symbolically, and alters the balance of flesh in the world of the living and in the world of the dead. It cannot be expected that from this act a precision of answers amenable to scientific measure and explanation will result. Killing another and absorbing or releasing his metaphysical substance is tantamount to raising a question about existence that follows the death of a close one. For the Amerindians most deaths are caused, and it is imperative to identify the face of the other that may be responsible for the killing. Death and murder are together perhaps the most pervasive processes of the play of difference, so much so that at times it looks like death and the Other are the same. But the Amerindians do not present themselves as those who are the opposite of death, although the worlds of the living and of the dead contradict each other.

One mythic tale after another explains that, much like the Judeo-Christian myth of expulsion from the Garden of Eden, humans lost their immortal condition in a clash with divinity. Existence in the here and now is mythic life. The present of mortality is transitory between the premythic time-space of immortality and the postmythic time-space of immortality, which is periodically visited by the shaman and brought to the fore on the occasion of the death (the killing) of each individual. Thus, it is life *zum Tod* ("toward death"), as in Heidegger; however, it is so with very different qualifications. For Heidegger, to live toward death constitutes an authentic form of existence, while to forget this fact, or to live as if it were not so, is a form of inauthenticity. Neither authenticity nor inauthenticity is a moral condition, nor is it subject to Dasein's choice. In what concerns the Amerindians, life is a matter of ritual appropriateness, of ritual propriety and etiquette. The world or time-space of the living is intertwined with the world and time-space of the dead. Killing enemies is part of the enormous funerary rite that life is.

"Cannibalism" is the next word to be discussed. It has had such an impoverishing use in the history of anthropology, I feel tempted to say, often as a counterphobic reaction to the horror of anthropophagy. For the Amerindians, the cavities of the body are portals through which metaphysical substances ebb and flow, come from the other and go to the other, or are wasted. Eating, copulating, and killing an enemy or animal are phagic acts of comparable nature. The physical acts of swallowing, of ejaculating, and of striking a mortal blow on another being cannot be understood outside of their metaphysical meaning. Life here and now is tragic, difficult, unfair, and temporary, that is sure. The repositories of thinking from which one can cull out sylvan epistemologies, moral systems, and gnoseological strategies is called in anthropology "cosmology," and it surfaces in the Amerindian mythic tales. Such tales vary from one group to the next, from one cultural and linguistic trunk to another (e.g., from a Carib- to a Tupí-speaking group), but the theme of a temporary life on earth is almost always present in the narratives. While mortal, the members of a particular group are diametrically opposed to the dead—that is, the immortal ones, those who were immortalized, who regained their premythic immortal condition. The Indo-European vocabulary and conceptual framework puts us in mired ground because, within the semantic sphere of those languages, what is understood as death has no correlation to the Amerindian expiration of the vital principle with the ensuing transformation of the invisible double of the being who abandoned the cosmic layer of earth. This double, the characterization of which of course varies from one group to the next, under no circumstance should be translated as "soul" or as "spirit," as it so often has in the anthropological tradition, thereby smuggling into the conceptual cosmos of Amerindians the foreign Christian notions of the life of the soul after the death of the body. Instead of just taking up the Christianized Indo-European words and using them to refer to the experiences of Amerindian existence, it would be a great deal more interesting for anthropology to establish a contrastive discussion between theology and Amerindian cosmological discourse about mortality and immortality.

For the Amerindians, life on earth is cruel because, as mortals, they have to kill in order to survive. The act of killing another being—a plant, an animal, or an enemy—for the Amerindians is an act of what anthropologists call "cannibalism," because it entails a change in the balance of metaphysical substances between the killer and his victim. The Amerindians often characterize the world of the dead, the world of the immortals, as a time-place where all the yokes of mortal life are absent—no sexual taboos, no need to work, no scarcity of food, no conflict, no death, and no need to kill. Cannibalism is a tragic condition of being mortal; it is more than eating the flesh of another human being, but rather eating at all from the flesh of the world, in the sense in which Merleau-Ponty used this expression.[3] For the Amerindians it is the lot of mortals as opposed to those beings endowed with immortality. Plants, also mortal, practice acts of cannibalism as well. The Achuar of Peru, for example, understand the red streaks in manioc tubers as traces of blood from children vampirized by those plants (Descola 1996). But again, none of these Amerindian beliefs, practices, and passions can be understood as straightforward interpretations of reality, practical and rational along the lines of any Western, Indo-European, Judeo-Christian, Euro-American, and cosmopolitan epistemology. What I claim to be at stake here is the need to be able to think a sylvan mode of thinking and to discuss it in contrast to cosmopolitan epistemology. Anthropology, in that sense, could be a debate between epistemology and cosmology.

Not only is the word "cannibalism" inadequate to refer to the flow of metaphysical substances among beings, but also "soul" and "spirit" are inappropriate to designate any of the dimensions of Amerindian philosophical anthropology. I find it illuminating to think about the Amerindian beliefs and practices relating to extensions of visible being in comparison to the Western ontology of Being, such as developed by Martin Heidegger in *Being and Time* (1962). Dasein, the being there, thrown *(geworfen)* in the world, like the mortal Amerindians, is rolling freely, in the middle of the world, in this and in that direction, amid endless possibilities. Dasein has infinite possibilities, but it is mortal, thus finite. The contradiction between the infinite possibilities of Dasein's being-in-the-world and its mortality—its finitude, or totality—makes it anxious. There is no logic or reason—no purposive rationality—showing Dasein how to balance out the knowledge that it lives toward its own death, confronted with endless possibilities. One of the most remarkable consequences of this line of reasoning—a consequence that has become prevalent in the intellectual history of the twentieth century—is that consciousness can no longer be regarded as the bottom line on which the questions of existence are examined. The Greco-Roman and Judeo-Christian self who seeks its identity in reflection, in the feelings brewing in the Augustinian *foro intimo,* and who obeys the dictates of its consciousness is evidently denied by Dasein, or perhaps one should say, continues to be denied by Dasein since Nietzsche, Marx, and Freud.

Not centered around itself—that is, not focused on its own consciousness—Dasein is not an assertion of identity, as the cosmopolitan tradition of philosophical anthropology has contended all along. As Heidegger puts it, Dasein is a question about the relation of its being with the Being of all beings. To say that this is a good way to describe the Amerindian existential quest in their beliefs, practices, and passions would be tantamount to engaging in the naïve assumption of transparency between cultural and linguistic traditions, that which is the object of my critique. The split of the Amerindian being between the visible and the invisible double can be equated neither with the Christian dichotomy between body and soul, nor with decentered Dasein, running ahead of itself, divided into authenticity and inauthenticity, anxious, confronted by the dissonance between its infinite possibilities and the finite means of its mortal existence. But there are interesting intersections between Western epistemologies and Amerindian cosmologies, which it is possible to discuss away from the ideological temptation of translation to reduce one to the other. The Araweté Indians, for example, regard themselves as forsaken on earth, living on the very last corner of the earth (Viveiros de Castro 1992), while twentieth-century philosophy has taken a turn in the direction of abandoning the humanism of man as presentation of self-identity, and replacing it with notions such as the Sartrean *delaissé* or the Heideggerian geworfen, or the Levinasian "persecuted."[4] It is these contrastive similarities that are interesting to discuss, rather than taking the meaning of one and trying to reduce it by translating it into something else.

The foregoing discussion brings us to an area of South American ethnography marked by extreme obscurity. I refer to the notion of myth. Although the books and essays defining the concept of myth are endless, a coherent treatment of the subject is not to be found in this extensive body of literature. It is not my intent to be drawn into the fascinating discussion of the meaning of myth, from Cassirer to Blumenberg, from Malinowski to Lévi-Strauss, or from classic theology to contemporary literary criticism. However, I want to focus on something that is central to articulating a proper notion of myth: the question of temporality.

Mythic tales always have a temporal reference. The stories relate events that took place in a remote era; as the Indians put it, "a long time ago." This of course has the sense of past in Indo-European verbal time. However, living Indians, like shamans, can visit this supposedly "past time," and at times, the narrated remote events are replicated in the present. This stands in strong indication that the mythic is not only a temporal frame, but also a spatial one. The mythic cannot be equated with the Kantian a priori categories of time and space. We need something resembling the Bakhtinian chronotope–a collapse between temporality and spatiality–in order to discuss the mythic in Amerindian beliefs and practices (see Maranhão 2000b).

In addition, if one heeds the content of many mythic tales, it becomes inevitable to conclude that the events narrated in the stories constitute a borderline and a border time between a cosmic time-space in which there was no ontological differentiation among beings and another cosmic time-space of ontological difference. The time-space of difference is violent and visible, while the time-space of ontological undifferentiation is pacific and invisible. Difference results from the absence of difference, and introduces mortal life, voracity, and cannibalism, dependence on flesh and ontological confusion between the immortality of divinity and the bestiality of animals.

The beliefs, practices, and passions outlined in the mythic tales do not belong to a past era, but to an adjacent time-space, an invisible time-space bordering the tangible visible. The eschatology of mythologies divides the cosmos into three time-spaces. The first is premythic and corresponds to the situation of generalized immortality and ontological undifferentiation. The second is the mythic—that is, the current difficult time-space of mortality, cannibalism, and strife. Finally, there is the postmythic characterized by the recovery of immortality by man, or perhaps, I should say, by the Amerindians belonging to a particular group of coresidents, cohunters, cowarriors, and coinseminators of women. I put it in this apparently awkward way because among the Amerindians, group identity is superseded by the question of the human against the divine and against the animal, and of the living against the dead. Now, it is inevitable that after 500 years of extermination of Indians and of the disruption of their cultural and linguistic traditions, the question of identity has undergone severe changes. It should not surprise us that in the sylvan world the question of the nature of humanity has been overshadowed by the quest for group identity and for Indian identity vis-à-vis the white man.

It is interesting to talk about the mythic, premythic and postmythic time-spaces with Amerindians whose beliefs and practices are deeply immersed in sylvan cosmology. Often, once the interviewer insists on questions about these three chronotopic situations, the Amerindians' replies begin to make no sense to cosmopolitan reason. The Indian will say about an event marking the beginning of the mythic time-space that he was too young to remember, or that he has not been there recently. The conversation about the pre- and the postmythic also sounds fuzzy and replete with logical inconsistencies. Cosmopolitan reason cannot help quiz Amerindian narratives. If before the split of cosmos into several layers all beings were immortal, how would one tell man from divinity and from animal? More specifically, if there was no ontological differentiation, why should there be a being called "human," or "Yanomami," or another called "divinity"? My speculation on this matter is that if there is no ontological difference there is no need for language. The experience touched upon by language is that of difference, which creates the conditions necessary for interpretation and translation. To talk about the premythic or the postmythic is to try and cover with language something radically refractory to that medium. The results of such absurd semiotic effort—namely, to try to appropriate with language something that has no difference—can only be awkward. Needless to say that such bizarre conversations are not exclusive of the conversational setting between ethnographer and Amerindian.

Finally, I would like to discuss the word "society" so commonly employed to designate groups of Amerindians. The pedigree of this technical term of the social sciences harks back to the cradle with Marx, Weber, and Durkheim. It is an eighteenth-century word that went in vogue together with the emergence of the nation-state with the French Revolution and the American War of Independence. Society is the body of the nation-state, it is the nation organized socially, politically, and economically toward the goal of a common production project. The founding fathers of the social sciences, and particularly Durkheim, conceptualized society as the root of sociality; there would be no difference between society and sociality. What I mean by sociality is the fundamental situation of self and other, always accompanied by the awareness that there is a third person. Sociality unfolds from this dyadic and triangular situation—that is, from the play of the proximity between self and other transformed into a distance by the third person, and back into proximity. In this phenomenology of the privileged setting of sociality it is important to distinguish the primordial movements, the possibility of harmony and disharmony, of loyalty and betrayal, of peacefulness and violence, of care and hostility, of vengeance and forgiveness. The intimacy of the pair constituted by self and other is permanently under the threat of the third person who can form a new intimate pair, breaking the original one, or remain excluded, therefore becoming a hostile outsider. The founding fathers of the social sciences ignored this fundamental situation, and assumed that primordial sociality was indigenous to society. Thus, the intimate setting of self and other was made to look like something already belonging to the social contract. However, from a phenomenological point of view, the social contract and society are possible only as developments of the situation arising of the triangle constituted by self, the other, and the third person.

Thinkers such as Max Scheler, Georg Simmel, Martin Buber, Jean-Paul Sartre, Maurice Merleau-Ponty, and Emmanuel Levinas developed a line of thinking about society from the privileged setting of self and other.[5] Alfred Schütz outlined a phenomenological social ontology between self and other from which the construction of society unfolds. Even Durkheim in his concern with individual and society was to a certain extent acknowledging that there was something more fundamental and prior to the historical processes of social solidarity. Such intellectual efforts and developments notwithstanding, the fact of the matter is that the discourse about society in the social sciences took the direction of the collective, the social contract, fueled as it was by the strong winds of nationalism (and Durkheim is an excellent illustration) under the banner of the political institution of the nation-state.

Anthropologists inappropriately call the groups of Amerindians they study "societies," echoing the original telescoping of society with sociality at the onset of the social sciences. The use of the word "society" smuggles into the understanding of the Amerindian groups several notions completely foreign to their beliefs and practices. When the word "society" is used, a search for collective identity is insinuated. The contours of the collective are drafted by a common production project, by a quest or construction of a common language, culture, religion, ethnicity, and so forth. But the ethos of the sylvan as characterized here is not that of a society, although the colonial process has destroyed most of this Amerindian way of being-in-the-world, transforming the Indians into marginalized minorities of the society of the nation-state. The Amerindian world that I try to cull out of history—the history of the colonial invasion of the New World—is one that was only given to be known with colonialism, but which however challenged colonialism, not politically, as something consciously other than colonialism, but as something that defied all modes of understanding of cosmopolitan and colonialist epistemological strategies. This is the Amerindian world steeped in the exchange of metaphysical substances, the community of substance that has nothing to do with society, the being-in-the-world consisting in being-in-this-world of earth and mortality, this mythic time-space defined by the mythic tales and so on.

The issues plaguing anthropology as a science of translation are naturally pervasive in all areas of the discipline and not typical of the ethnography of South America, which I am using here in illustration of the broader difficulties of translation, and especially of intercultural translation. The trust in the possibility of intercultural translation and the efforts to refine its techniques overlook the fundamental difficulty residing in the fact that there is a dialogical process of communication that can never be entirely captured by a given language or a given culture as a homeostatic system. It is true that cultural, linguistic, and social systems do shape everyday conduct, but the human freedom to elude that determinism cannot be ignored.

The claim of anthropology is that it can make sense of the extremely unfamiliar in familiar terms. The recent decades in the history of the discipline have witnessed several movements of critique such as dialogical, confessional, and critical anthropology, to mention just a few. However, anthropology cannot come to grips with its translation problem as long as it remains fastened to its nineteenth-century descriptive vocation. The alternative is obviously a dialogical anthropology, not one, however that textualizes and therefore kills dialogue, but one that takes part in a live dialogue. This is a formidable intellectual project, which has been taken up several times in the past century, in different disciplines and from different points of view. I would like to briefly review an intellectual tradition aspiring to overcome the incongruities of conflicts between identity and difference and their textualized representation. The three examples to be discussed are those of the Buber-Rosenzweig translation of the Hebrew Bible into German, of Paul Celan's German poetry trying to capture the traumatic memory of the Holocaust, and Heidegger's efforts to develop a philosophical language in absolute refusal of any philosophical anthropology.

The Buber-Rosenzweig translation of the Hebrew Bible to German is a landmark in the reflection on translation. The goal of the endeavor was to revitalize German by allowing the spirit of Hebrew to sprout in the translation, thereby freeing the biblical text from its Lutheran Christianization. Thus, words translated as "altar" became "place of slaughtering," "burnt offers" became "the offer of a present that ascends," and "I am the Lord" or "the Lord God" became "*ICH*," with all letters capitalized (Reichert 1996, 179–80). But this project, spanning almost three decades of work, was a great deal more ambitious. It aimed at uniting German and Jew, self and other, without appropriation by either. Rosenzweig sums up the scope of the project, writing: "If the voice of the Other has anything to say, then the [target] language must afterwards look different than before. . . . Language will experience a renewal" (quoted in ibid., 174).

The translation was not well received. Criticisms were legion, from Scholem to Benjamin. Siegfried Kracauer made the most devastating comment by pointing out similarities between the philosophical grammar of the translation and the then-nascent National Socialist appeals to *völkischer Tonfall* ("racial inflection") and *völkische Romantik* ("racial Romanticism") in the German language. The problem was that the translators assumed that they could transcend the abyss between Hebrew and German and create a new hybrid language. It is interesting to note that the notion of Being was central to the concerns of the two translators. They wished to capture the dimension of transcendence of time of the Hebrew *ihyeh*. The proposed solution was a phrase centered on the neologism Dasein: "*Ich werde dasein, als der ich dasein werde*" ("I shall be here as the one who shall be here"). The redundancy of the Septuagint in what concerns the question of identity ("I am that I am," or "I am the being one") is also broken by the use of the future—something which, by virtue of the use of the first person pronoun, has presence and announces itself as something to be in the future. The Buber-Rosenzweig formula evidently resonates with Heidegger's Dasein. The "*ICH*" replacing "I am the Lord" reminds us of Buber's "*Ich*" in "*Ich und Du*": the one who says "ich" is already saying "du" (Buber 1970 [1923]).

For Heidegger, it is impossible to develop the reflection on Being without thinking about language, which is "the house of Being," and outside of which Being cannot be given notice. In addition to this fundamental role in rethinking the ontology of Being, language has another importance for Heidegger to express his ideas. Philosophy and science would have been contaminated all along by the forgetting of the question of Being; it was not enough to remind his audiences of this fact, but also to do so in a language expunged of the misleading tendencies of tradition. What was at stake for Heidegger was nothing less than to generate a new language in which to talk about something entirely new. However, the new language and its subject matter had roots in classical Greek and in the mutterings of the fragments of Greek philosophy (Heraclitus, Parmenides). More than translation, Heidegger's project amounted to a restoration. Nevertheless, the goal was not to restore to its original appearance something that had already been, but to engage in a discussion with the remnants of the ruins of language and of thinking.

Perhaps the main interlocutor of Celan's poetry is Heidegger. His philosophy was very appealing to Jewish thinkers like Celan himself and Emmanuel Levinas, among others. However, Heidegger's politics shed doubts over his philosophical project. Indeed, Celan's poems constitute one of the most provoking reactions to Heidegger's philosophy. He engages in the same language game of the Heideggerian philosophical grammar. Celan wrote his poetry in German and perhaps fulfilled to a larger extent than Hölderlin or Georg Trakl the Heideggerian reflection on the role of poetry in breaking ground for fresh new thinking. In one of his poems, Celan refers probably to Germans whom he both admired and feared and among whom one could find Heidegger, as "long-muzzled axes in lowland" *(Tüllenäxte im Tiefland)* (1986, 24–25), a metaphor referring to an allegorized Germany. In another poem more generally understood as referring to Heidegger, Celan writes: "Left back for me/cross-beamed/One:/ the riddle I must unravel, while you, in hempcloth, knit the stocking of mystery" (ibid., 64–65), in which "hempcloth" alludes to the hangman's rope in knitting "the stocking of mystery." This is perhaps an allusion to the peasant hats Heidegger wore in several pictures during his period of retreat in the Black Forest.

Celan's poetry maintains and retrieves the memory of the Holocaust, but it attempts to do that avoiding trivializing, distancing itself from the banal of the cry of victims. In the post-Holocaust history of European Jewish thinking, Celan stands out as one of those voices fearing that the bemoaning of the symbolic and concrete example of Auschwitz could render threadbare the powerful and painful memory. Writing between speech and silence, Celan raises the stakes of Adorno's rhetorical question, asking what kind of poetry could be written after Auschwitz. The language in his poems is reminiscent of a concealed experience, evocative, hermetic, and alliterative in an almost kabbalistic and cryptic sense, projective, inquisitive, replete with semantic and morphological anagrams. His style is marked by a "lacerated syntax, by lacunae, hesitations, aphasic fumblings and epileptic halts" (Washburn in Celan 1986). He pursues the Heideggerian poetic and philosophical strategy of having an experience with language, while engaging in saying. In his poetry, language and signification clash with one another in a difficult dialogue with each other. Language does not match experience; experience in turn does not flow through language. The incompatibility between the two thematizes difference, insinuating a certain perplexity before that which is refractory to identification.

Understanding is not an operation between the speaker/listener on the one hand and the said on the other. Understanding is dialogical as first Buber and then Gadamer have argued. This, however, is not the hermeneutics proposed by Heidegger. For Heidegger, language is the home (Heimat) of man. Speaking, man asks where he lives. To understand what to speak/listen means would be tantamount to understanding what is the Being of Dasein. Faced with this impossibility, man still raises the question and toys with different possibilities by speaking in tongues (that is, saying the saying of another with his own mouth), by assuming that every saying can be conveyed in another saying (the presumption of translation), by speaking/writing poetically, and so on. For Heidegger, saying is "a freeing that conceals while bringing into the unconcealedness of the clearing."[6] Saying conceals at the same time that it reveals. The science of translation and its subdisciplines naively assume that once said, the saying completely reveals, and thus it would become possible to translate one saying into another. But the said already has a problematic relation with the saying. Translation ignores what the saying conceals.

In the hermeneutic tradition that grew in the wake of Heidegger's philosophy, with Ricoeur and Gadamer, for example, it is the semiotic potential for surplus signification that triggers thinking and constitutes the trait of the openness of thought. But for Heidegger, it is the withdrawal from the conventional sign that opens thinking to surplus signification. Whether the extra of the unspeakable, of the invisible, lies in the occult face of the sign, or in its eclipse, is of little importance, if one, unlike Heidegger, places the decision of this question in the proximity language is in relation to the other. This of course brings Levinas's thought into the picture. This turn of thinking from Heidegger toward Levinas, however, does not deny Dasein's hermeneutical self-presentation ("Who am I?" "What is my relation to Being?"). The question is partial, incomplete, but finds its extension in the situation in which questioning being finds itself questioned by the Other, the Levinasian Other who so persuasively complements the Heideggerian mysterious and almost mystic Dasein. Dasein cannot discover by itself the full meaning of its Being, but the Other surprises Dasein, making it understand itself as a totality of meaning. Thus, the unspeakable, or the invisible, is not that which is kept away from me because of my hermeneutical limitations; it is that which has not yet been told or shown to me by the Other. Here I am extending a reading of Heidegger with texts by Levinas (1969). For Heidegger, proper, it is solitary Dasein that faces the mystery of Being in its solitary death.[7]

The idea that man generates language, rooted in psycholinguistics, is as extravagant as the idea that language creates man. Language is not a being. The biblical "first there was the word" and Heidegger's assertion that "language speaks man" both point to a clear separation between man and language. For Heidegger, language is, among other things, the house of the being of man. Loosely paraphrasing Heidegger, man comes to language, while language, in turn, calls things. More than indexical or referential, language is vocative; it calls the things that its naming practices do not describe, but only address obliquely, because things are not sitting out there, waiting to be called. There is a life and an interrelatedness that precede language with complete independence from it. On the other hand, language is a privileged way of pointing to things and of addressing people—in short and paraphrasing Austin, of doing things with words.

Heidegger adds that language and things penetrate each other.[8] Between the two there is intimacy, in-between-ness, an interrelatedness leaving no doubts that language and things are separate and different from each other. This proximity between language and things, which is also a penetration, thematizes difference. If one thinks that difference begs for identity, then the intimacy between language and things is a deferral. But if difference does not need to be reduced to identity, then the intimacy of the proximity between language and things is a copresencing of both. By pointing to and calling things, language establishes a copresence with them. There are measures and ideal measures of this proximity/distance between language and things, but the copresencing is not bound by any means to such measures. Words can kill and can be listened away, as they can call mistakenly or entirely miss their call.

The difference characteristic of the proximity/distance of the intimacy between language and things is also the site of pain, as notes Heidegger (1971), adding that difference also presents itself as a rift. Why does Heidegger introduce this chain of thoughts going from proximity/distance to intimacy, to difference, then equating difference with the rift, and ultimately with pain? Could it be the case that difference is not a "natural" condition, that it is a sort of tear in that which originally would have been one—that is, word and thing? Or even a marker of the many striving to be one? Heidegger cautions his reader against thinking in sentimental terms about the site of pain that is difference. Does he mean by this that the pain of difference cannot be understood in terms of the logic of cause and effect that could be converted into a discourse about perpetrators and victims (ibid., 205)? I think this is a plausible reading. The pain of the rift between language and thing is not moral; it does not outrage. In fact, adds Heidegger promptly, difference "stills the thing" (ibid., 206).

The stillness of the difference between language and thing suggests passivity, conformity, acceptance of the fact that neither can language substitute for world nor vice versa. Even if there is an anxious curiosity about the order and relationship among things, difference has the power to calm down that anxiety and to still the rift.

The advocacy of translation as the only means to overcome the Babelian hubbub among languages reflects a trust in reason and in the rationality of the said above and beyond the saying. Only that which is said would be capable of promoting peace. The unsaid would be an ally of war and the end of reason. This modernist ideology persists, although, as I have very briefly shown, after the intellectual developments of the twentieth century there is little in support of the continuation of that cultural ideology. The many crises within anthropology as a science of translation testify to the debacle of the belief in the correctness and in the usefulness of rendering something from a sylvan source language in a cosmopolitan target language. Anthropological theory and theoretical debates are by and large a rationalization of the failed translation practices.

In face of such categorical statements, the question is begging of how to proceed and do anthropology in a direction opposite to translation—in other words, how to engage cosmopolitan epistemologies in a debate with sylvan cosmologies. If the debate is to remain confined to cosmopolitan readers and speakers, then a spokesperson must be appointed to "explain" the meaning of the cosmological issue to be debated. Anthropologists have liked to appoint themselves to that role of Hermes, but they have found themselves speaking only to the believers, not to the gods; thus the debate has not taken place. Among so many other contentious issues for discussion—such as social justice, sovereignty, freedom, and the like—on which the curtain of the twentieth century was closed, lies the fairness, or the justice, or the respect and responsibility for the voice of the other so persistently thematized by the discipline for one and a half centuries. I am suggesting that the opening of anthropological discourse be sought in the closing of that curtain by those thinkers who questioned the cornerstone notions of intellectual traditions, such as Paul Celan, in his poetry written between speech and silence, or Heidegger, for whom the saying conceals at the same time that it reveals. Having positioned myself in the uncomfortable corner of the critic who has no alternative to offer, and recognizing the powerlessness of criticism, I would like to conclude with just a few remarks far away from the ambition of constituting a recipe for an anthropology against translation.

First, anthropology has worked all along with the assumption of conventional hermeneutics according to which the interesting meaning of what it studies lies in the surplus of signification, although more often than not it has been forced to settle for something a great deal more modest than the potential full meaning of a word or expression. Against that, I would like to propose a counterstrategy consisting in the withdrawal from the sign, and patience with the immediate meaninglessness of the said. That can be accomplished only if the saying is valued above the said.

Second, anthropology has worked primarily with the referential function of language, and when it turned to the pragmatic functions such as indexicality, it did so in an effort to subsume the observed usages of language into explanatory totalities. But language calls things in the world. There is a difference between language and things. The testimonial of the fieldworker is that there are things and there are words; they are co-related and in copresence. Dwelling in this difference between word and things is already an unfathomable and interminable practice.

Third, the difference between word and thing is not static or fixed. Words and things pierce and penetrate each other, they lacerate each other, and hurt each other not only in their mutual invasions but also in the stillness of difference and distance, which I have called above, after Heidegger, the rift. This is a painful condition of difference, but it is not a moralized pain that aches and begs for alleviation.

Fourth and finally, the saying is a proximity/distance that cannot be covered by the said. The hubbub of Babel is a true condition of proximity/distance between self and other; it is the foremost trait of the proximate other man or woman. Living this proximity/distance does not require translation to the said, but perhaps a series of other gestures belonging to the ethical.

~

Notes

1. After criticizing Sahlins's (1972) introduction of the concept of economic productivity to discuss practices in sylvan groups, Descola proceeds using the same categories of economics, such as "work force" and "productive potential" with regard to the Achuar (1996, 318–19).

2. For my discussion of the use of the concept of Dasein in anthropology in connection with the work of Ernesto de Martino, see Maranhāo 1998b, 2000a.

3. For Merleau-Ponty's concept, see his *The Visible and the Invisible* (1968); and for my use of the concept in conjunction with the ethnography of Amerindian Amazonia, see Maranhão 1998a, 2000a.

4. The main work of Levinas to which I refer here is *Totality and Infinity* (1969). The notion of "persecution," however, is developed in his *Otherwise than Being or Beyond Essence* (1981). It means that in living for the Other, regardless of his or her will, the person cannot help but feel persecuted. Persecution inheres in passivity and unfolds in another one of Levinas's key concepts, that of substitution. Regardless of whether the person is focused on his or herself, the fundamental orientation of self is toward the Other, so much so that self is responsible not only for the misery of the Other but also for his or her crimes, even and especially when those crimes target self. It is interesting to establish a discussion between the Amerindian fear of alterity and the Levinasian notions of persecution and substitution.

5. For a study on social ontology see Theunissen's (1984) brilliant essay discussing the attempts of Husserl, Heidegger, Sartre, Buber, and Schütz to develop a fundamental philosophy of the social encounter. Regrettably, Theunissen's study leaves out the work of Levinas.

6. See Heidegger 1971, 200; and Marx 1972, 240.

7. See commentary by Theodore Kisiel on Heinrich Ott's paper "Hermeneutic and Personal Structure," p. 185, n. 18.

8. See Heidegger's essay, "Language," 1971, 202.

References Cited

Albert, Bruce. 1985. "Temps du sang, Temps des cendres: Représentation de la maladie, système rituel et espace politique chez les Yanomami du Sud-est (Amazonie brésilienne)." Ph.D. dissertation, Université de Paris X, Nanterre.

Buber, Martin. 1970 [1923]. *I and Thou*, trans. W. Kaufmann. New York: Charles Scribner's Sons.

Celan, Paul. 1986. *Last Poems*, trans. K. Washburn and M. Guillemin. San Francisco: North Point.

Da Matta, Roberto. 1982. *A Divided World: Apinayé Social Structure*, trans. A. Campbell. Cambridge, MA: Harvard University Press.

Descola, Philippe. 1996. *In the Society of Nature: A Native Ecology in Amazonia*, trans. N. Scott. Cambridge: Cambridge University Press.

Heidegger, Martin. 1962 [1927]. *Being and Time*, trans. J. Macquarrie and E. Robinson. New York: Harper and Row.

———. 1971. "Language." In *Poetry, Language, Thought,* trans. A. Hofstadter. New York: Harper and Row.

———. 1982. *On the Way to Language,* trans. P. Hertz. New York: Harper and Row.

Levinas, Emmanuel. 1969. *Totality and Infinity,* trans. A. Lingis. Pittsburgh, PA: Duquesne University Press.

———. 1981. *Otherwise than Being or Beyond Essence,* trans. A. Lingis. The Hague: Nijhoff.

Maranhão, Tullio. 1998a. "The Adventures of Ontology in the Amazon Forest." *Paideuma* 44: 155–68.

———. 1998b. "Ernesto de Martino und das Geheimnis des Daseins." Pp. 172–76 in *Wegmarken: Eine Bibliothek der ethnologischen Imagination.* Wuppertal: Edition Trickster im Peter Hammer Verlag.

———. 2000a. "Heidegger and Levinas in the Amazon Jungle." Pp. 283–300 in *Moderne(n) der Jahrhundertwenden,* ed. V. Borsò and B. Goldammer. Baden-Baden: Nomos Verlagsgesellschaft.

———. 2000b. "The Temporalization and the Spatialization of Time." Pp. 85–106 in *Zeit-Zeitenwechsel-Endzeit,* ed. U. G. Leisle and J. Mecke. Regensburg: Schriftenreihe der Universitat Regensburg.

Marx, Werner. 1972. "The World in Another Beginning: Poetic Dwelling and the Role of the Poet." Pp. 235–60 in *On Heidegger and Language,* ed. J. Kockelmans. Evanston, IL: Northwestern University Press.

Merleau-Ponty, Maurice. 1968. *The Visible and the Invisible,* trans. and with Introduction by A. Lingis. Evanston, IL: Northwestern University Press.

Ott, Heinrich. 1972. "Hermeneutic and Personal Structure of Language." Pp. 169-94 in *On Heidegger and Language,* ed. J. Kockelmans. Evanston, IL: Northwestern University Press.

Overing (Kaplan), Joanna. 1975. *The Piaroa, A People of the Orinoco Basin: A Study in Kinship and Marriage.* Oxford, UK: Clarendon Press.

Reichert, Klaus. 1996. "'It Is Time': The Buber-Rosenzweig Bible Translation in Context." Pp. 169–85 in *The Translatability of Cultures,* ed. S. Budick and W. Iser. Stanford, CA: Stanford University Press.

Sahlins, Marshall. 1972. *Stone Age Economics.* Chicago: Aldine-Atherton.

Theunissen, Michael. 1984. *The Other: Studies in the Social Ontology of Husserl, Heidegger, Sartre, and Buber,* trans. C. Macann. Cambridge, MA: MIT Press.

Viveiros de Castro, Eduardo. 1992. *From the Enemy's Point of View: Humanity and Divinity in an Amazonian Society,* trans. C. Howard. Chicago: University of Chicago Press.

Translating "Self-Cultivation"

Ellen B. Basso

Defined as the rewriting of an original text, translation involves the creative and manipulative power of one culture over another. Much more is involved with translation than language. But is it appropriate to think of translation as something that can take place intraculturally—that is, interpersonally? If so, how is this accomplished, and how are specific instances of such translation remembered within an oral culture? These are questions that underlie my thoughts on translation and the interpersonal in this paper, which ranges across work on certain narratives told to me in their Carib language by the people called Kalapalo living in several communities in the Alto Xingu region of central Brazil.

These Kalapalo narratives focus thematically upon important figures from the past who are connected with "self-cultivation," an expression I use to write of an embodied and ever changing understanding of one's humanness that emerges with body techniques involving repeated form practice.[1] These are body techniques that involve people learning to pay attention to what is happening to their bodies, and in turn communicating these processes to others in a variety of linguistic forms and genres: technical vocabulary, declarations about meaning, narrated descriptions of personal experiences, and ultimately through enactments of those experiences in performance. Stories also exist that include memories of occasions of translation connected to self-cultivation, during which a person's private and personal experiences are made to reach others, at times entering more collective and public understandings. The subsequent effects on the thought and action of a community may have significant historical consequences.

Alongside the creation of meaning outside or beyond but still through an individual's own experiencing, communication of this same kind takes place across very different personalities, often between a specially "trained" personality to a less, or differently, skilled one. Different experiential frames are thus posited as equivalents in a middle zone of "translation" that becomes the very ground for changes involving a cultural process or production in language, occupied by what Lydia Liu calls a *neologistic imagination* (Liu 1995, 137).[2]

Commenting on a very early use of the figure of "self-cultivation" by Confucius, in which the idea of "self" is not essentialist but contextual, free from specified goals that give it a special flexibility and creative range, Hall and Ames observe that a person is characterized in terms of events, in such a way as to pre-clude considering agency or act in isolation from the other. In this way of thinking, they write: "[T]he agent is as much a consequence of his act as its cause" (1998, 15). Thus self-cultivation is not something that directly has to do with an essentialist "self," or even an "identity," but it can often be centrally related to the experience of performance and enactment. Self-cultivation does not, then, carry the European sense of "refinement" or "education" but rather of strengthening and enhancing the human personality to a higher than normal or ordinary state, through training the body. "Self-cultivation" cannot therefore carry the European sense of a disem-bodied "self." The Japanese philosopher Yuasa tends to write of self-cultivation from the point of view of individual practice and experience, but the contexts of that practice and the Confucian emphasis on self-cultivation as ritual expressions of "propriety" raise questions regarding the emergence of a community of practi-tioners.

I have adopted these Asian connotations of "self-cultivation,"[3] because I find the expression serves well for understanding some important aspects about Native American practices that seem to have been neglected. First, self-cultivation is the foundation of particular "communities of practice," such as exist throughout the region of central Brazil known as the Alto Xingu, where these communities have long contributed to the complex social matrix we still see in that place. Xingu communities of practice transcend "kinship," "settlement," and language group membership. Second, "self-cultivation" is useful for talking generally about formal practices among Kalapalo that were (in some cases, still are) designed to shape dis-tinct embodied personalities having special connections to professionalized skills. Among the Kalapalo, embodiments often were the substance of biographical nar-ratives from which we learn how these subjectively interesting activities became more objectively significant, public, and shared. Such stories are particularly clear about the events involved in individual form practices. Kalapalo narrators can devote much time to connections between the private and personal on the one hand, and specific form practices observed in seclusion by initiates on the other. Even more interesting, stories describe in considerable detail the means by which an individual's embodied disciplines were reshaped into directives for a collective observance or ritual performance (a realm of social life more accessible to others). To call these stories "origin myths" is to oversimplify their import considerably. The interpersonal configurations that constitute dramatic contexts for translations of enacted and performed embodiment in these Kalapalo stories are shaped by various discursive conventions used by people to talk about such matters in biographical and other "documentary" genres, to use an expression from Lydia Ginzburg. In Amazonia, these conventions seem to differ rather markedly from those appearing in more informal speech genres, and especially conversational speech, contributing to a "tradition" that transcends chronotypic boundaries.[4] With this in mind, I want to especially take up the question of the work of translation as imaginative communication within such a community of practice, arising when people attempt to share experiences of "self-cultivation."

Most pertinent to our concern in Leipzig with "translation" is that Kalapalo stories describe *translation events*—that is, how someone translated their embodied knowledge from their privately held imaginative understanding into another, "not private," shared, and visible discursive form. More complicated acts of translation by shamans involved the opportunistic construction of dramaturgical frames, the creation of "rituals." In response to the shaman's orienting people to one another in settings of intense emotional enactments, the participants reassessed their previously held interpretations of their own place in the world. These interpretations were in keeping with the intentions of the shaman. What he translated was the meaningful experiencing of "self-cultivation" from his own interpersonal contexts of psychosocial reality into those of others around him. Translation events such as these offer the opportunity for a discourse-centered approach to the subject.

My concern with "embodied experience" participates in the current anthropological interest in how the material body, serving as both an idiom and a medium for expression, becomes crucial for understanding the interpersonal world, for communicating people's experiences of others and, in turn, enabling them to receive information about the world around them. Embodiment helps people to "explore the intersubjective construction of meanings related to body experiences and their use in negotiating responses to social and cultural tensions" (Collier et al. 2000, 21).

Some of the most important discussions of embodiment meanings and representations have been concerned with experiences of affliction and suffering (as in the work of Kleinman, Csordas, Scheper-Hughes, and Crapanzano). My own interest here is not directly with meaning and representation but rather with practice that involves emulation of paradigmatic individuals appearing in narratives as "standards of value," attempts to follow idealizations of doing and becoming. Kalapalo self-cultivation seems to replicate the practices of exemplary models or heroic personages from the past, figures that (as Hall and Ames point out concerning those in Chinese texts) thereby function very differently from the transcendent structures of meaning (such as "Reason" or the Trinitarian God) to provide understandings of what it means to be human. Like Asian mind-body theory, Kalapalo interest in work upon the body is focused upon the problem of human ways of living as they pertain to the development of particular aspects of intelligence and personality and the transformation of their understanding of "humanness." Idealization of this kind is not focused only upon figures from the past who are modeled in their biographical richness but also on oneself in the present—more concretely in Kalapalo stories, an experiencing of oneself as continually seeking to be validated and verified. The imagining of this ideal is envisioning the other as an active embodied understanding, an experimental, changing awareness.

More specifically, self-cultivation practice involves repeated ascetic exercises and attempts at mastering a form. More important than the ascetic nature of the exercises themselves, though, in keeping with self-cultivation as ongoing practice, "cultivating one's person" refers to the person as a "doing" or a "making," not a sort of "being." There is no final goal to a final "identity," although people will easily become identified with their form practices. Rather, it is an ongoing project; one's abilities ebb and flow, are judged important or not, in very precise contexts. While the forms may be practiced in isolated circumstances (as in a seclusion chamber), they involve interpersonal, even ritualized relations within a community of practitioners, a "community of practice." Not only are there a shared set of moral values and embodied understandings, but even more interesting is that discursive frames exist for the narration of creatively new information that opens up for reception and discussion privately held meanings of new and more seasoned practitioners.

I turn now to a more detailed exploration of these questions by discussing a few examples of translated self-cultivation among Kalapalo. Regimes of often highly ritualized embodied practice are particularly salient for understanding some personality differences among these people—and therefore the processes of interpersonal relations in which they are involved. Kalapalo understandings of their regimes are also frequently constitutive (through quoted conversations) of important personal narratives. Like the better known self-cultivation techniques of Asian cultures, Kalapalo practices are connected with the goals of shaping, controlling, and channeling feelings in particular ways, as well as development of certain skilled habits of thought and of technical practice. Some of these "goals of habitus" are given to young men and women who are secluded during puberty. The Kalapalo describe other dispositions as if they were virtually professionalized personalities. In their biographies, men called *tafaku oto* ("bow masters") and *fuataū* ("knowers" or "shamans") are described as if they had a heightened consciousness of themselves as embodied and engaged in repeated practice throughout their lives.[5] This is notable with respect to their distinctive ways of participating in relations with others; the particular forms and content of their memories; their discursive and nondiscursive use of esoteric knowledge; physical appearance, gestures, and body-acts (e.g., the detachability and reattachment of body parts in the case of shamans, the ability to fly in the case of some bow masters); and their particular habits of speech.

Elsewhere I have described how Kalapalo shamanic knowledge, coming in moments of sudden and surprising insight and associated with unconscious contact with fearsome and powerful beings, can be contrasted with the much more deliberate, procedural, practical knowledge acquired by a person who was training to become a warrior (Basso 1995, 1998). What is of particular interest here is the essentially experimental action and perhaps experimental subjectivity in which shamans are involved, and hence their compelling need to "translate" their experiences to others, to offer them the chance to participate in their own imaginative understandings. I call this activity "translation" because Kalapalo do not directly narrate a shaman's representation of his experience to others (since that was not told with the goal of having it shared in narrative). Rather, the shaman reshapes his experiences into something very different: his personal understanding becomes a public performance. A story about the shaman known as Posa, told by the late hereditary leader and shaman Kambe, illustrates several instances of how this man's private—and perhaps (from the point of view of the rest of the community) unconsciously embodied—experience was translated into, first, instructions for a ritual performance, and, on another occasion, performance instructions to a warrior, and then a Jaguar.

Let's look more carefully at these examples. First we learn about Posa that he is a shaman who actively makes things happen by discursive and performed acts of translation. The narrator Kambe treats Posa's acts of translated self-cultivation as historical events. Put differently, as it is described to me, Kalapalo history emerges from particular intelligences and insights, decisions and choices, that together constitute enactments of specific persons (such as Posa). In the following segment of Kambe's story (A1), a particular masked ritual is introduced. But first we must hear something about the shaman himself.

~ 5

A1   *Then another time he went back there so he could watch the undufe*
ceremony, at a meander in the river, in the deep, dark water, where all those
powerful beings were performing. Performing undufe like Zhakwikatu.

"I'll go watch that," Posa said. He could say that because he was a
brother of those powerful beings, this person known to us as Posa.

Ndom, *he dove into the water and* ndik, *he stood in a place looking*
just like where we are now, the entrance to a settlement.

The house where those powerful beings live lies ahead.

As he looks, he sees what appears to be an undufe performance, Zhak-
wikatu, just what he's going to teach the other people later on. That's why he's
come there to watch.

He himself was the one who first began to teach how to make those
masks.

And he was the first to make Zhakwikatu, Atugua, Kwambe, all of
those undufe things.

~   *The next day they make bread for him. The powerful beings make a*
huge stack of bread, and as the sun begins to set, Posa feels like drinking some
manioc soup for a while. He doesn't have to worry about poisonous things.

Bread is wrapped up for him, after which putsi *he rises up to the*
surface, and then he carries the bread home to his wife. "Here's some bread,"
he tells her. He can eat the bread because he's the brother of powerful beings,
this person known to us as Posa. The brother of powerful beings.

~   *Later on he called to the others and told them that they should all*
make a performance. This was the time to teach them about what he had
seen.

"What are we going to have to do for that?"

"We're going to make undufe." That means, Zhakwikatu.

"All right. How are we going to do that?"

"What we have to do now is go get some wood. Let's collect some
wood."

That means, "Go cut wood." Cut takisi *wood.*

Then they worked on that wood, and because of what was going to
happen next, the powerful beings came there. Atugua the Whirlwind came
there, because of what they were going to do next with that wood. They
shaped the masks, and they were ready.

"Let's do it." They went to get palm fiber. And they worked on that.
And that was ready.

Next he painted the mask.

"What design will be made here? What can be used for this one?"
"I want to see this one right now," Posa said.
Then he holds the mask up before him, and as he does that the power-
ful beings—right there in the ceremonial house—the powerful beings appear
before him. None of the people can see them. He's the only one who sees them
when they appear. He and his little daughter. He sees the design, he puts it
on the mask, and then all the others also put it on. Then again after that one
is finished, he looks at another powerful being, a different one this time, and
once more he looks at the design. "Put this one on, it's a Fish's design." This
way everyone gets a design to put on his mask, until they're all done, finished.
They're ready.

~ *Now that they were painted, "Let's go," they went outside. You must*
have seen it yourself, when Pidyu *came outside here. "All right," he showed*
them how to arrange themselves, he Posa, the brother of powerful beings. The
brother of powerful beings.

This segment appears superficially to be little more than simple didactic speech: a listing of the techniques involved in making, revealing, and then performing with the masks. Yet this lesson is enabled by the manner in which Posa is actually translating his shamanic experience of contact with these powerful beings into a ritual performance. First he translates his underwater experiences, then what he learns from the powerful beings as they appear to him right there at the settlement where he is sitting with the other men. The human settlement provides the others with a concrete reality they can use to imagine what Posa saw, just as the people listening to the story in 1982 also had the same concrete image in mind to aid in their own imaginative understanding. Posa's brothers, the powerful beings, have allowed him to visit them (the story tells us) because Posa wants to teach the others about these masks. The preliminaries are of course important, because the men are learning to make objects that only Posa has seen up to this point. But what is most important, in the end, is their full participation in the performance, a "revealed" performance that Posa has brought from underwater (they are told) and which he has helped them to re-create. Kambe reminded me during his narrative that this first "above ground" performance is the ancestral event of the very same observance I witnessed in 1981, a year before he told me the story.

Another kind of translation event appears in this same narrative when Posa encourages the warrior Matega to perform like the killer he has been trained to be. He does this while a Jaguar (which he earlier wounded in self-defense while hunting monkeys in the forest) lurks behind the shaman, hoping to take revenge. Posa has the idea of frightening the Jaguar.

> **A2**   *Later Posa told them that all this time the Jaguar had lurked behind him, hiding in his shadow, watching Matega. He was watching as the warrior walked around shouting over and over about how he was going to kill his enemy, kill his enemy the Jaguar.*
>
> *And Posa reminded the Jaguar that this warrior was dangerous when he showed himself that way. He let us know how frightened the Jaguar became at hearing that, how right away the Jaguar began to leave that place. "But I told him to come back the next day, that I had something to tell him." So the next day the Jaguar did come back to Posa, who reminded him how he had almost died because of our bow master.*

I now contrast this translation into performance with the examples below, the story of Tamakafi. The Kalapalo *tafaku oto* "warrior" or "bow master" was a very different sort of person, one whose intelligence was oriented toward hunting and war. While described as exceptionally beautiful, competent killers of other men and animals, and what I have called "readers of signs" (Basso 1995), they also seem to have distanced themselves from the rest of their communities, suffering unresolved conflicts with male relatives and problems with women. Resignation and bitterness are often seen in the speech of warriors whose stories are the subject of Kalapalo biographies. Translations of self-cultivation are usually admonitory didactic discourses, in which embodiments are given special meanings, but on some occasions, meanings given to events by others are cynically rejected by the warrior.

My example here is taken from a story told to me and his family by the ritual song leader Kudyu, about an ancestral figure named Tamakafi. First is my interpretation of Kudyu's introduction of Tamakafi the warrior:

> **B1**   *I'm standing by the fire I've built on the edge of the water, using the stomach medicines that had been prepared the night before, when I see my uncle paddling from across the lake. He's carrying a big pile of arrows in his canoe, and he's staring at me as he paddles toward me. He greets me as he pulls in, but I'm not happy to see him. What does he want of me? Why had he come over this way? He wants me to go with him to collect arrows at the arrow-cane place. I try to get out of it because my dreaming has warned me of just this kind of thing. At night especially, I find myself surrounded by wild pigs, charging at me with their tusks. Other times while I sleep, I'm carried away by horrible female beings—the Yamurikumalu—who keep beating and*

beating me, over and over. That was what I've been going through. But Uncle won't listen to me. He wants to take me away. Because I've been seeing his wife. In the end, I give up arguing with him and agree to go with him. As I walk away to get my own arrows, I can feel him staring at my body. My massive calves. My enormous arms. After all, I'm Tamakafi, the warrior.

There are a number of places in the story where translation events seem to be taking place. There is an entire series of incidents involving his sign readership—for example, in a conversation with his uncle as they cross the lake on the way to a dangerous place. Tamakafi shoots at a fish, but his aim is not accurate and the fish is able to throw off his arrow, a very bad sign. However, Tamakafi interprets the event differently:

B2   *As we traveled out on the middle of the lake, some fish came toward us, some sahundu. Tik. I shot an arrow right at one of them, and as I did that mbuh, the fish fled with the arrow still in its side, and as it did that it shook the arrow off popopo. I managed to spear it. "Leave it, Kid," Uncle told me. "Throw it away." "Let it be," I answered. "Throw it away," he kept telling me. "No, let it be. What happened was my arrow sliced right through here, through its head," I lied. Now I was angry.*

Another translation event takes place as a friend of Tamakafi's is about to die:

B3   *While I'm shooting around me in all directions, Waga dies from his wounds. None of us are going to make it. I realize I can't stop thinking about that. Just then my uncle tells me he's got to leave. My answer to him is he's got to wait until later. He has to wait. Why? Because he's brought me so that some of us will be killed. This time he doesn't try to argue with me.*

    Kuh, kuh, kuh, kuh, kuh. As the arrows keep flying around me, again Uncle tells me he thinks he should go tell the others. Does he think he can get away with that? Again I ask him why he thinks now's the time for him to leave. After all, he's brought me here so that some of us can be killed. Doesn't he want to watch me being killed? Why should he go now? Shamefully, he admits I'm right.

And a third occurs after another friend is left helpless when his weapons are destroyed:

B4   *I can't stop thinking how we're all going to be killed, how we're all going to die right there, just as we are. I realize that the old man had brought us to this place for no other reason than to have this happen to us. I am sure that's the reason. Why else would he have done that to us?*

The next thing I see, Kafagikatu's bow cord snaps. And look, he's the only other one of our group who is left. I'm alone when he comes up to me. I see that he's really frightened because his bow cord has snapped in half. But I remind him that he shouldn't talk about it that way. That he should think carefully how he's eaten the jelly left over from cooking fish. I tell him some-one can die from eating that. That he should think about how he had eaten fish jelly. How he likes to eat hot food. Monkey heads. I remind him that it was the food he had eaten that had done this to him. He tells me he didn't remember about those things. "You spoke with your back to people more than once," I remind him. He's forgotten about that as well, but he never really knew that if he turned away when he was speaking to people, an arrow was going to hit him. He had forgotten that could also make a difference. Speak-ing with our backs to people.

    That was all.

⁓ *(Kudyu's thirteen-year-old son Katsïgï asks from behind his seclusion wall: "Why was he saying that about their speaking?" "Because it affected how fiercely he fought," Kudyu explained. Said Katsïgï fearfully: "It was dangerous to do that." Kudyu: "It certainly was dangerous to do that.")*

Tamakafi's teachings have a moral authority different from those of Posa, who seems (at least in the example I've given) more like a creative artist seeking to have others participate in his imaginative visual understandings. Tamakafi embodies, has embodied experiences of, and also speaks "truths." When Tamakafi comments to Kafagagï about his bow cord, he translates his friend's alarm at the loss of his weapon into a somewhat dispassionate symbolic code. (Remember, they are about to be killed.) In this story, the translation moves from embodied experience into discursive explanation, in which embodied practice is given symbolic meaning. This example actually combines enacted embodiments with the explanation, so to some extent it shares the event of performance with the Posa example. Here though, the didactic context is a critical one, and it takes place in the setting of a battle in which the interlocutors are shortly to be killed. In Tamakafi's story, the warrior serves as a visual model of exceptional strength and prowess in war, and also verbally instructs his fellows in "appropriate" interpretive behavior. Even when he is cynically lying, he teaches them how to make the correct explanatory connections between things.

    The incident thus becomes closely tied to the personal life of that speaker, and Tamakafi then can explain what just happened in a meaningful way; what is more, he can give reasons for what they both know is about to happen. This recording of explanations of events is, I believe, characteristic of many Native American narratives, in that explanations do not appear in the form of conclusions or precepts, and it is left up to the listener to put the pieces of the puzzle together to arrive at an understanding. The Kalapalo is a particularly dramatic example of how interpersonal relations involve learning about oneself through the reporting of experience to another.

In both these stories (Posa and Tamakafi), the leading speakers are shaping and then translating exceptional experiences of self-cultivation into a more public and collective frame. When the shaman speaks in these events he is making accessible to others entirely new experiences reshaped in ways they can understand and embody themselves. The bow master reshapes poorly understood or less skillfully interpreted body techniques. Translation within each of these stories moves from one embodied experience to another, accompanied by didactic, sometimes explanatory discourse that appears to function rather like footnotes in translations between highly incommensurate written languages.

While in neither example are the translations treated as "proposals" that are disputed, clearly in each case the authority of the central figure is respected by his companions of lesser status; these relations of power implicitly shape the reception of what is offered. If we were to look at other instances in which there are real differences of opinion about the choice of equivalents (for example, where Tamakafi rejects the "correct" interpretation of bad signs and insists on continuing with the adventure), we might see the importance of political grounds for reception. Other examples of disputed translation in Kalapalo stories involve tricksters who persuade others to adopt what appear to be self-cultivation practices but which lead to their destruction (Basso 1987).

⁓ I also want to say something about how I am now translating from Kalapalo into English. While my earlier more literal translations of Kalapalo narratives adhered closely to the discourse strategies of Kalapalo storytellers, particularly their considerable use of quoted speech and repetition, my later experiments with translation have come about because many readers have had trouble "finding the story." Earlier, I followed the practice of ethnographers who were beginning to apply some of the ideas of Dennis Tedlock and Dell Hymes in their search for formal poetic structures in oral texts. This certainly was successful for learning how Kalapalo structure their narratives and the various meanings conveyed by conventional structuring devices. Kalapalo quoted voices are highly colored by evidentiality and complex pronouns that help position narrated persons. They are often differentiated from each other by these grammatical features, while narrators only very rarely glossed emotional configurations. But, as much we tried to pay tribute to the conventions used by the original speakers, and in that sense claimed a certain ethnographic "authority" as we worked directly from narratives taped during the story telling, these translation practices can make the stories turgid and difficult to read.

Knowing that I was going to make vast concessions to the very different expectations of American readers, I turned to more European conventions. So far I have experimented with psychonarration, free indirect style, autobiographical voicing, and present-tense narration. As it turns out, I find these have done very little violence to the Kalapalo originals, and in some ways have improved on my more direct translations, in which quoted speech and structures of repeated remarks were organized into lines of poetic-looking texts. While A1 is a translation that often faithfully replicates the patterns of quoted speech, I shift between past- and present-tense narration in order to contrast Posa's experiences of "ordinary life" with his hallucinatory, dreamlike encounters with powerful beings. The second translation style, in A2, uses the first person voice framed by a third person narrator, who we might imagine is someone descended from one of the "ordinary men" present at the revelation of the Zhakwikatu. This translation seems commensurate with the Kalapalo in that the first person narrative style during quoted speech makes it somewhat easier to convey in English the subtleties of biographical "processes" contained in the story. Posa has the experiences he does because of his shamanic skill; he can penetrate the watery barrier and reach powerful beings. He can survive eating their food and return safely home, carrying the gift of food to his wife (so it was real, after all). And later the fact that (unlike "normal" people) he can see (and survive) a visit from these same beings all indexes his shamanic identity. To represent this amazing personage from the perspective of a one-time participant in his personal visions seemed to be a good way of translating this story. After all, those others he told his stories to seem only to have needed to be believers, and this is an important component of the objectified third person voice of the story, as well as of the narrator Kambe. A shaman himself, Kambe never questions, but only describes and in this sense repeats, what he has been told by his own teachers. A contrast has been built between Posa and the other men of his community, including his descendants.

In the Tamakafi story (B1, 2, 3, 4), the tension that dominates this warrior's interpersonal relations suggested to me an autobiographical voicing strategy, with present-tense narration. Together these have really brought out the differences in personality that in the Kalapalo are very clearly represented by the evidentials in the various quoted conversations. Tamakafi is made to appear filled with tension and anxiety, aware of everything and everyone around him. He is impatient and somewhat arrogant toward others, who in turn are incompetent at best, but often unthinking and selfish. Tamakafi's awareness of the effects he has (as an embodied subject) upon the others who share his adventures emerges very clearly as he narrates his story. This also clarifies the reactions he has to the other men around him. To translate the story so as to show Tamakafi understanding his personal power and differences from the others is entirely in keeping with his highly "empiricized" personality, for as a warrior, his training has been designed to develop a heightened awareness and understanding of his body and his surroundings. Hence his particular abilities as a reader of signs.[6]

These examples of Kalapalo translations of self-cultivation and their emergent approach to social life through the translated interpersonal may also serve as the basis for questions about the circulation of meanings in a diasporic and multicultural world, and the consequent shaping within the wide range of transnational negotiations and localizations of what Appadurai calls "mass-mediated sodalities" and "communities of sentiment" (Appadurai 1996). With a focus upon questions of performance, assertion of principles, and protest against their interpretations, of teaching and learning, of matters of witnessing, sponsorship, affirmation, approval, and assent, as well as rejection of an earlier generation's principled life, we go beyond Appadurai's "communities of sentiment" to something more. "Communities of practice" also emerge through the circulation of practice techniques in such multicultural, multisited, and transnational contexts in which performance arts, sport, "self-improvement," and revolutionary, religio-educational movements of all kinds appear. In this regard, Kalapalo practice offers some contributions toward answering questions asked by writers concerned with the ideological grounds that condition the historical production and reception of translations, including Liu's "translingual practice," the proposals of "equivalence" and "commensurability" between languages. Translating self-cultivation, concerned as it is with different ways of communicating knowledge about practice from one domain to another, is a matter of seeking to establish commensurability. Whether this takes place within an existing community of practice, in which something new is introduced by a creative thinker like Posa, or across nations and languages when a new transnational and translingual community is forming, and in the context of developing a postnational organization or "neighborhood" (another Appaduraianism), the translation of self-cultivation involves people in a special effort to link their form of practice to a witnessing self.

What is involved, then, in the development of basic terminologies and specific discursive frames and practices that contribute to a "community of practice"? How do local practitioners recontextualize their own "form texts" into translocal contexts, so that others are taught how to pay attention to what is happening to their own bodies? What are the operant translation factors when the guidance of skilled practitioners is still needed for successful self-cultivation in newly sited contexts? In the Kalapalo examples, we see how two very different personalities offered distinctive and personal translated versions of self-cultivation. One version became a ritual observance still practiced in 2000 in central Brazil. Another (at least in narrative form, maybe in other forms) became a reminder and a warning to future generations of how seriously and carefully warriors were supposed to practice their self-cultivation; self-cultivation practices served explanatory functions as well as other, more manifest functions of skill development. Kudyu's thirteen-year-old son, who listened to his father's story from his seclusion chamber and commented on this very point, seemed aware of this (B3). I suggest we look to other examples of this kind that may be involved in transnational creation of communities of practice that also involve translingual practice. How do people translate such embodied disciplines and imperatives of practice across a range of languages and national sites? I suggest that important contexts for the development of such "communities" involve translingual practices in interpersonal relations. Here I call particular attention to the idea of translations as the invention of performative frames. By enacting these, people can achieve reassurance from the commentary, performances, and narrative explanations of particular others, which in turn may help clarify their own place in the world.

"Translation" has become a metaphor for a wide range of transcultural and transnational negotiations—particularly regarding the languages and practice of East Asian modernities. The word "transcoded" has been used similarly by Stuart Hall to refer to a process of localizing, at different sites, goods, media, and information-processes of marketing consumer lifestyles. It is in this sense that I am particularly concerned here with recontextualizing form texts, form talk, form practice, and form performance. While embodied experiences like those of self-cultivation may not in themselves always be articulated through speech, they constitute interpersonal sites of the doubly translated: a process of communication from the personal and privately embodied into another's accessible and enabling understanding. The kind of translation I have been discussing is speech-centered and interpersonal. "Communities of practice" arise, are debated, spread, and dissolve in the course of such events.

~

Notes

1. The expression "self-cultivation" is itself a perfect example of a neologism, translated from Chinese and Japanese sources, translating the character *(xiu),* as in "cultivating oneself" *(xiuji)* or "cultivating one's person" *(xiushen).* Hall and Ames write: "The character *xiu,* translated 'cultivate,' is most commonly glossed as 'effecting proper order' *(zhi),* in a sociopolitical rather than an organic sense. . . . [T]he cultivation of self as a cultural product allows for a greater degree of creativity than the more restricted horticultural or husbanding metaphors might suggest . . ." (1998, pp. 190–91). "Self-cultivation" in Confucian writings involves the expression and performance of the body. "Self-cultivation" is also offered as a commensurable equivalent to translate the Japanese *shugyo* or simply *"gyo."* A connotation of shugyo, according to the Japanese philosopher Yasuo Yuasa, "is that of training the body; however, it also implies training, as a human being, the spirit or mind by training the body"—a kind of "meditation in motion" (1993, 8).

2. Liu (1995, 1999) describes commensurability as a trope occupying the middle space between two languages, where neologisms are invented within the space of linguistic creativity. See also Bassnett and Trivedi (1999).

3. See discussions by comparative philosophers David L. Hall and Roger T. Ames (1987, 1995, 1998) for Confucian China; Yasuo Yuasa (1993, 1996) for Japan, especially Zen; and Joseph S. Alter (1992, 1999) for India.

4. Returning to the Asian traditions from which I have taken "self-cultivation" as a model, Zen koans, written and oral biographies, and even ink portraits of famous practitioners function in part as teaching aids, and communicate across vast boundaries of language, time, and culture.

5. Bowmasters (tafaku oto) are no longer cultivated by Alto Xingu communities, but they are remembered in especially dramatic biographical narratives. Also, their self-cultivation practices, in much attenuated form, are still occasionally seen during the puberty seclusions of youths (although it seems that this, too,

will be lost with the current generation). Shamans are still important figures in Kalapalo life.

6.   I describe this in greater detail in Basso 1995.

References Cited

Alter, Joseph S. 1992. *The Wrestler's Body: Identity and Ideology in North India.* Berkeley and Los Angeles: University of California Press.

———. 1999. "Heaps of Health, Metaphysical Fitness." *Current Anthropology* 40(suppl.): S43–58.

Appadurai, Arjun. 1996. *Modernity at Large.* Minneapolis: University of Minnesota Press.

Bassnett, Susan, and Harish Trivedi, eds. 1999. *Post-colonial Translation: Theory and Practice.* London and New York: Routledge.

Basso, Ellen B. 1987. *In Favor of Deceit: A Study of Tricksters in an Amazonian Society.* Tucson: University of Arizona Press

———. 1995. *The Last Cannibals.* Austin: University of Texas Press.

———. 1998. "'Interpersonal Relations' in a Kalapalo Shaman's Narratives." Pp. 315–29 in *Theorizing the Americanist Tradition,* ed. Lisa Valentine and Regna Darnell. Toronto: University of Toronto Press.

———. n.d. "Memory and Self-Cultivation." Dinner address, Memory Disorders Research Group, Tucson, 1999.

Collier, George A., et al. 2000. "Socio-economic Change and Emotional Illness among the Highland Maya of Chiapas, Mexico." *Ethos* 28(1): 20–53.

Hall, David L., and Roger T. Ames. 1987. *Thinking through Confucius.* Albany: SUNY Press.

———. 1995. *Anticipating China.* Albany: SUNY Press.

———. 1998. *Thinking from the Han.* Albany: SUNY Press.

Herdt, Gilbert. 1992. "Selfhood and Discourse in Sambia Dream Sharing." Pp. 55–85 in *Dreaming,* ed. Barbara Tedlock. Santa Fe, NM: School of American Research Press.

Liu, Lydia. 1995. *Translingual Practice. Literature, National Culture, and Translated Modernity: China, 1900–1937.* Palo Alto, CA: Stanford University Press.

———. 1999. "The Question of Meaning-Value in the Political Economy of the Sign." Pp. 13–41 in *Tokens of Exchange: The Problem of Translation in Global Circulations,* ed. Lydia Liu. Durham and London: Duke University Press.

Sapir, Edward. 1994. *The Psychology of Culture: A Course of Lectures.* Edited by Judith Irvine. Berlin and New York: M. de Gruyter.

Turner, Terrence. 1995. "Social Body and Embodied Subject: Bodiliness, Subjectivity, and Sociality among the Kayapo." *Cultural Anthropology* 10: 143–70.

Yuasa, Yasuo. 1993. *The Body, Self-cultivation, and Ki-Energy.* Translated by Shigenori Nagamoto and Monte S. Hull. Albany: SUNY Press.

————. 1996 *The Body.* Albany: SUNY Press

Waiting for Light in the Jungle

The Patience of a Koranic School

Mark Münzel

 6

NO POEM IS FOR HIM WHO READS, NO PAINTING FOR HIM WHO VIEWS,
NO SYMPHONY FOR HIM WHO LISTENS.
—Walter Benjamin (1981, 9)

With these words, Walter Benjamin comes to the conclusion that no translation can serve to enlighten the reader as to the original intentions of the author. My paper is about South American Indians. The Koranic School mentioned in the title is merely of metaphorical character, an image of a translation whose intention is not simple, quick comprehension.

I am no specialist in Islamic cultures, and my understanding of them is quite cursory. I have come to know them through various readings, in particular those Koranic Schools in Muslim, but not Arab, countries such as in West Africa, where children learn to read *surahs* by heart despite their not understanding Arabic. This image is surely superficial to the point of being false, for in reality Arabic is also taught in the aforementioned Koranic Schools. But I want to use it only as a metaphor. The image of children patiently studying an incomprehensible text in a foreign language, their fingers gliding over letters they cannot decode, seems to me a liberating, antipedagogical vision over and against the terror and intent of modern educational theory in transmitting clarity and enlightenment.

I consider the pedagogy of these (somewhat simplified for the sake of my argument, and from Islamic reality distant) Koranic Schools of my imagination as "pedagogy of hope." It is pedagogy founded on the hope that what is learned mechanically today may one day make sense, by way of holy enlightenment.

Naturally this reactionary, religious didactic style stands in opposition to modern didactic methods. The Koranic Schools of West Africa are only waiting, desperately, for modern Western educational theorists who will replace the rote memorization of nonsensical formulas with fun learning games. The teacher, wielding an edible Barbie doll, will ask, "Is this the Prophet?" and when a student answers, "Yeah!" he will be rewarded with the doll, which he will eat, proof that learning is fun. It is the fun that matters, and the quick realization of simple comprehension.

- Despite their opposition, both educational methods, the Pedagogy of Fun and the Pedagogy of Hope for Holy Enlightenment, can be seen as two sides of one coin: In the Koranic School the student will learn that he does not understand everything. One hopes that this state of mind will someday help him to understand.
- In the nonconfrontational school where learning is fun, the student is given the illusion that he understands something, and one hopes that he does not later realize (someday, should he ever read a book) that he hasn't learned a thing.

The point of both learning systems is not so much to *induce* understanding as to develop a *specific state of mind* that can help the students either to open themselves to understanding (in the case of the West African Koranic School) or to close themselves off (in the case of the nonconfrontational school). Neither system has the intent of instilling in students immediate understanding, or the ability to repeat an idea in their own words.

I would like here to plead for the pedagogy of the Koranic School, with this one difference: that I am more interested in enlightenment—not through the grace of God but via thoughtful consideration in combination with a type of translation that Frobenius first termed *Ergriffenheit* ("passionate surrender"). The term later developed, in the course of other translations, into *ilinx* (Caillois 1967 [1958], 67–75); *appréhension concrète du réel* (Duvignaud 1973, 129–67, in his chapter on Frobenius); or "surrender" (Wolff 1994, summarizing Wolff 1976 and earlier papers). With Wilhelm Emil Mühlmann (1981, 15–18 *et passim*) it became *pathologische Betrachtungsweise* (from *passio* = "suffering") or *passionierte Erkenntnis*, and finally *passiones* with Fritz Kramer (1984), in philological variation on and reference to Lucien Lévy-Bruhl.

⁓ "Kaa! Kaa! Kaa!" *Our ancestors, the old Kamayurá ran yelling through the forest, they were searching. The wood answered them, "Ka'a! Ka'a! Ka'a! Ka'a!" The Kamayurá listened, "He is there! That must be him!" They ran there to see. They ran yelling. The humans were looking for the moon. (free translation after Münzel 1973, 52)*

In the language of the Kamayurá (a small Tupí-speaking community on
the southern edge of the Brazilian Amazon region) the exclamation *kaa* indicates
anxiety and sometimes despair. The sound is a single, drawn-out "a." If one pro-
nounces the word with two short "a" sounds, *ka'a*, then it means "forest" and to
a degree "wood."[1] So at least I was told in 1968, while living among these Indians
and tape-recording the myths they told me. The narrator (named Snake)[2] spoke
the word with a single, drawn-out /a/ and expressed thereby the desperation of the
search for light. But it becomes clear, in the course of the tale, that they were in fact
rather looking for wood (spoken with two short "a" sounds) and that the initial
pronunciation misleads him who listens to the tale.

Just like the ancestors who were being misled because they were searching
for wood (instead of the moon), I was misled because I was not looking for it.
Snake demonstrated to me my ignorance in the course of the tale: he suddenly
spoke so quickly that I hardly had a chance to understand him. Later, as I was
listening to the tape with the help of a translator, I discovered that he had asked if
I understood: "If yes, then answer me!" I did not understand him and did not answer. No longer was the ignorance of the ancestors (searching in the wrong place)
the theme of the myth, but rather the ignorance of the researcher, who only later
understood what one was trying to tell him.

The myth tells of the ancestors, blinded by fear, running through the dark
forest looking for light. They are looking for the moon, and he shouts to them,
"Here I am!" But the humans would not hear him. Instead they heard the wood
of the trees calling. Maybe it was only the echo of their own desperate calls, their
kaa! kaa! being returned as ka'a! ka'a! ("Forest! Forest!"). One has to understand
that the humans themselves are in fact made of wood, and the voice of the wood is
actually their own. The moon warns them not to follow the wood, but they do not
hear him in time. Too late they realize that they are on the wrong trail.

The fateful mistake will forever repeat itself. The moon is made of stone,
and stone is immortal. Since the people chased after the wood and not the stone,
they gave up the chance to be immortal (see Münzel 1990). Actually they chose
themselves, since they too are made of wood. They felt comfortable there, where
the wood grows. Ever since then the people are alive and warm like the wood;
they enjoy life, are not cold like the stone. But ever since then they are also mortal
like wood, suffer pain, and eventually die. They never became like their heavenly
models, the moon and the sun.

This narrative continues with a series of episodes in which the mistakes
of the people are illuminated. Moon and sun try again and again to make them

immortal, but their attempts are always undone by failings of the humans, who one time lie, another time lack sufficient bravery, and whose men always choose the beauty of the women over immortality. The ancestors were right in the end, say the narrators of the myths, because life is much nicer now, and we could not live as cold stones.

> God defeated the night by sending out godly light. He collected this light in a special clay pot. This pot broke, unfortunately. Potsherds fell to earth and were spread all over the earth. The light spread, as did the shards, all over the earth in the form of (no longer a single bright light, but:) a singular dispersed glittering light. It was a great misfortune. The original godly light was lost.
>
> But: In fact it was good so. We people could hardly live in the whole glowing light of God. Our life is so beautiful because we always see single sparkles of God's light. And further: If these sparkles of light were all bundled together instead of spread out throughout the world, then we would not be able to see the Evil (that is as everyone knows dark). One would not be able to find it, and that will be necessary when the Messiah comes:
>
> Then it will be necessary, with the help of the sparkles of light spread all over the earth, to hunt down and destroy the Evil in the dark. One could not do that if the original clay pot of godly light were not destroyed. Only when the Evil has been hunted down can the pot be restored and the Eternal Empire of Peace be restored.

Walter Benjamin based his work, "*Die Aufgabe des Übersetzers*"—which can be translated as "The Task of the Translator," but also as "The Translator's Surrender"—on the myth of the Jewish Cabala just recited (Scholem 1983, 66–67; see also Moses 1992). The translator can never end a translation; he never manages to grasp the whole light—only single sparkles.

From Jewish mysticism to a mythology of the Indians of the Amazon is quite a distance. Only on the outer edges can one find similarities, connections that are naturally not historical but rather of universal human thought or a misunderstanding on the part of the reader.

Both myths are about godly light that people are searching for but can no longer find, because it is spread out in the darkness. And in both cases it is better that way. If Michael Pauen's (1997, 346) interpretation of Benjamin, and mine of the Kamayurá myth, are accurate, neither Benjamin nor the Kamayurá draws that radical line so familiar to Western dualism that we often accuse the (in fact more liberal) Jewish and Islamic traditions of it, between the dark present and the bright empire of light almost impossible to reach.

Walter Benjamin transcribes the image of light (and the clay pot for the light), dispersed on the earth but not lost, to the problem of translation and the understanding of a foreign text. Just as in the Cabalist teachings (which Benjamin never explicitly mentioned, although they were familiar to him) of the breaking of the pot and the spreading out of the light, only to be collected again at some distant time together with the clay pot, a "messianic end" of history will one day come when a translation will reveal the deeper meaning of the (until then mutually incomprehensible) languages (Benjamin 1981, 14). That will nonetheless never be possible if the translations attempt, long before the messianic end, to elicit meaning too clearly, instead of following the original so literally that it will remain incomprehensible. Only through incomprehensibility can the deeper quality of the original be maintained. The shattered pot can be reconstructed only if the individual shards are returned, piece by piece, to their original place, and not through an attempt to build a new, more beautiful, but different vessel.

Benjamin demands patience from the translator and his reader. The meaning can not become immediately apparent, but at some time in the future and in hindsight, because "all translation is only a temporary way of dealing with the otherness of a language" (ibid.). In that time the conception of that otherness changes and affects the original. The reader of a translation may understand it differently and (sometimes) better than it was originally intended: "Because in the course of its continued existence, which could not be named thus, if it were not the change and renewal of a living object, the original changes. There exists a fermentation of the written word, even after it has been written down" (ibid., 12).

Samuel Weber combines Benjamin's sentence with a section of Laurence Sterne's novel *The Life and Opinions of Tristram Shandy, Gentleman,* in which the reversal of time is thematized: it is the law that things do not rise, but fall; the father is not descended from the son; and therefore, the son is legally related to the father, and not the reverse. Yet to deny this relationship is nonsense. For Benjamin the father is related to the son. The one-dimensional nature of the legally recognized direction father to son "undermines the very continuity it seems to create," because in reality the original also changes over time, "because it belongs to a medium that is always changing: language" (Weber 1997, 132, 133; cf. Sterne 1996 [1760–67], 230–31).

⟋⟍ Indian mythology has become an example for me of this principle of understanding foreign texts that can only be understood over time, whose meaning becomes clear in the course of a continuously expanding, changing translation in one's own mind.

Similar to the Cabalistic, and, generally speaking, all myths, the Indian myth presents images that we may first think are the whole story. But behind them are concealed further images and deeper meanings, like Russian dolls, whose smaller, hidden incarnations (the surface of which cannot match the glitter of its immediate predecessor) nevertheless make it superfluous.

To return to Snake's tale: the search for the moon hides a whole philosophy of Light. Light (in the way of speaking of that Indian culture) also has the meaning of "Truth," perhaps also of "contemporaneousness." While these (still relatively simple) connections are apparent for most Indian listeners and only create initial problems for us Western researchers, some of the secondary meanings might remain a mystery even for some members of the narrator's community. It is not a question of secret knowledge, but rather of various interpretations that do not interest everyone. A youth, fresh from his initiation into the world of adulthood may be interested in discovering in the myth ways of climbing up the social ladder and be less interested in speculation on the nature of Knowledge or Truth.

In the story, humans are looking for the light in the form of moon, who nonetheless does not shine the brightest. He is but younger brother to sun. Moon is clumsy. Something always happens to him (that is why he dies again and again), and sun has to help him out of the mess, returning him to life. The humans, in searching for moon (much less the wood) are right from the beginning on the wrong path to finding sun and thereby finding true knowledge.

The word for "sun" in the language of the Kamayurá is *kwat*. This word sounds (linguistically by chance, but that does not bother the riddler, who is less interested in linguistics than in sound) very much like the word for "knowledge," *kwa'ap*. This sound is again similar to the already mentioned ceremonial word for "wood," ka'a.

When humans search for the wood they are almost looking for "knowledge," except that they make a mistake at the beginning of the word: they forget the "w." If on the other hand they were looking for the sun, they would again be near the right path, only this time they make a mistake at the end of the word. Here they end on "t" instead of "ap." Ka'a—kwa'ap—kwat—knowledge is neither wood nor sun but somewhere in between. Humans can search only for one thing or the other; never will they be able to find both at the same time.

~ I am not sure if this is what Snake really meant as he was telling me the myth. I do know that he loved such word games and that later, a relative of his drew my attention to the similarity of the three words to one another. The longer I thought about it, the more questions I had. Only I cannot ask them, as Snake has since passed away. His younger relatives and members of his community know the myth, but they tell it in nonidentical versions. I have not since heard the beginning with the searching calls in the dark forest. Questioning the people today about what Snake meant, or playing them the tape recording, is not possible, because the Kamayurá refuse to remember the dead.

A strange dialogue took shape, because the Indian side did not "really" participate, except in my own head. Other Indians did "really" speak in the place of Snake, but they left Snake himself (whose text was at issue) out of the "real" conversation, because they would not and could not talk about the dead, much less even think about them. They gave me clues as to what Snake might have meant, but always without mentioning him personally. Thus I could never be sure.

Snake's story has remained with me over the years. It is no longer what it once was when I heard it for the first time. Instead, its meaning has changed for me again and again. The story and I, and maybe Snake in my mind, have moved on.

~ Three years after I heard the story, I was doing research in Paraguay among the Aché (a Tupí-Guaraní group related to the Kamayurá) and spent much time in conversation with another researcher, León Cadogan, who had delved deeply into the philosophy of the Guaraní (another Tupí-Guaraní group related to both the Aché and the Kamayurá). I read all the works of Cadogan and others I could find—authors who had written about the Guaraní—and I listened to Cadogan speak, slowly and quietly, in a darkened room, rocking to and fro in his rocking chair, hiding from the midday sun.

The locus of the Guaraní philosophy, I learned, was the Word, the Guaraní equivalent of what we would call our *soul* (see, e.g., Cadogan 1952). Cadogan spoke slowly because he was very sick. He sat in the rocking chair because he was very tired. He died soon after.

Eighteen years later I was again in Brazil and met the former administrator of the reservation where the Kamayurá lived. Orlando Villas Boas (and his brother Cláudio) had lived with the Indians of this reservation for twenty-five years, had heard innumerable myths, and had published some of them (see esp. Villas Boas 1970).

Now we were sitting in the comfortable chill of a subtropical evening on the veranda of the retired administrator's São Paulo house, and he was telling me about the meaning behind the myths. Behind the colorful mythic creatures stood an ultimate deity, and that is: Knowledge.

I mention the context in which I learned from these experts because they have influenced my understanding. The atmosphere in the room of the old Paraguayan academic (darkened because of the midday heat) was sad and made one think of death, but it was at the same time peaceful and protected from the heat and the blinding light. On the veranda of the Brazilian administrator I found the approaching darkness beautiful. The hectic noise of a city inhabited by twenty millions ebbed away to leave a freshness—and a view of the moon. There was a contrast between the bright, oppressive sun and the (although less lively) comfort of darkness. And as I thought back to the Indian myth, I remembered not only the meaning of "knowledge" but also the contrast of Light and Night.

～ At first I was interested only in the more general philosophy of the myth. I had studied anthropology in the 1960s, and no one had bothered to tell me that Indians could think philosophically. Of course, several pioneers of African ethnography, such as Placide Tempels, Marcel Griaule, Geneviève Calame-Griaule, and Germaine Dieterlen, had earlier written about abstract and very complex philosophical systems, but they were accused of building up primitive African religions with European philosophical concepts.

To my naive questions—along the lines that, might there not be something to it, and might it not be the same with South American Indians—I received the response that Indians think on a more practical level. From someone who knew his way around Amazon fishing, whom I asked about Indian ideas about fish (their important source of food), I was told to go back home: Indians didn't think about fish, they only ate them.

After all these answers, which angered me and left me defiantly looking for philosophy, I was told myths by Amazon Indians that were (for me quite obviously) philosophical. The already mentioned narrative is obviously about transience and eternity, about the nature of humankind, who are cheerful liars, and about truth.

~ 6

⌒ᴗ Having returned from the Indian village, I lived for several weeks in a zoo-logical garden (in Bélem, where residences had been arranged for scientists who were visiting the Ethnographic Museum on the same property). I saw otters here for the first time and could observe them easily: they hunted fish. And the scales fell from my eyes: the myth, which is also about fish and otters, describes very realistically the behavior of these animals, which can be understood without any philosophy.

This does not necessarily contradict the previous philosophic interpretation: the mythical fish represent the ancestors of the Kamayurá, and the otter is, for the fish and thereby the people, an archenemy. In the end, opposed to zoological reality, the fish defeat the otters, but the threat remains because the fish (and the humans) chose mortality.

⌒ᴗ Later, while I was deep in the philosophy of the Guaraní and the Aché, who at that time had been much better researched than the Kamayurá, I turned my attention to the meaning of the "Word," which is like the "soul." It is possible to read the religion of the Guaraní as a philosophy of words in which one has to differentiate carefully between types of words and of speech, inasmuch as each has something to do with other aspects of human existence (see, e.g., Meliá et al. 1976; Chamorro 1998).

Only now I became aware, as a process of memory, of the importance of the wordplay and the difference between the right and the wrong Word among the Kamayurá. The myth begins with the confusion of words: the people yell "wood" instead of "knowledge," "moon" instead of "sun," and are thereby searching for transience and darkness. They lie later and say the wrong thing; give sun and moon, who want to help them, the wrong information; and thus expose themselves to the possibility of death. Again and again the people say the wrong word at the right time.

⌒ᴗ I read Walter Benjamin much later. Only then did I remember that the word kwa'ap in the language of the Kamayurá means not only "knowledge" but also something along the lines of "understanding." In Benjamin's text the good translator not only helps with the comprehension of a story but also estranges the language that he is translating. He delivers words that one cannot understand because the strange, incomprehensible language is maintained to such a degree that "the meaning is touched on but like harp is by the wind" (Benjamin 1981, 21).

The reader needs patience: he must wait until one day the meaning opens itself to him. The original text is changed thus, because we understand it differently. Perhaps that is what Snake meant to tell me, when he put me to the test already mentioned, from which I learned that I had understood nothing—and that little that I had understood, I would understand much later.

Of course I am reading Benjamin from an anthropological and not a "benjamin-ological" perspective. Although he is thinking about texts of a religious or philosophical nature "above all the religious" (ibid.), and thereby about the European or Asian equivalents of Indian myths, he nevertheless refers only to written texts. The myths of Amazon Indians are of a completely different, oral medium.

Snake's narrative was not meant to be recorded, nor to be interpreted anew in the process of a century-long *interpretatio verbi sacri*. The narrator had come to know the tape recorder as a technical device only a few years earlier, and he was not yet conscious of the consequences of fixing a text for eternity. He spoke for the moment, and the joke he made (of asking me to prove that I could understand and translate his words) was meant to provide laughter only slightly removed in time.

The difficulty for me is that I do not want to stop understanding his text, even long after his death, when he can no longer explain anything. This is also the difficulty with understanding a European holy text, whose authors are just as dead, but those men had thought during the course of their lives about the immortality of their texts. Snake, on the other hand, can be understood only if one considers that he never wanted to live forever.

Moreover, Benjamin wrote only about the problem of translating a text, while I am interested in the translated understanding of a whole culture. Anthropology (as Wolfdietrich Schmied-Kowarzik writes) developed out of "Georg Forster's [that is, its founder's] intuitive oscillating between observation of the other and one's own interpretation thereof," and grew to become Clifford Geertz's recognition of the "responsibility of the author" (Schmied-Kowarzik 1998, 22). We cannot ignore our own subjectivity. But this sometimes depressing observation is not the theme of my paper. It is more about the theme of hope for future enlightenment that we find in Benjamin: "No poem is for him who reads, no painting for him who views, no symphony for him who listens." Actually, I prefer to understand this confusing rejection as a recognition: the poem is for the *future* reader of its translation, the picture for the *future* viewer.

Of course Snake was not thinking of me thirty years in the future, or of my descendants, but nevertheless at least a few hours later. And the teller of a myth knows that his text may, generations later, develop new uses. The anthropologist can learn patience here. He is subject to the expectation that he will understand a new culture very quickly. The happy revelation of having understood something is intoxicating, and he thinks to be able to understand a culture if only he can make a clear and simple translation of it. This may work superficially for some functional relationships, if one keeps the observed area small and consequences of further developments vague (for example: "if the animals die, the shepherd will most likely be unhappy"). But for complex texts, this would be too cocksure and presumptuous. My gradual understanding of Snake's myth has taken decades. And I have not understood more, only differently.

If we replace Walter Benjamin's "sacred text" with an Indian myth, and his concept of translation with interpretation, then the meaning of an anthropological "translation" (the attempt to understand) becomes clearer. Paul de Man teaches us about Walter Benjamin's text that we should not take "the relationship between translation and original as an analogy of natural processes of similarity or of derivation through formal analogy" too lightly, or accept easy explanations; "rather we should understand the original from the perspective of its translation" (de Man 1997, 183).

 Educational experiences, readings, and conversations have changed my understanding of the (apparently unchanging) text. But I remain patient. The older I become, the better I understand Snake—possibly because I forget how it really was.

Notes

1. This refers not to the common language but to the ceremonial idiom.
2. As the names of dead Kamayurá must not be spoken out, I do not indicate here the full indigenous name, but its approximate translation.

References Cited

Benjamin, Walter. 1981 [1924]. *Die Aufgabe des Übersetzers*. Pp. 9–21 in *Gesammelte Schriften*, vol. 4., ed. T. Rexroth. Frankfurt am Main: Suhrkamp.

Cadogan, León. 1952. "El concepto guaraní de 'Alma'—su interpretación semántica." *Folia Lingüística Americana* (Buenos Aires) 1: 31–34.

Caillois, Roger. 1967 [1958]. *Les jeux et les hommes: Le masque et le vertige.* Folio essais, 184. Paris: Gallimard.

Chamorro, Graciela. 1998. "A espiritualidade guarani: Uma teologia ameríndia da palavra." Teses e Dissertações, 10. São Leopoldo: Sinodal.

de Man, Paul. 1997 [1897]. "Schlußfolgerungen: Walter Benjamins 'Die Aufgabe des Übersetzers.'" Pp. 182–228 in *Übersetzung und Dekonstruktion,* ed. A. Hirsch. Frankfurt am Main: Suhrkamp.

Duvignaud, Jean. 1973. *Le langage perdu: Essai sur la différence anthropologique.* Paris: Presses Universitaires de France.

Kramer, Fritz. 1984. "Notizen zur Ethnologie der Passiones." Pp. 297–313 in *Ethnologie als Sozialwissenschaft,* ed. E. W. Müller et al. (Kölner Zeitschrift für Soziologie und Sozialpsychologie, Sonderheft 26/1984). Opladen: Westdeutscher Verlag.

Melià, Bartomeu, and Georg and Friedl Grünberg. 1976. "Etnografía del paraguay contemporáneo: Los Paï-Tavyterã." *Suplemento Antropológico* (Asunción del Paraguay) 11(1–2): 151–295.

Mosès, Stéphane. 1992. *L'ange de l'histoire.* Paris: Seuil.

Mühlmann, Wilhelm Emil. 1981. *Die Metamorphose der Frau: Weiblicher Schamanismus und Dichtung.* Berlin: Reimer.

Münzel, Mark. 1973. *Erzählungen der Kamayurá, Alto Xingú—Brasilien.* Wiesbaden: Franz Steiner.

———. 1990. "Mythisches Bewußtsein (am Beispiel einer Erzählung brasilianischer Indianer)." Pp. 174–85 in *Wie alt sind unsere Märchen?* ed. C. Oberfeld. Regensburg: Erich Röth.

Pauen, Michael. 1997. *Dithyrambiker des Untergangs: Gnostizismus in Ästhetik und Philosophie der Moderne.* Berlin: Akademie.

Schmied-Kowarzik, Wolfdietrich. 1998. "Vom Verstehen fremder Kulturen: Philosophische Reflexionen zur Ethnologie als Kulturwissenschaft." Pp. 1–24 in *Georg-Forster-Studien,* vol. II, ed. H. Dippel and Helmut Scheuer. Berlin: Berlin Verlag.

Scholem, Gershom. 1983. *Walter Benjamin und sein Engel: Vierzehn Aufsätze und kleine Beiträge,* ed. R. Tiedemann. Frankfurt am Main: Suhrkamp.

Sterne, Laurence. 1996 [1760–67]. *The Life and Opinions of Tristram Shandy, Gentleman.* Herfordshire: Wordsworth.

Villas Boas, Orlando, and Cláudio. 1970. *Xingu: Os índios, seus mitos.* São Paulo: Edibolso.

Weber, Samuel. 1997. "Un-Übersetzbarkeit: Zu Walter Benjamins Aufgabe des Übersetzers." Pp. 121–45 in *Die Sprache der Anderen: Übersetzungspolitik zwischen den Kulturen,* ed. A. Haverkamp. Frankfurt am Main: Fischer Taschenbuch Verlag.

Wolff, Kurt H. 1976. *Surrender and Catch: Experience and Inquiry Today.* Dordrecht: Reidel.

———. 1994. "Surrender and the Other." *Anthropological Journal on European Cultures* 3: 155–68.

Linguist and Anthropologist as Translators

Volker Heeschen

Translation and Antitranslation

Man transposes, transforms, and translates. The phenomena of *Sprachbund* presuppose translation practices in everyday life, such as occur in multilingual areas like Northwest Amazonia, some Pacific islands, or special areas in Aboriginal Australia. Translation chains of fairy tales and sacred and nonsacred narratives show how speakers and narrators move from one language to the other (Roth 1998). In these chains, narratives of one community are made public in the neighboring one. Style, contents, and meaning are inevitably changed, embellished, elaborated, pidginized, reduced to plot structure, and so on. In everyday talk the speech of one speaker or narrator is repeated, corrected, clarified, and translated from the speaker's code into that of the hearer or the audience.

In the encounter—or clash—of cultures, misunderstandings occur. Time and again mountain Papuans are accused of murder. Missionaries or administrators have heard that someone was killed when, in fact, he was only beaten, the corresponding verb meaning "beat, hunt (marsupials), kill (pigs)." For murder the idiom "beat sufficiently or up to the end" must be used. After conversion, and while still keeping to their traditional understanding of managing conflicts, these Papuans turn "What? shall we receive good at the hand of God, and shall we not receive evil?" (Job 2:10) into "We receive good at the hand of God, why shall we receive evil?" And the famous verse (Matthew 5:39), "Whosoever shall smite thee on thy right cheek, turn to him the other also," is immediately turned into "If somebody smites thee on thy right cheek, do not turn to him the other also."

Natural translation, then, is a way of moving across all kinds of boundaries, boundaries that are established consciously through a kind of antitranslation. Man's thriftiness with new information in small communities, secret languages, identity as a process of pseudo-speciation, the ubiquitous techniques of irony, allusion, veiled speech, and figures of speech put barriers between individuals, clans, men's house communities, members of different hamlets and inhabitants of neighboring valleys. Aesthetic forms require translations of everyday talk into enigmatic structures. Texts can be reduced to strings of proper names without any necessary translation. Songs and poems are likely to show both simple grammatical structures and rich imagery, making translation difficult or even impossible.

Under these conditions, understanding requires much explanatory comment and evaluation of differing interpretations. Translation is no longer a way of looking for equivalences, but a method of teasing out culture-specific information related to words, pairings of words, the sequence of verses, and the technique of the *parallelismus membrorum*. The richness of commentary and interpretation may lead to appreciation of yet more reasons for what is called provisionally "antitranslation" (cf. Heeschen 1990). Small societies impose reserve, discretion, and unobtrusive speech behavior in face-to-face communication; in order to express one's own desires, needs, and ideas, one has to use the aesthetic and artistic means suitable for exclusive communication (cf. Heeschen 2001).

Transforming and translating, then, form part of man's everyday communicative behavior. Anthropologists transform observations, nonverbal symbols, behavior, and rituals into texts. They textualize oral performances, and, as a result, isolated texts are transferred a second time into the framework of the original culture. Clements (1996, 11), summarizing Asad, Lienhardt, and Shaw, says that translation and "textualization should definitely be regarded as part of the ethnographic enterprise." Furthermore, following from the ethnologist's experience of learning to live another life, "worldview differences" and cultures—that is, different symbol systems—must be presented in order to establish equivalences, approximations, "cultural translations," and a descriptive metalanguage. Modern authors strike Humboldtian and neo-Humboldtian positions in which each translation moves from one worldview to another (cf. Gipper 1972, 90–91).

The "dignity of translation work" is recognized by Clements and the authors he quotes and by, for example, the contributors to Swann's *On the Translation of Native American Literatures*. It can be traced back to Schleiermacher and Humboldt and (re)discovered in modern hermeneutics (Gadamer) or its postmodern opponents (Derrida). However, the importance of translating is reflected neither in linguistic fieldwork nor in ethnological practice (see below). There may be at least two reasons for this—namely, the apparent irrelevance of theory for translation practice in the field, and the seeming irrelevance of discovery procedures for the final, textualized presentation of the data.

This contribution follows the course of these discrepancies. First, it is almost too great a distance from Schleiermacher's *Dialektik* or Wilhelm von Humboldt's translation of Aeschylus' *Agamemnon* to translating from a Papuan language into English, Indonesian, or German.[1] Second, I think that philology mediates between theory and practice (see next section). In order to know the meanings of words and idioms, the fieldworker and translator must collect and use all kinds of information, especially if the meaning is hidden in nonverbal symbol systems (see elsewhere in this chapter). Third, the fieldworker and translator experience uncertainties whenever they hear a new word, evaluate metaphors and idioms, or translate myths, songs, or fairy tales. A self-account of his or her competence in the source language is a prerequisite for accurate presentation of data (see below). Giving a self-account by showing the construction of the data reduces the second kind of discrepancy.

In the communities where I have worked, the languages were initially unknown. We had to begin by translating and understanding even simple words, gestures, and all other kinds of communicative behavior. Translating was an everyday practice that slowly enlarged the language islands in the sea of nonverbal behaviors and culturally defined situations. It is this unique experience that assigns the status of philological mediation and that of self-account of the participant's competence to translation work. I will hint at some examples of my practice: looking for equivalences of so-called abstract notions, working on fragmentary texts, and talking about ephemeral speech.

Some Preliminaries: Understanding and the Philology of Ephemeral Utterances

When the author was asked after his periods of fieldwork which of the linguistic theories had been most useful to him, he could only point to the university courses on Middle High German or the Iguvine Tablets. The difference between an autonomous linguistic science and one that regards language as embedded in culture, sociology, and the principles of speaking appears immediately. Philologists prepare translation work. Fieldwork cannot form part of autonomous linguistics. The translator has to use all kinds of information given by neighboring disciplines. The philologist enlarges all the questions that the field researcher or the descriptive linguist, interested in ethnological problems, excludes from his examinations because they are historical. The field researcher elicits the meaning of speech acts just enacted, which he nevertheless has to present in written grammars or independent compilations of texts. The philologist interprets old texts, the language of which either has completely perished or, because it comes from an earlier period in the development of the language, is no longer understood without commentary. It is her or his task to restore the cultural and social environment so that what appears as a detemporalized work can again be understood as a contextually occurring "speech act."

In the opinion of Anttila (1973, 177), linguists, in contrast to philologists, occupy an extreme position in that they "hold the view that all connections between language and nonlinguistic matters can be disregarded" (my translation of the original German). That is exactly what the philologist does not do: "for he studies language in the totality of its cultural references including all possible relations to the way of life of the people (customs, objects of art and of daily use, etc.). That is, he uses language and linguistics in connection with history, archaeology, folklore, the science of comparative religion, and so forth" (ibid., my translation). The attempt to establish linguistics as an autonomous science with an object exclusively its own is at the same time an attempt to free it from the traditional connection with philology and auxiliary disciplines (Jäger 1987, 198–200). The contrary process—namely, the interweaving of an autonomous linguistic science with other disciplines—took place during the last three decades without including philology. "What philologists have always done is only now penetrating into synchronic linguistics as a theoretical necessity. Through sociolinguistics, anthropological linguistics, ethnolinguistics, and psycholinguistics the cultural sphere has become part of linguistic theory. In other words, these disciplines are synchronic philology" (Anttila 1973, 184–85, my translation).

Although Ehlich (1981), as well as Anttila and Jäger, attacks the idea of linguistic autonomy with the help of the insights of philology, he defines the differences between field research, philology, and autonomous linguistics more exactly. The field researcher who starts to work at a language unknown to him uses the classical type of "native speaker": "This type of native speaker bridges the gap to an alien world. . . . [He] opens the doors to the linguist's destination, the treasuries of unknown languages and culture" (ibid., 154). The second type of "native speaker," according to Ehlich, is the linguist himself: he himself answers for "the fundamental capacities and competences that are in play when people talk." The philologist cannot call on either type of speaker for assistance but must instead deal with "detached texts"—that is, texts the understanding of which is not aided either by an immediate context of speaking or by the contemporary cultural setting. Ehlich defines the philologist as a secondary hearer—that is, a reader: "We may say, then, that the philologist is a *contingent hearer/reader* of a text, the term 'contingent' being taken in its exact philosophical sense" (ibid., 159). In order to overcome the distance between himself and the text, the philologist proceeds in two different ways: as a field researcher who undertakes to elicit the meaning of a speech act with the help of other disciplines, and as a linguistic "native speaker" who proceeds introspectively and can rely on his competence. The difference is that the philologist has to take great pains to build up his competence with the help of those other auxiliary disciplines.

In the practice of research the differences between philologist and field-worker are obscured. On one hand, the real "native speaker" cannot explain and clarify everything that interests the linguist, so that even in the foreign speech community he continues to depend on assumptions and intuitions. On the other hand, a lot of work has to be done by the field researcher far away from all the informants. Not only does he or she have to construe a grammar out of the chaos of field notes, but, in addition, the translation and interpretation of collected texts often is little different from the work of the philologist. In the case of the philologist the temporal gap is wide, while in the case of the field researcher it is small. But both may be aided by works on botany, comparative religion, or kinship systems. At home an arsenal of libraries assists him. In the field he is assisted by the questions he asks the informants in ever varying form and in growing despair, and often he does not even understand the answers.

All the authors herein agree that there is no direct approach to the data, whether they are historical texts or utterances by speakers of "exotic" languages in the ethnographic present. A direct approach could exist only if one could eliminate the disparity between general laws of cognition, which at the same time are considered a prerequisite for each act of cognition, and utterances that are historically conditioned and that differ between speech communities and individuals.

This also would presuppose a timeless point of view, independent historical processes. Each translation and each interpretation of a foreign text or of an utterance, taken down as example, comment, or text, can only proceed hypothetically. It presupposes meaning and devises a general conception that guides the comprehension of single sentences and words in order either to confirm or to dismiss the presupposed meaning. This process can be repeated again and again, with all available aid. It is a process of approximation that may never end. It is, in fact, the hermeneutic cycle.

The philological process of understanding in which subject and object are not thought to have timeless validity, but rather consist of a dialogue between speaker and hearer "caught in the web" of their own subjectivity, was first and most thoroughly thought through by Schleiermacher, the translator of Plato and interpreter of the Holy Scripture. Cognizing and understanding are inseparable from speech. As early as 1804, even before Wilhelm von Humboldt's great works, Schleiermacher pointed to the identity of speaking and cognizing. Cognizing and understanding, however, are not only bound to single languages or, in Schleiermacher's words, to certain *Sprachkreise*, but also to certain epochs or even to singular speech acts during the life of one individual or author.

The problem of understanding becomes salient not only when speaker and hearer want to understand each other despite linguistic and epochal differences, but even between two individuals speaking the same language and belonging to the same culture. Every understanding is an act in which meaning is negotiated. Seen from the ability of humans to speak to and understand other humans, this restriction of the initial position, the unalterable difference, is no absolute obstacle. Thinking and understanding proceed from concrete, ordinary events and coincidences, and they remain inseparable from speech. Pure thinking and advanced acts of understanding only gradually liberate themselves from engagement with what has accidentally developed from the subjectivity of speaker and hearer or author and reader.

The irrationality of linguistic differences, however, cannot be abolished by logical constructions or rationalized by making the plurality of languages itself the subject of a theory of cognition. In the same way, the differences between two individuals cannot be eliminated merely by their common culture and language. The annihilation of differences is inherent in dialogue and, in fact, dialectics. But this annihilation can only be conceived as a historical process of never-ending approximation. In the end, Schleiermacher has to return to an ontological principle embracing all mankind in order to be able to set up a concept of truth. Leaving aside the epistemological problems, one can claim for philology that it is the art and the science of annihilating differences between a text and its reader or between speaker and hearer. For this process Ehlich coined the very fitting expression "dealienation." It can be applied to the fieldworker as well as to the philologist.

Given the tasks of the field researcher, I would point out one thing regarding dealienation. The cyclical nature of knowledge begins with the understanding of a foreign utterance and grows more certain through reconstruction of the general setting and subsequent returns to that utterance. This cycle is repeated in the work of the descriptive grammarian and the ethnologist as long as both of them collect information, and observe and categorize data. Each act of speaking is, above all, individualized, appropriate for certain situations, and embedded in the special methods of achieving understanding within a culture. In Schleiermacher's words:

> When regarding language as an object we find that all acts of speaking are only one manner in which language comes to light in its proper nature and that each individual is only a place in which language appears, just as when reading eminent authors we turn our attention to their language and find out their differences of style. In the same way, each utterance can only be understood from the totality of the life to which it belongs, i.e., as each utterance is perceivable only as the speaker's moment of life, with the same contingency as all moments of his life, and this only from the totality of his surroundings, which determine his development and his further progress. Thus each speaker can be understood only through his nationality and the age he lives in. (1977, 78)

The field researcher has to remain aware that all utterances are such unique life-moments. The vocabulary of single groups or speakers, the interplay of language and other codes, the openness of texts and some grammatical principles are instances of such life-moments. Linguist and ethnologist alike as translators realize mediation between remote or irrelevant theory and dominant practice in the field as they systematize such life-moments and work toward dealienation or "cultural translation."

Still, induction is stressed in Schleiermacher's annihilation of differences and in Ehlich's dealienation. Insofar as the translator's work is still reminiscent of practices in the field, discovery procedures may survive in description and translation, along with moments or features of understanding based on dialogues between subjects and cultures. These should persist as accounts of how we get the data and how we justify texts and descriptions detached from the "other" culture.

Weltansicht and the Lexicon

When a fieldworker—that is, linguist or ethnologist—works on utterances and textualized discourse and is asked for the best theory for manifold practices in the field, he or she is led away from theory to mediating devices. Other questions the fieldworker is asked concern words: "Do the people have a word for, for instance, 'love,' 'Schadenfreude,' 'shame,' 'guilt,' or 'home'? Do they count?" Indeed, from pre-Humboldtian times up to Lévi-Strauss and cognitive anthropology, a worldview is said to be contained in the lexicon. The best-known examples concern lexical terms referring to snow, horses, date palms, sweet potatoes, and so on. They refer to a presumed morphological precision and concreteness in exotic languages. Conversely, one observes a paucity of words referring to abstract meanings, which are supposedly abundant in the languages of research. Or, with respect to syntax, a preference for temporal sequences instead of causal relations is observed. Here I will illustrate richness, gaps, uses, and the ways gaps are bridged.

Work on the Mek languages started with compiling wordlists and a dictionary (cf. Heeschen 1992; see Heeschen and Schiefenhövel 1983 for details). From the start all work proceeded through finding equivalences, paraphrases, and translations. Four patterns emerged from this work as far as the lexicon is concerned.

First of all, there is a constant shift between vagueness and idiomatic richness and concreteness. The lexicon extends into grammar. In the Yale language, *ba-* signifies, among other meanings, "go, run, fly," but speakers also can be concrete—for example, *mededo balamla,* "he goes rushing(ly), he runs"; *lamlam al balamla,* "it flies with quiet wings." The flight of birds, arrows, spirits, and airplanes can be differentiated. Vagueness is characteristic of face-to-face communication, as things and movements are within the perceptual field and need not be distinguished. Concreteness turns up in stories, especially all kinds of nonsacred narratives. Idiomatic richness here contributes to a kind of proto-aesthetic form independent of perceptual cues from the setting.

Second, languages must be vague and abstract, supplying a means of generalization. Languages have what Bühler (1934) called the *abstraktive Relevanz* ("relevance for abstracting"). Humans use symbols detached from ongoing interaction and perception, and not always as icons or indices referring to the real and perceptible environment. Accordingly, seemingly concrete terms have abstract meaning contrary to the many prejudices one may have against exotic languages. In Yale, *kon denakna* refers to a snake sloughing its skin, while in reference to people it means "revival" or even "eternal life." Going the straight or direct way expresses (universally, I suspect) right or good behavior or life. Newly initiated boys' "shining skin" also symbolizes "growth, happiness." In Eipo *se* is an interjection meaning "alas" that hints at paraphrases for "pity" or even *Heimweh* ("yearning for home"), as in *se, na me tenen arebmal,* "alas, thinking it could be my child he gives" or *se, na motokwe dibrenun tenen welebinun,* "alas, in order to see my land (mountains), I will climb up (a tree, a hill)." The concrete "preparation of a building-place for a hut or a men's house" also means "settlement, finding a home, being at home."

Third, the assumption that there is a universal set of meanings rationalizes the discovery of idiomatic and paraphrasal equivalences for words. Besides meanings like "happiness" or "pity" that can be extracted only by chance from paraphrases and utterances, the comparison of indices and dictionaries is a systematic means of working at translations freed from the burden of singularities and peculiarities. Comparison points out gaps: I found "accept" and "thank" in the indices of some dictionaries of Papuan languages. I remembered that Yale *wali alamla*, "he says well," must be an equivalent for "accept, approve, thank." Indeed, this enriched the translator's possibilities in a number of texts. If you receive a gift in Eipo society either you may say nothing (and return a gift days or months later), or you will say "my father" or "my elder brother." Thus "say my father or my elder brother" signifies "thank."

Fourth, the use that speakers make of ties between lexical and other symbolic systems is often neglected. Papuan languages usually have two or three color adjectives. The apparent descriptive paucity is augmented by ostensive reference to materials showing color and used for ornaments and body paintings. The beauty of young men or women or the appearance of an ancestor is expressed by images referring to such materials, the colors of the morning sky, the feathers of the bird of paradise, the brightness of rivers, teeth, kinds of soils, fruits, and so on. Speakers are fully aware of the "colors of the world."

A similar conclusion applies to numeric adjectives. Sometimes I had the impression that even adults were not able to count up to three, if asked inappropriately in interviews. Although the counting system seems to be restricted among the Eipo and Yalenang, members of the Mek people love to count. In fairy tales, up to one hundred *cuscus* (tree-living marsupials of the genus *Phalanger*) are mentioned. Wounds, arrows, casualties, the number of hits, and earth-ovens are counted. Counting the number of mornings after sleep and the number of moons or seasons is essential for measuring distances and sequences of events. After a dance, the *taros* (edible roots of a tropical plant) and other gifts are carefully counted. The speakers are fully aware of the quality of countability of objects and living beings as well as the flow of time. Style and ways of speaking make the best out of a set of words that superficially seems to be poor if one looks for numbers as abstract mathematical concepts that are used for calculations.

A similar relationship between the paucity of the linguistic material and the richness of rites, the degree of awareness, and preoccupation with topics shows up in references to sexual antagonism and the strict separation of the sexes that is said to be common in other Highland societies and throughout Melanesia. Eipo and Yale have only two words to refer to this distinction, "man, male" and "woman, female." Beyond language the antagonism is shown in taboos, rites, and ceremonies. Women came from and danced at the periphery in primordial times, while men established themselves in the center. The men's house, which women should neither approach nor enter, is thought of as the very center of one's world. Coming and going in the hamlet, as well as the use of certain paths in the garden areas and in the hunting grounds, is strictly regulated. Initiation is, above all, a separation of the boys from the women and their fertility. Dirt, dust, and foods characteristic of that sphere are ritually driven out of the body of the boys during initiation. Men are reborn by cultural means, and the food they eat, the objects they handle, and the actions they perform while constructing a hut or making a new garden are purified by rites—that is to say, by cultural acts. The antagonism is transposed into nonverbal behavior and ritual action. The corresponding Weltansicht could not be guessed from lexicon or grammar. Conversely, we know societies the language of which constantly classifies nouns according to gender, but in which the antagonism is absent or far less developed.

The notion of honor is expressed by "a person who should be given" respect by "a person who is looked at, who stands in the middle or center"; generosity, by "giving quickly, giving with two hands"; and stinginess by "giving with thumb and little finger" or "turning one's face to the wall." My own people are those "who give me" and a poor man is "alone, eating alone, covered with dust, ashes on the skin and in the hair, being excluded from the flow of gifts." It is easy to say that this or that language has a multitude of words for this or that object, or that it does not have a word for this or that concept. Yet interactions and nonverbal behavior and reference to these interactions and that behavior replace words. Paraphrases and descriptive sentences are as important as ready-made words. Just as universal needs and universal rules structure human interaction and face-to-face communication, the absence or the presence of a single word does not tell us anything. Words for more abstract concepts are the outcome of a long history. A rich imagery and elaborate metaphors precede this generalized means of reference. The concepts are hidden in, and covered by, metaphors, idioms, paraphrases, references to nonverbal behavior, and so on.

Translating requires an evaluation of the specific functions of language, its task specificity in a society, and its relationship to other symbolic systems. In addition, a *Weltbild* cannot be derived from language alone, but only from the whole symbolic means of a society at a given time. Translation, then, is always also an act of situating speech and language within culture-specific sign systems that supplement each other. Core notions and concepts can be translated into pantomime, dance, rites, and enacted knowledge, and all this can be retranslated into language proper by description and narration. In the latter instance language functions reflexively, following the logic of other signs and relying on the meaningfulness of symbolic behavior. Translation, then, is an attempt at discovering the meaning of words by reference to nonverbal codes and symbols, extracting abstract notions from paraphrases and whole texts, and switching one's awareness from universally presumed notions to special uses, idioms, and collocations in a single language. Indeed, in the original sense of "hermeneutics," it is an exploration of the ties among lexicon, grammar, and texts, ties that lead from one symbol system to another.

Weltansicht, Local Languages, and the Dignity of "Texts"

The dignity of texts may be due to the fact that grammar and lexicon do not correspond easily with a given worldview. Texts are much more "manipulable": explanations can be inserted, alternatives can be given, and idioms replace words and vice versa. Each translation develops into a cultural translation—that is to say, it is also a metacode that monitors differences in content and balances formal differences. Such a translation, then, would mean the destruction of differences at word- and sentence-level unities and the creation of global equivalences on the level of whole texts.

Wilhelm von Humboldt also relied on structures larger (or less formal) than words or sentences in order to construct and define a people's Weltbild. Contrary to expectation based on the famous defining passages of the linguistic relativity hypothesis, he says, "The true grammatical structure cannot be separated from what has been called literature, which is just one name for a good number of phenomena" (Humboldt 1903–36, VI, 396; my translation). Grammar and lexicon are nothing but assurances of the freedom of use in connected speech. The parts that are supposed to determine thinking cannot easily be detected. "If this [discovering a worldview] is everywhere a difficult work, it will be possible only where people have put it [the worldview] down in a more or less extensive literature and where they have fed it into their language by connected speech" (Humboldt 1903–36, VII, 173; my translation). In one of his lectures in the Berlin Akademie, "Über die Sprachen der Südseeinseln," Humboldt introduces Weltansicht and character of the languages by presenting and interpreting a myth. Cultural translations are metacodes relying on the "freedom of use" ensured by the formality of structural means.

Many, including Malinowski as well as Humboldt, maintained the dignity of texts not only as literature but also as tools of research and as documents speaking for themselves. However, high-quality, extensive text editions are rare and sometimes of questionable reliability. On the other hand, there is a lack of requisite theory in linguistic and anthropological fieldwork.

With respect to the languages and cultures of Melanesia, one could say that cultural translations qua metacode hardly exist. Texts are given in a "reduced" language, and one may cast doubts on the researcher's language capacity (cf. Franklin 1992; Schild 1977, 262). The original texts are rarely given. They were collected in English, Dutch, local pidgins, Melanesian pidgin or Indonesian; they were told by informants dealienated from their own cultures, collected by researchers dependent on such informants and staying only some days in one area; and so on. From the viewpoint of philology, even famous collections like Wirz's concerning Marind-anim myths are, to put it mildly, somewhat incomplete (cf. Schmidt 1998, 207–10). Collections of texts (as well as examples taken from corpora) have almost completely vanished from descriptive linguistic studies. Short sample texts added to grammars, however, are usually well edited and commented (cf. Foley 1991). I have also found elegant and well-documented cultural translations without the texts in the local language (e.g., Voorhoeve 1986).

Besides that (and besides studies like that by Urban [1996] or the recent discourse and entextualization studies [cf. Silverstein and Urban 1996]), the reliability of texts, editorial work, and translation were never evaluated. Fischer (1994, 239; my translation), after examining text editions from fieldwork in New Guinea, concludes: "In view of the importance of text recordings in ethnography and the importance assigned to myths in culture (and in all cultures) the most noticeable feature of all publications inspected here is that recording and publication are not sufficiently systematized and not carefully realized." With respect to translation theory, Roth (1998, 243) says: "However, the problem of how the narratives and songs [collected in the beginning of folklore studies] had crossed all these linguistic boundaries [e.g., from Gaelic or Serbian into German or French], the process of translation itself, went almost entirely unnoticed, both in folkloristics and, as Axel Schmalfuß noted (1972, 288), in cultural anthropology as well. Translation was obviously taken as self-explanatory and unproblematic." Again I would conclude that there were no mediations between field practice and theory.

In my experience, the process of translation was always too problematic, incessant, shamefully incomplete, and aesthetically unsatisfactory. After translating one text I felt like having done the ride across Lake Constance: do not look back, otherwise . . . one has to start again. Linguists and anthropologists are not used to giving account of their language learning and speaking claims (cf. Franklin 1992). A hundred years ago only Gabelentz proposed a self-account and reflections on one's own competence: "Only he who masters the language in practice is equal to this task [that of describing a language]; scientific knowledge, cognition and judgment presuppose competency; the scientific presentation will be nothing but a correct explanation of this competency. . . . Thus grammar becomes a description, contemplation and analysis of one's own self" (Gabelentz 1984 [1901], 82; my translation). Apparently, describing a language and writing a grammar presuppose translation capacities.

Besides the quite understandable fact that, in a first contact and monolingual situation, I could never be sure of the meaning of words, utterances, pieces of information, genres, and so on, I was constantly plagued by the essential elliptical character, the incompleteness, and the dependency on the deictic field—that is, on the perceived or imagined space. Listen to the utterance of a child: "Redcurrants. Kernels. But cherries, you cannot eat them." The child eats, tastes the kernels, remembers the kernels of cherries and the fact that these, in contrast to those, cannot be eaten. The translator was always faced with reconstructing the context. What was said could only be interpreted by what was unsaid. The meaning of each utterance always goes beyond the linguistic form. We create meaning in taking the scanty linguistic material appearing in the sound as an opportunity to transfer that which has been referred to into known contexts.

Thus the acts of speaking and of understanding have to be regarded as "the materialization of a semantic horizon which is generally already in existence prior to the utterance heard" (Hörmann 1978, 395). A little later Hörmann says (ibid., 398): "[T]he original function of using language consists in an 'improvement and a complementing' of the orientation already achieved at a non- and pre-linguistic stage." From a host of nonverbal interactions clarified by short utterances, deictic acts, question-and-answer games, fragments, and finally more complex, but still incomplete, sentence structures arise Bühler's "language islands" as texts, elaborated pieces of information. The corresponding rules of production should be those of expansion, clarification, and paraphrase. Indeed, the text, the original utterance, the story and its meaning have to be extracted from ongoing discourse. They do not exist as self-contained entities, but they are produced during processes of expansion, clarification, and enlargement because each utterance qua sentence is defective compared with the whole of Hörmann's semantic horizon.

A myth, for example, is the compilation and the piecing together of a good number of fragments. In an account of a boys' initiation the narrator said, "And they stepped over." Question-answer games, in another word: a kind of metadiscourse yielded the concept of rebirth. The boys come back to the village, step over the thighs of the women into the men's house, which is wrapped up with banana leaves. In another myth the narrators only said, "And they missed it." The *kisang*-pumpkin, which was red and hanging in a tree, alarmed the men by the thundering noise it uttered. They tried to kill it, but all of them missed it. Only a skink from the west hit it with a special bow. The ancestor of one western clan, who appeared in the shape of the pumpkin, was hit, and he fled, creating on his way valleys, rivers, garden soil, and his remnants turned into birds hunted by men and into cultivated plants.

In regard to texts one could summarize the preceding as follows. There is a discrepancy between the dignity of texts and the absence of thoughts on translation (not on theoretical translatability and equivalence) within the fields of descriptive linguistics and anthropology. The dignity may be due to Humboldt's proposal that a Weltansicht can be deduced only from connected speech, not so much from the lexicon and grammar. The absence can be explained by linguists' and anthropologists' failure to conceive of translation as a test of their competency and to mediate between practice qua discovery procedures and theoretical ambitions. Furthermore, translation of texts requires, to a certain degree, the capacity to evaluate problems of style and artistic form, to be an artist oneself (cf. Berman 1992 on Boas's translation capacities). One assumes that texts in grammars or ethnographic works are more or less complete entities, but they come into being by piecing together fragments, individual production, comments, clarifying remarks, and interpretations. Translation, then, is the product of a kind of metadiscourse. Texts form part of *la parole*, not *la langue*.

The problems of understanding, finding equivalences, and translatability probably come into being by looking back from an open generalized system like the scholarly languages into a closed or hermetically delimited system. A local language is a means of creating limits, definitions, and specificity—or, said otherwise, it creates relativity and worldview. Such specificity becomes visible only in texts or the connected speech of local languages. Consequently, translation is a means of opening and destroying the specificity of delimited systems, which may survive only in comments and metadiscourse and carefully displayed postnative competence. Collections of texts are a step in the construction of data. They must not mirror anything but the life-moments of a language.

Talking about Speech

In the same way that texts are pieced together by expansion and clarification to finally yield a recognizable genre, real-life utterances that depend on semantic clues from the deictic field are pieced together, expanded, and clarified until they develop into self-contained sentences that delight the grammarian. Each word and each sentence to which the field researcher refers in his descriptions is implicitly the result of the art of translating. The field researcher, whose aim it is to pin down his results, is bound to the process of understanding foreign life-moments and referring to foreign environments and strange "belief systems"—that is, to the never-ending process of translating and adequation. This part of the construction of data, which is also a transition from observation to experience, is hardly noticed by linguists. It is philosophers like Quine (1960) and linguistic-philological "outsiders" like Wandruszka (1984) who, concerning this part of the descriptive task, doubt the validity of abstract grammatical statements.

In the reality of everyday conversation and during the linguist's interviews with his native grammarian-colleagues, the grammarian's clauses and sentences emerge, are made, and are assembled. Instead of a more or less elicited ditransitive sentence like "The inhabitants of the hamlet of Dingerkon gave the pigs to the guests," you invariably hear unelicited minimal narratives, such as "the people of Dingerkon had pigs, they invited the guests, they came, (they danced), and the former ones (prepared the earth-ovens and) gave the pigs to them." Discourse is an endless series of such expansions—for example, "The boys ate pork" becomes "The initiated boys ate pork"; "The pig gave birth to man" becomes "The mythical pig gave birth to this clan's ancestor"; or "They came from over there" becomes "They came from Larye, the Larye people came." Clarifications can be inserted at any point; thus the roles in "The Dingerkon people gave the guests" are clarified: the subject, as in "The Dingerkon people, as to them, they gave the guests," or the beneficiary, as in "The Dingerkon people gave, they gave to the guests." If you have a structure like "They came, they ate," in which Papuan languages may indicate by a special (verb or conjunct) morpheme whether the subjects are different or remain the same, speakers expand and clarify: "All of them came from Larye, and those who came ate," or "Although they arrived, the strangers, they ate, my people alone ate, because they did not like the strangers (or because the strangers refused to eat)." Sentences are expanded into minimal narratives, and narratives can be resumed by sentences.

Short versions, the resumé versions of narratives, are condensed structures.

They are clarified by canonical paraphrases, by reference to named participants, by being inserted into a minimal narrative. I believe that the interaction among condensed structures, expansions, and clarifications not only forms part of, but constitutes, grammar, while condensed structures are a late abbreviation for semantically defined structures. Only some forms and some syntactic means make sense to native speakers if they can be translated into utterances and paraphrases that establish a minimum of context and that refer to concrete examples. Condensed structures only make sense as part of the grammar if the means of clarification are taken into account. They do not exist independently. The linguist learns by translating genuine utterances that seemingly rigorous rules of grammar fade into matters of style and individual use; the means of explaining, situating, and directing constitute the reflexivity that is inherent in each utterance.

Grammatical means come into being by constant metalinguistic monitoring. The linguist has to follow and translate the movements from utterances to self-contained grammatical structures and from condensed structures to minimal narratives. The transformation from sentences that still rely on clues from the deictic field and context into self-contained sentences, from Bühler's *Zeigfeld* to the *Symbolfeld*, are the grammar. In the same way discussion of fragments of texts constitutes textuality, the logic of producing texts and entextualization. Finally, seemingly complete pieces of information and talk about structures are inherent in everyday talk and lead to abstract sentencehood. Parole, use, and individuality kindle the difference between ideal form and utterance, between a prototype and utterances. Only linguists and anthropologists, who are aware of the life-moments of speech, consider these differences that pose problems to understanding and its correlate, translation. Sentences and texts are incomplete; understanding and translation are means of continually re-establishing completeness.

For me, although postnative competence has improved, sentences and texts remain enigmatic, sometime precarious. In order to understand the contents, a translator has to know the meaning of single words, phrases, and whole sentences. He or she tries to guess at and outline the basic idea of the whole (Schleiermacher's *Divination*). Speaking, understanding, and translating result from the totality of life to which they belong, but this totality consists of single utterances that are perceivable only as the speaker/hearer's moments of life. In accordance with Schleiermacher, Quine (1960) maintains that there is a fundamental vagueness between original and translation. By looking at the logic of producing texts and sentences, difference and vagueness are no longer theoretical notions, but concrete otherness revealed in acts of understanding and translating moments of life and speech.

In many ways the tasks of a philologist working with "dead" languages and of the linguistic or anthropological fieldworker are comparable. Both are involved in understanding life-moments and in translating ephemeral speech acts. Each is at least open to questions of individual style, parole, and use. Understanding does not result from the mere fact that two speakers belong to the same speech community. It always results from a process of understanding during which speakers and hearers fill gaps, establish concrete differences, and negotiate vagueness—all the while taking into consideration that talk about speech and texts involves "the continual re-establishment of a communication, which is structurally disturbed and always remains precarious" (Jäger 1987, 203, my translation).

Texts and sentences are assembled in a metadiscourse in which translation from the vernacular into a generalizing code is a means of pointing to, maintaining, finding, and revealing concrete differences. Translation serves to avoid cultural preconceptions and limited typological experiences. Thus, following Humboldt, a foreign language is not a barrier, but a means of eliminating barriers. It is a means of dealienation and of developing postnative competence.

The translator, moving from the vernacular to his own language and back, discovers the complementarity of symbolic systems. The translator's language should not develop into a metalanguage: its difference, vagueness, and otherness are maintained by the vernacular and evaluated along with growing postnative competence. Yet each language, because of the reflexive function of language with regard to nonverbal symbolic signs, may be used as a kind of metacode. With respect to Weltansicht—that is, to closed cultural sign systems—the use of a generalized language like English or German breaks up the uniformity *(Geschlossenheit)* of the vernacular (cf. Camartin 1992). This breaking up seems to be unidirectional.

Translation, along with the inherent reflexivity of the languages involved, should mirror the incompleteness suggested by the unalterable differences of speaker versus hearer, text versus reader, observed language versus language of description, and language versus other symbolic codes. All these considerations and observations will not help the translator in the field, but ideas concerning difference, vagueness, and incompleteness may help to overcome sadness and shame resulting from insufficient postnative competence. Furthermore, linguist and anthropologist alike as translators may, at least momentarily, refrain from theory in order to remain close to the data or give an account of how the data are discovered and constructed. Perhaps she or he will look at translation as a means of (philological) dealienation, of defining the task specificity of speech in different cultures and of bridging gaps within and between speech communities. As for the anthropologist, translation develops into a metacode pointing to gaps, balancing differences, and requiring devices that mediate between observations in the field and experiences transposed into theory. Translation as a metacode becomes apparent when the translator moves across the boundaries in both directions, from the vernacular to one of the widely spoken national languages, and from these back to the local language. The asymmetries are another field of research.

Note

1. The present writer has done research on German language philosophy and, subsequently, realized fieldwork in the eastern mountains of West Papua, where the Mek languages, members of the Papuan Trans New Guinea Phylum languages, are spoken. See references in Heeschen 1998.

References Cited

Anttila, Raimo. 1973. "Linguistik und Philologie." Pp. 177–91 in *Linguistik und Nachbarwissenschaften,* ed. R. Bartsch and T. Vennemann. Kronberg/Taunus: Sriptor.

Berman, Judith. 1992. "Oolachan-Woman's Robe: Fish, Blankets, Masks, and Meaning in Boas's Kwakw'ala Texts." Pp. 125–62 in *On the Translation of Native American Literatures,* ed. Brian Swann. Washington, DC, and London: Smithsonian Institution Press.

Brockmeier, Jens. 1998. *Literales Bewußtsein: Schriftlichkeit und das Verhältnis von Sprache und Kultur.* Munich: Fink.

Bühler, Karl. 1934. *Sprachtheorie: Die Darstellungsfunktion der Sprache.* Jena, Germany: Gustav Fischer.

Camartin, Iso. 1992. *Nichts als Worte? Ein Plädoyer für Kleinsprachen.* Frankfurt am Main: Suhrkamp.

Clements, William M. 1996. *Native American Verbal Art: Texts and Contexts.* Tucson: University of Arizona Press.

Derrida, Jacques. 1972. *La dissémination.* Paris: Seuil.

———. 1987. "Des Tours de Babel." Pp. 207–45 in *Psyché: Inventions de l'autre.* Paris: Galilée.

Ehlich, Konrad. 1981. "Native Speaker's Heritage: On Philology of 'Dead' Languages." Pp. 153–65 in *A Festschrift for Native Speakers,* ed. F. Coulmas. The Hague: Mouton.

Fischer, Hans. 1994. *Geister und Menschen: Mythen, Märchen und neue Geschichten.* Berlin: Reimer.

Foley, William A. 1991. *The Yimas Language of New Guinea.* Stanford, CA: Stanford University Press.

Franklin, Karl J. 1992. "On Language Learning Claims in Ethnographies." Pp. 589–97 in *The Language Game: Papers in Memory of Donald C. Laycock,* ed. T. Dutton, M. Ross, and D. Tryon. Canberra: Australian National University.

Gabelentz, Georg von der. 1984 [1901]. *Die Sprachwissenschaft: Ihre Aufgaben, Methoden und bisherigen Ergebnisse.* Tübingen: Narr.

Gipper, Helmut. 1972. *Gibt es ein sprachliches Relativitätsprinzip? Untersuchungen zur Sapir-Whorf-Hypothese.* Frankfurt am Main: S. Fischer.

Heeschen, Volker. 1990. *Ninye bún: Mythen, Erzählungen, Lieder und Märchen der Eipo im zentralen Bergland von Irian Jaya (West Neuguinea), Indonesien.* Berlin: Reimer.

———. 1992. *A Dictionary of the Yale (Kosarek) Language (with Sketch of Grammar and English Index).* Berlin: Reimer.

———. 1998. *An Ethnographic Grammar of the Eipo Language Spoken in the Eastern Mountains of Irian Jaya (West New Guinea), Indonesia.* Berlin: Reimer.

———. 2001. "The Narration 'Instinct': Everyday Talk and Aesthetic Forms of Communication (in Communities of the New Guinea Mountains)." Pp. 137–65 in *Verbal Art across Cultures: The Aesthetics and Proto-Aesthetics of Communication,* ed. H. Knoblauch and H. Kotthoff. Tübingen: Narr.

Heeschen, Volker, and Wulf Schiefenhövel. 1983. *Wörterbuch der Eipo-Sprache: Eipo— Deutsch—English.* Berlin: Reimer.

Hörmann, Hans. 1978. *Meinen und Verstehen: Grundzüge einer psychologischen Semantik.* Frankfurt am Main: Suhrkamp.

Humboldt, Wilhelm von. 1903–36. *Gesammelte Schriften: Hrsg. von der Königlich Preußischen Akademie der Wissenschaften.* 17 vols. Berlin: de Gruyter.

———. 1981 [1816]. "Einleitung zum 'Agamemnon.'" Pp. 137–45 in Humboldt, *Werke in fünf Bänden. V. Kleine Schriften. Autobiographisches, Dichtungen, Briefe, Kommentare und Anmerkungen zu Band I–V.* Darmstadt: Wissenschaftliche Buchgesellschaft.

Jäger, Ludwig. 1987. "Philologie und Linguistik: Historische Notizen zu einem gestörten Verhältnis." Pp. 198–222 in *Zur Theorie und Methode der Geschichtsbeschreibung der Linguistik: Analysen und Reflexionen,* ed. P. Schmitter. Tübingen: Narr.

Quine, William Van Orman. 1960. *Word and Object.* Cambridge, MA: MIT Press.

Roth, Klaus. 1998. "Crossing Boundaries: The Translation and Cultural Adaptation of Folk Narratives." *Fabula* 39: 243–55.

Schild, Ulla, ed. 1977. *Märchen aus Papua-Neuguinea.* Herausgegeben und übersetzt von Ulla Schild. Düsseldorf: Eugen Diederichs.

Schleiermacher, Friedrich D. E. 1977 [1838]. *Hermeneutik und Kritik: Mit einem Anhang sprachphilosophischer Texte Schleiermachers,* ed. M. Frank. Frankfurt am Main: Suhrkamp.

Schmalfuß, Axel. 1972. "Übersetzen." Pp. 285–90 in *Kulturanthropologie,* ed. Ren König and Axel Schmalfuß. Düsseldorf.

Schmidt, Andrea Elisabeth. 1998. *Paul Wirz: Ein Wanderer auf der Suche nach der "wahren Natur."* Basel: Ethnologisches Seminar der Universität und Museum der Kulturen/Wepf.

Silverstein, Michael, and Greg Urban, eds. 1996. *Natural Histories of Discourse.* Chicago and London: University of Chicago Press.

Swann, Brian, ed. 1992. *On the Translation of Native American Literatures.* Washington, DC, and London: Smithsonian Institution Press.

Thouard, Denis. 1998. "Verstehen im Nicht-Verstehen: Zum Problem der Hermeneutik bei Humboldt." *Kodikas/Code* 21: 271–85.

Urban, Greg. 1996. *Metaphysical Community: The Interplay of the Senses and the Intellect.* Austin: University of Texas Press.

Voorhoeve, C. L. 1986. "We, People of One Canoe—They, People or Wood: Two Asmat Origin Myths." *Irian* 14: 77–125.

Wandruszka, Mario. 1984. *Das Leben der Spachen: Vom menschlichen Sprechen und Gespräch.* Stuttgart: Deutsche Verlags-Anstalt.

Trance and Translation in the *Zar* Cult of Ethiopia

Antonio Luigi Palmisano

There is more in common between trance and translation than the Latin preposition *trans*—above all, something more that takes place in both processes. An Ethiopian ethnographic case allows for some observations on the processes of trance and opens the possibility to reflections on the concept of translation.

Defining the Cases

Often we have been invited to consider translation as "a process of appropriation and recontextualization," "a metaphor for the process of bridging differences," or "a practice dealing with difference." All these definitions are effectively stimulating, and each leads us to the recognition that at least two cultural and social worlds, those of speaker and listener, exist with intentions to communicate. Thus they rely on traduction processes. These worlds appear obviously different, else they would manifest identity.

We read about altered states of consciousness, as in the possession trance, visions, and ecstatic trance. The perspective of a social actor who is suffering supplies us with the protagonist of the trance (Palmisano 1996). He or she seems "acted upon" by another entity—a spirit, force, Divinity, and the like. In the *zar* movement in Ethiopia (Reminick 1974, 1975), the social actor or *ye zar faras* ("the horse of the zar"[1]) is said to be "ridden" by one of the many spirits of the sect (Palmisano 2000).[2] This experience, painful and overwhelming as it is for the social actor (Kramer 1984, 1987), takes place during a state of trance. But how is it experienced by the specialist and professional practitioner of the ritual trance—the *bale zar* or *bale wuqabi*,[3] "the master of the zar"—who presides over the zar session and acts as the incarnation of Divinity, who is priest and master of the trance for new adepts and for the person identified as sick (Palmisano 2001)? And what about other attendees at the ritual, who serve in various ways as coactors?

The Ethnographic Case: Garesu and Wofa

⌒ The case of Garesu and the cult of Wofa are especially relevant for the theme of trance and translation.[4] This zar movement in the highlands of Ethiopia practices in a clearly defined interethnic situation in which speakers of Oromo are numerically prevalent over speakers of Amhara. The leader, Garesu, who is a powerful bale wuqabi, embodies the Wofa Divinity and speaks an unintelligible sacred language that is consecutively translated into Oromo and Amharic by another specialist, the *aggafari*, for those in attendance. The translation occurs during the aggafari's trance, as he faces the crowd of believers in a temple, sited in a sanctuary that was founded by Garesu and his numerous followers.

The village-sanctuary lies a few hours' drive from Addis Ababa.[5] It is not visible from the highway, but it is the center par excellence for the ritual practice of Garesu's followers, who constitute an ethnopolitical community.[6] A tangle of tall thorn bushes embraces and reinforces the village's stone wall, some three to four meters high and two to three meters thick. The wall marks the untrespassable limit of a place, and at the same time it defines the man Garesu and those who are associated with him. Entrance inside the perimeter is permitted only through Garesu's approval. He sits on a kind of throne, a comfortable three-legged stool called the "throne of health," awaiting his usually numerous guests beyond the gate.

The gate stands out surprisingly in the middle of the countryside, interrupting the monotony of the Ethiopian highlands. The social, economic, and religious microcosm founded by Garesu starts here. He is a great charismatic leader who has been invested with the honorific title *gashe,* meaning "shield" and protector of persons and goods. Only someone who is invited can come through the gate. Men can be seen outside the doorway, waiting sometimes for weeks to be invited inside. The door is a double door consisting of an entrance portal with a roof and a second, smaller inner door.

At this point a paved road leads to a piazza, a small open space, on either side of which are stables for horses and cattle. Garesu's house and a large kitchen capable of feeding hundreds of people are here. There are also vegetable gardens and plots of cereal and other seed crops considered locally to be of high quality.[7] Pastures are found outside the powerful boundary wall, while herders and farmers work peacefully inside and outside of it. The whole complex is very impressive, especially in its social and economic activity. Men and women, burdened with enormous survival problems in an unpredictable setting, are attracted by the polarity of wealth and welfare, further feeding Garesu's capacity to identify and transform social and other resources.

This "urban" system contrasts with other rural settlements of the highlands. The impressive enclosure clearly marks the specificity of the place in the rural social and ecological space. The boundary wall is an effective border, delimiting the inner space and asserting it in juxtaposition with the outside. Its perimeter cannot be trespassed without prior approval from Garesu. Whoever enters through the door has been initiated de facto into the path of the adept.

Inside a kind of wonderland, a "Paese di Bengodi," is constituted as a place of health, safety, and welfare. It is an ideal place from which there is risk of expulsion, as from paradise. Everyday words express this utopic realization. The sick and suffering find shelter in such places, endowed as they are with transmundane and apotropaic attributes and suggestions. In fact, village-sanctuaries of this kind, which are sometimes situated on the highest peaks of the Ethiopian highlands, are actually called *gennet*, "paradise."

Within the village-sanctuary there is the *gelma*, a cult-house of about fifteen meters in diameter, with an enormous central pole that supports the roof, and a masonry structure inside, divided by curtains. A few people are usually waiting there for the protagonists of an extraordinary performance—Garesu, who, when he becomes God on earth, is called Wofa; and the aggafari, his helper, the so-called "guardian of the doors." Each performance starts with a process of translation. The Divinity, protected and hidden behind a wall, speaks an incomprehensible language. Beyond the inner wall-border, which marks the strictly and absolutely sacred space—the nonplace par excellence—are the adepts; the aggafari, seated on the ground within the limits of the sacred space, but nonetheless close to the door-curtain and thus closer to the adepts, translates into two comprehensible languages.

Man and God: The Author

The mark of the village border clearly creates a sacred place. Trance cults, engaged in possession trance, are practiced here. The God Wofa comes down on Garesu. Other spirits also often come down on him, but they are less complex and easier to understand in their wishes, and communication with them is thus simpler. Garesu, a powerful *bale wukabi*, is able "to ride all of them."

The gashe could—and still can—also become a *ras*, a political-military leader of a descent or local group. He is a "shield" whose capacity to protect the community is associated with his capacity to get in touch directly with a Divinity, Wofa, having a very difficult character. Wofa is the main Divinity of a minor pantheon. The followers of this cult are numerous, as are followers of the Ethiopian Orthodox Church and Islam. There is in fact a strong presence of believers who practice local cults; we can legitimately define the extended constellation of cults and religions that stands beside these two Confessions as the Third Confession of Ethiopia.

The Divinity in question, Wofa, manifests itself on particular days of the ritual calendar. Garesu becomes the Divinity and speaks. When he speaks he judges, and his judgments become sentences. Two litigants go to the temple to consult with Garesu; they ask for advice, opinion, and intervention. The man, Garesu, goes into a trance, and when Divinity comes down on him he becomes de facto the Divinity, Wofa. In his mind then, only God exists, and he can judge "the case." He can define and resolve moments of disorder and suffering inside the community whether caused by inside or outside contingencies; he settles disputes and controversies. The judgment formulated by Garesu during these precise liturgic and ritual situations is definitive, without any possibility of appeal. Obviously once Divinity has spoken it can not be put in discussion. No words create as much as divine words.

> *Garesu is coming! gashe Garesu! A man with deep flaming eyes carved in an impassive face. He is of medium height, sturdy with a broad chest, not fat, with his shaved head set on a bull's neck. An actual seventy-year-old "shield." He sits down: all the people attending bend down and kiss the ground before they dare to come any closer than five meters. As they approach they kiss the tip of his foot and then his ankle, starting with one foot and then proceeding with the other. If he allows them, they kiss his hand after having kissed his feet. He has nevertheless the kindness to stand up from his "health-throne" and greet me, shaking hands in European style. His expression changes from mildness to severity when the faithful greet him. Everybody brings a present: sometimes money but usually coffee and sugar. Strange, rare, or curious objects that he might have asked for: a full ostrich egg, a wig, a Swiss knife, a picture of President Clinton . . .*[8]

Garesu is represented by people as authority, a man of mystical power, a "shield," a protector of his own and others' communities: "He is a wise man. He knows everything, he speaks many languages." Besides Oromo and Amharic, the bale wuqabi speaks a language of symbols and unequivocal gestures. The aggafari does not attend these occasions. But when the Divinity Wofa manifests itself in Garesu or for Garesu, the presence of a deep and upsetting alterity requires the intervention of an interpreter, a mediator—tout court, a medium.

Two o'clock in the morning. I enter the gelma, which is already filled with people for the supplications. They let me go through, but there is almost no room left: there are 100 to 120 faithful in a temple of about fifteen meters in diameter. I stop a few meters from the aggafari. After waiting for some days, Wofa finally came down. Garesu's assistants woke me up suddenly.[9] Wofa judges, Wofa answers, Wofa sentences and removes any kind of hindrances. The suppliants are helped to answer by the more expert among them or by an attending bale wuqabi. The song of Wofa is very fast and rhythmical. It is followed, before he has finished, by the aggafari, who repeats in Oromo and then Amharic at the same high speed, musicality, and rhythm. The suppliants attempt to join in the rhythm when asking questions, but they do not always manage. The supplications are reported in the same manner by the aggafari to Wofa. Then the answer goes from Wofa to the aggafari and from the latter to the suppliants. The entire process repeats: the first words belong to the suppliants; the last word, always and only to Wofa.

The song is incredibly melodious, pressing, fascinating and hypnotic. Some suppliants cry. The faces show suffering, a heavy pathos is in the air. Some of them lie during the supplication. They do not have the courage to confess their guilt or their problems publicly. They are afraid to make mistakes. A young woman accompanied by her mother lies. Her lie is immediately discovered by Wofa, and she is stricken with terror. The young woman throws herself on the ground, crawls desperately between our legs and under our feet; she crawls begging for forgiveness . . . which she will not obtain. "You will die soon," says the voice of the aggafari, who adds then in Amharic, "Or your mother will die in your place"[10]

〜〉 The cult of Wofa substantially consists of great moments of community, of mutual understanding: it founds the premises for the efficient construction of a common language; it designs the Tower of Babel before its fall. But what is the object of this communicative exchange? The suppliant, in this case a young woman, seems to have committed a serious crime: she is suspected of having "poisoned" her husband's mother. In this social and religious context "poisoning" has many meanings, and this verb has multiple meanings that are decidedly different from the ones evoked by persons in our world. Nobody knew of the true or false "poisoning" until that night, although we cannot exclude that some rumors were already circulating. The woman asks about herself, about her own life, about what she will do some day or other, what will happen, how her relationships with the community will be, how things will go with the community. This is what she asks the Divinity, Wofa, who for the moment takes the shape of the man Garesu and stays in Garesu's body. His honorific title is gashe, and the shield is in fact behind the curtain, behind the wall: it is the defense of the community. A God, not a man, is seated behind the wall. In the social and existential hic et nunc Garesu is a god.

The Languages of Man and Divinity

The gelma is the temple of divine speech. Divinity speaks in a nonhuman language, not accessible to man. It is simultaneously translated by the aggafari so that it becomes understandable to everyone. But the supplicant is not able to understand perfectly what has been translated. Complex symbologies, bold metaphors, and barely accessible cryptograms permeate the language. All those present contribute to the interpretation, above all those who actually have or claim a major experience in the field of liturgy and ritual. The answer, or rather the continuation of the formulation of other, more specific questions, is shaped by the supplicant with the de facto help of those who have assisted her during the interpretation phase. Divinity sings a rhythmic song that is also sung by the aggafari when he brings the supplicant's words back to Divinity, endowing them with a musicality and a rhythm that they did not have when the supplicant spoke, his voice often broken by emotion if not by tears. Musicality, words and translation. But a woman has lied and is stricken by terror.

The two protagonists of this cult are Garesu, who, as God on earth, is called Wofa, and the aggafari. The process of translation is quite peculiar. Divinity speaks in a language that is not understandable and that is pronounced from the inside of the temple, the holy part, which is not accessible to the public. The group of adepts is on the other side of the wall. The aggafari, who mediates between the two places linked by the sound that becomes voice, speaks in Oromo and Amharic to the public.[11]

These cults are the paradigm of different forms of social and political organization of society, of structuration and interpretation of the world, of a "different" world. In a country such as Ethiopia, with great social, cultural, and linguistic variety, interethnic relationships are not always easy. In a place of this kind a meeting of people of different ethnic backgrounds is itself an event of relevant social, cultural, and political significance through the presence of the gelma on the territory. Inside the gelma a moment of extraordinary community construction takes place, more precisely of territorial community, that is able to transcend other forms of categorization of interpersonal relationships. But the two places are only apparently two, for both the researcher and the social actor.

The translations start from a divine language into two different human languages. While the results in other political and social contexts could be in juxtaposition, in this case they both contribute synergistically to the creation of a community through the double interpretation allowed to the suppliants through the construction of the world: a particular prestation given by two different languages that are spoken, albeit with differing proficiencies, by all those present. We have then a kind of upside down Tower of Babel: two human languages defined in juxtaposition to a divine language allow a moment of profound unity among the believers. This cult founds deep moments of cultural, territorial, and social community. How does this communicative exchange take place? What are the dynamics of this process?

The Summoned Lady: Judgment and Translation

The suppliant, a desperate young woman, is now suspected of having "poisoned" her husband's mother. Nobody knew of it, at least officially, until that night. She innocently asks Divinity about her future as if Divinity were a diviner. During the liturgical and oracular action, Garesu is not a man but God. During such performances we can only try to understand now this particular microcosm works, met as it was on the Ethiopian highlands—a world in which thousands of people follow a leader during a situation of exception that is defined through the participation of a group of believers. We want to define the inner rules of this situation and thereby uncover elements that are meaningful for a comprehensive anthropology in which we discover how judging and translating coincide.

The young woman, accompanied by her shaking mother, asks questions before the community of believers. The work of translation *vis-à-vis* Divinity has started before the end of the woman's speech: through the aggafari the words finally reach the man-God. He answers immediately, and, before his answer is finished, the aggafari has already started the double work of translating these sounds of the divine language for the outer part of the sanctuary's center. He usually starts by translating in Oromo and then proceeds in Amharic. The woman receives an answer. The answer is sometimes clear, but the use of metaphors is intense: "You will return with a perfumed lemon . . ." An outside observer might wonder if this

request-prophecy is similar to the apparently absurd wishes and requests of Garesu: "a picture of President Clinton," "a Swiss knife," "a full ostrich egg," and so on.
Or is it something quite different?

In any event we are facing one or more messages. The sentence in question,
as oracular as it might be, in this case means: "Come back with your lover, not with
your husband . . ." Divinity gives an order, enunciated in the shape of a self-real-
izing prophecy: "Next time I want you to come back with your lover!" Wofa either
suspects or knows that there is a lover in this business and so summons him for
judgment. The suppliant goes through a crisis for this answer. What does she ask
now? The young woman, presumed adulterer and "poisoner," finds herself in an
unusual situation of expectation. She has already been waiting for the manifesta-
tion of Divinity for days, and the situation has become almost unbearable. She
is breaking down. This is a *Grenzsituation,* and she is psychologically dependent.
Supported by friends and advised by assistants of the aggafari, she is ready to free
herself from the weight of guilt or error.

In the local language, all specialists of the cult are called bale wuqabi, or "riders of the spirit." There are men and women considered able to exorcise spirits and
to induce them to go where the bale wants them to go. These men and ladies invite
and encourage the woman to ask other questions that, once translated, will reach
the Divinity through the aggafari. This extraordinary work of social construction
proceeds according to this paradigm.

The local reality is built socially, and not only during these specific moments
and situations of the cult. Offenses, crime, and deceit make trouble that disturbs
the order of everyday life. The order of the universe is thus revealed and, at the
same time, defined and stated by the local community of participants. This community intervenes in the definition of the infractions and in their re-establishment, rather than in the discovery of the crime. At this point even the answer is
given by the group. The last word belongs to Divinity. "What is to be done with
this woman?" This is the type of question arising to all those who have perceived
and felt the event as problematic. This is why they use the word "judgment" and
the phrase, "day of judgement." The group process of construction ends on that
day.

"You will die!" does not mean that the woman has been sentenced to death
or that she will be executed by someone who will take charge of the executioner's
work. The psychological pressure is extraordinary in these contexts. There is a
kind of self-isolation, as if the woman had been ostracized, as if she had been so
powerfully cursed that her closest relatives seem to maintain their distance care-

fully. To live under such conditions is difficult, especially in communities of this size. It means to be abandoned by all, to be banned. Social death can also become physical death by a kind of self-renunciation or self-destruction. It means to lose oneself in a heavy and deep depression, in an absence of social life. Under these circumstances, leaving the community can be a solution. But abandon, exile, or migration cannot be realized in every community.

Before the resolution to forsake one's own world is taken, there is a process that one could call "repentance" or "reviewing one's actions." There is an attempt at the reintegration of the woman and her family by the community; there is also the incumbent threat on her mother's head: "Either you will die or your mother!" To include the mother clearly implies that the whole family of the suppliant is involved in such a way as to seek the mediation of the conflict. The whole community participates toward the resolution of this conflict that was born inside the community.

How do the witnesses of the social drama respond? Those present are believers; they also might be friends or relatives of the woman and her mother, but also enemies, or friends of the one who is thought to have been poisoned by that woman. The poisoned victim could be a daughter, mother, sister, cousin, aunt, lover, or wife of one or more persons attending. The same may be true for her friends and relatives, as well as for friends and relatives of her suspected "poisoner." Which one of all these roles can we imagine to take priority over the others? A precise answer is impossible because it depends on the situation, and the situation is defined in social-political terms. In some cases the articulation of roles is so obvious that there isn't any priority to discuss. It is a continuous game, a synergy of these different roles, in the person of the believer. He is not only a follower of this particular cult but also a member of the community, and someone who will take an interest in solving the potential conflict. The attempted "poisoning," successful or not, leads toward the destruction of interfamily relationships, and this in a way so serious that it could undermine the peace of the whole community. There will then be an effort to solve this potential conflict as soon as possible.

But one or more social actors could wish, for political or egocentric reasons, to exacerbate the potential conflict situation. The game will then follow the rules and dynamics already demonstrated inside the temple. Many persons are attending, and each of them potentially can perceive particular sentences and understand in what direction someone, more or less consciously, is trying to lead the interpretation process. The woman can now be manipulated easily and answer contingently in a situation created ad hoc by the manipulators—that is, by all the social actors attending the ritual. They strike again, supporting one type of social construction rather than another. It is a game of roles that we, as actors, cannot define before the game starts. We can only define them as the game proceeds—and, best of all, when it is about to end—but we can certainly foresee some of its dynamics. The game actually ends with and for the complete and effective definition of the roles.

The Interpreter and the Translator

⌒ Aside from the context of trance and divine possession in the temple, the *elfigna*, the main role of the aggafari is that of distanced adviser. The aggafari never stays close to the leader; he generally occupies a rather withdrawn position in comparison with the leader's centrality. In everyday life he confirms and builds up this position, as he himself represents it, of strengthened marginality—as man of the margin, as the one who does not want to play the "prima donna," as a protagonist in the shadow. The aggafari is so much associated with the "margins" that even in the elfigna he stands far from the throne,[12] on the threshold of the door that leads outside. He is not always visible, even though present, during public occasions, apparently busy with the kitchen and the supplies. He remains in touch with the leader through gestures and eye language, making distant comments on what is taking place. The aggafari, a kind of secondary bale zar, a co-medium, acts as an interpreter—that is, a translator.

The language used by the spirits to communicate with the patient-suppliant during the trance session, like the general liturgical language of the bale zar, has two main attributes: it has, first of all, an extremely complex lexicon and syntax and, once translated, works only through difficult and complex metaphors (hyperboles, metonymies, synecdoches, etc.) that are sometimes surrealistic. Second, although a complex language—from the lexical and semantic point of view it is an "other" language—the main point is that it is divine. It is neither Oromo nor Amharic, nor is it any other language spoken in the Horn of Africa or on this earth. It is neither the language of Yahweh nor that of the Bible, nor is it the language of Allah and the Koran. It is instead the language of the minor God Wofa, who is able to kill with his own words. Wofa is *Waq' fa*,[13] the language of God worshipped as a Divinity and embodied in man. The word of God, Waq' fa, has transformed itself in spirit, Wofa, and has made himself man, Garesu.

This language therefore requires a double translation: from divine to human, and from metaphors to binary thought. It is not a translation that concerns the *topos* of glossolalia—that is, the translation of foreign languages. Two questions arise now: the first one regards from what and into what the bale zar translates. Certainly he translates from one language to another, from one linguistic world to another, but that is only an initial answer. The second question is, what precisely, in addition to words, does the bale zar translate?

The Etymological Case: Trance, Translation, and Traduction

Trance, translation, traduction: these three words all share the same Latin preposition *trans*. The first is a noun formed by the verb *trans-ire;* the second is a past participle of the verb *trans-fero;* the third is again a past participle of the verb *trans-duco*. The fact that they share the preposition *trans-* is not the only element that the three words have in common.

The substantive "trance" derives from the verb *trans-eo, -es, -ii, -itum, -ire*. This verb in its intransitive form indicates "to pass, to bring oneself to go from one condition to another," and thus "to transform oneself to change one's state," as well as "to cross" or "to go through something." The transitive form expresses even more clearly the meaning of "to go through, to cross over" when speaking of places, conditions, or time itself. This verb seems to manifest clearly the effort of the subject in his action of modification, in his overcoming and transformation of a changing condition (the English substantive "transition" derives from this verb), hence attempts by the subject to effect a passage.

The substantive "translation" derives from the verb *trans-fero, -fers, -tuli, -latum, -ferre*. Its more restricted spectrum of meanings include, above all, to "transfer, transport, transplant" something or someone from one place to another, both physically and figuratively. The Latin word *translatio, -onis* directly indicates the action of "transfer, transport, transplant," often referring to agricultural activities, and only in an absolutely secondary meaning referring to the passing from one language to another.

Finally, the substantive "traduction" derives from the verb *trans-duco, -ducis, -duxi, -ductum, -ere*, which has as its first meaning "to let cross, to lead beyond, to carry across, to transfer from one state to another," or "drive, lead someone or something across something," or even "to drag it, to expose it in front of someone or something." These meanings are even stronger in the Latin substantive *traductio, -onis,* and kept almost integrally in the English "traduction."

The verbs formed with the preposition trans- are thus verbs of motion. The first one, trans-ire, expresses the movement of the subject. The other two, trans-fero and trans-duco, express the fact that the object is being or has been moved. Not all suppliants are able to go into trance (-ire); not everyone is able to reach another world of communication, or another place—a particular nonplace— unless they are brought to it (-fero) or conveyed there (-duco) by a peculiar actor, the bale wuqabi.

Concluding Remarks

⌒ The wall-curtain separates, from social actors' perspectives, the two linguistic worlds of sacred and secular. On one side there is a sacred language with fragmented tunes and exasperated rhythms, a peculiar low and deep sonority, a lexicon that is absolutely not understandable to the believers or to humans. On the other side are spoken the Oromo and Amharic languages of everyday life, the Semitic and Cushitic languages of peasants and stock-breeders, of petty traders. Between one world and the other, a mediator—a translator or a *traductor* in Latin terminology—transforms the sacred language into secular languages. His way of speaking echoes the fragmented tunes and faithfully reflects the rhythm of the sacred language. His lexicon is clear in both Oromo and Amharic, the first and second languages of translation.

These languages are articulated in very elaborated images that are sometimes easy to understand ("You will come with a perfumed lemon in your hand!"), but more often obscure in meaning, such that the whole community of those present must construct a possible interpretation.

The most courageous and those with more experience, others who are possessed and other "riders of the spirits," will help the suppliant to understand and ask other questions more "useful and meaningful" in that context. But those who do not manage to keep silent will also speak. And there will be reproaches. Interpretation and ambiguity in the oral sacred text as translated are strictly related: without ambiguity in "Wofa-aggafari," no interpretation and no social and religious construction of the community's identity would be possible. Without interpretation, no other question to Divinity, maybe no other communication with Divinity at all, would follow. The oral sacred text is translated . . . actually: trans-lated!

But this means "transferred," "transported," "carried across," "driven beyond." Trans-: across, beyond . . . what? This wall, this curtain. The sacred oral text is transported and transferred from that place to another place, from the sacred place of the body in trance to the secular place of the crying community. There are boundaries of sacred places: the body of the person in trance defines the place of residence of the spirit. And this means that the body, the earthly place par excellence, becomes *ou-topos,* "nonplace," the worthy house of the spirit.

No one can legitimately think to be able to move with his own body beyond this wall, in the sacred space. No believer can be transported. Only the voice can cross the borderline, this wall-curtain. Revelations, interpretations are born through it.

Body or geographic space are, or can be, included as matrix of identity. If body and geographic space are or can be understood as identity, then it is all the more true that transport, the translation of bodies, persons, or text (even simple words) partake in the modification of identity.

Ethnographic travel is actually a translation, a *trans-latum,* a coming out of the geographic space, a place, in order to enter another space, another place.[14] The ethnographic problem is in fact linguistic—that is, a problem of translation and communicability of alterities, of being different. Moreover, the specific case of translations during trance states is a metaphor for how everything is potentially understandable; these translations demonstrate the triumph of communicability.

In the situations of "crisis of presence," of existential crisis that can be manifested by the suppliant who goes to practice the cult, the successfully completed game of the translations (moving from nonunderstandable to understandable, from Wofa through aggafari to suppliant), asserts itself as metaphor for an ineluctable and nonrational healing process. When facing manifestations of the negative in history and life, the successful translation is a countermanifestation of the "positive": what was not understandable is now understandable. The miracle of communicability has been achieved once more.

The sound, the nonexisting word, has become sacred word in the temple. The sound acquires meaning and becomes word. This word of Divinity has been translated, traduced, traducted, transferred still in the segregated place of the temple, which is all to say, communicated—in a state of trance. There is and there isn't a consciousness, there is and there isn't a liability on the part of the group of believers. In this sense, the gelma is the place of translation par excellence. Together with the believers, this word—already translated and interpreted in chorus in the temple—has come finally out of the temple and then of the sanctuary, to be manifested to the world: a translation as the word/will of the Divinity.[15]

It is as if words were born from the nonword in the sanctuary. The sound is transformed into word when it is transported to the world of men: sound, musically "articulated" sound, language of Divinity, human language, communication of a message to the outside, community language, my language. This is translatio.

The inside of the sanctuary is a world; a world that is extremely closed and intimate, in which meaningful words are born, in which truth is born to be translated, traducted, traduced, and taken outside;[16] a world out of which revelations are transported and diffused into everyday concerns in the political and social world of people.

Translation here is an *Aufhebung* of borders, of boundaries, but not of difference; translation is the cofounding process of differences through new and previously unthought of relationships and bounds. The process involves sound, transformation in words, translation of these words, interpretation of the words, statements of ambiguity, and life, social life without any colonization of everyday life. Translation is interpretation. To opt for a translation means to opt for a policy, for a political choice. In this sense, philology is the art of identifying ambiguities, an ambiguity that is at home in the vast spectrum of meanings possessed by each root. The technologization of translation implies the renunciation of communicative art; the cancellation of multilingualism means to abdicate politics; the race toward monolingualism is to precipitate toward the existential dictatorship of being one. This amounts to translation as a political performance and not as a technical happening.

⁀

Notes

1.   Zar may be related to the Semitic root *zar,* meaning "to visit." In other forms, it indicates someone who "comes," "reaches," or "comes down," but it also may mean "to afflict." In classical and modern Arabic, the verb *zara-yazuru* may mean "visiting," as well as "afflicting someone."

2.   Zar possession trance is also found in Somalia (Lewis, I. M. 1969, 1989), Eritrea (Conti Rossini 1943, 1946) and Sudan (Boddy 1988; Böhringer-Thärigen 1996) under the same name, and in many other countries.

3.   In Amharic and other Semitic languages, the term *bal* means "owner," "master," and so forth. In poetry, the word *bale* means "messenger."

4.   I have done fieldwork for four years in Ethiopia on religious movements, notably zar cults. The impact of these groups on Ethiopian politics and economy has been appreciable. Participants in one such group estimated that there were between 100,000 and 300,000 adepts. This group was led in the 1960s and 1970s

by Lijj Taye, who was very popular. He disappeared during the time of Mengistu Hailemariam, who considered him to be a dangerous political opponent. The disappearance of leaders who have such influence can provoke economic collapse in large rural and urban areas because of the activities associated with the leaders, the foundation of sanctuaries, and the dynamics of pilgrimage to key sites.

5. The exact location and name of this forlorn village are not given for reasons of confidentiality, in part to avoid a potential wave of tourism that might result from anthropological research.

6. My access to this village was obtained through Liliana de Martini, the extraordinary granddaughter of Lijj Yasu, himself the legitimate heir to Menelik's throne and acting emperor from May 1911 to September 1916. Lijj Yasu, son of Choa Regga, Menelik's daughter, and of Ras Michael, governor of the Wollo Province, died in the jail (1935) in which Ras Tafari Makonnen kept him before he could be crowned emperor of Ethiopia as Haile Selassie I. As granddaughter of a highly esteemed emperor, de Martini was deeply respected and well like by many of these groups. As a result, she was given free access to the cult areas by their leaders. She was of great help during this study, both for access to the field site and for her illuminating descriptions of Ethiopia. This chapter is dedicated to her memory.

7. *Teff* is cultivated, as are pulses and other plants, such as *ensete*. Not all are ideal for the local climate and soil. Teff is eaten mainly by the Amhara throughout Ethiopia, but they are a linguistic minority in this village.

8. This is the transcription of my first impressions taken from my field notes. I wrote them on the evening of the first day I spent in Garesu's gelma, the culthouse.

9. During those days I spent hours in the gelma, the place of worship of Divinity and the spiritual residence of the bale wuqabi, along with other believers. I walked around in the village, ate, and gossiped. I slept in the *elfigni*—the mundane residence of the bale wuqabi—on Garesu's *alga*, a kind of bed-sofa that he generously offered me.

10. I am still transcribing extracts from my field notes.

11. But the two places are only apparently two, for both the researcher and the social actor.

12. In the leader's living room there is a large sofa; some guests are there, all rather interested to show themselves as potentially close to Garesu, while the aggafari is sitting apart from the others, or is standing close to the door or on the threshold

of the elfigna's kitchen's door from where he winks and signals to the leaders. Mamo Abba Ruski, another important bale wuqabi who has come to honor Garesu, is also sitting in the elfigna.

13.   *Waq* is the sky Divinity of the Oromo pantheon, who is also worshipped by other ethnic groups that speak Cushitic or Semitic languages. *Fa,* an abbreviation of *afan,* means "tongue, language" in Oromo.

14.   The bale zar translates bodies or objects from one place to another, from one physical world to another. The master of zar, the powerful bale wuqabi, as well as the aggafari, translate one world to another, but above all they transport a man to another world, beyond the limits of this world, and then again back to the social world, to everyday life.

       This cult shows then that the translation performed by the master of the zar is not at all linguistic but rather social, political, and existential: *trans-latum.* This allows us to reflect on the meaning of translation in the field of literature and linguistics.

15.   The true translation is the conveying of Divinity to the temple. It resembles the concept of translation of the saint's body in the Roman Catholic canon into sacred relics. Nothing could be lost or changed; the displacement had to be effected as a whole and in toto in order to preserve and to found the holiness of this body or those relics and to manifest the presence of Divinity in human history.

16.   Each physical-social transition is a translation, and each translation, a physical-social transition. Two languages, languages of neighboring ethnic groups, are the institutionalization and the fixing pro tempore of two different paradigms of transition.

References Cited

Al-Shahi, Ahmed. 1984. "Spirit Possession and Healing: The Zar among the Shaygiyya of the Northern Sudan." *British Society of Middle Eastern Studies Bulletin* 11: 28–44.

Baxter, Paul T. W. 1969. "An Arsi Woman's Neighborhood Festival." In *Colloque International sur les Langues Couchitiques et les Peuples qui les parlent.* Paris: Centre National de la Recherche Scientifique.

———. 1979. "Atete in a Highland Arssi Neighborhood." *Northeast African Studies* 1: 1–22.

Boddy, Janice. 1988. "Spirits and Selves in Northern Sudan: The Cultural Therapeutics of Possession and Trance." *American Ethnologist* 15: 4–27.

Böhringer-Thärigen, Gabriele. 1996. *Besessene Frauen.* Wuppertal: Edition Trickster im Hammer Verlag.

Conti Rossini, Carlo. 1943. "I camminatori sul fuoco in Etiopia." *Rassegna di Studi Etiopici* 1: 94–110.

———. 1946. "Magica." *Rassegna di Studi Etiopici* 4: 73–76.

Kramer, F. 1984. "Notizen zur Ethnologie der passiones." *Kolner Zeitschrift fur Soziologie: Soziologie als Sozialwissenschaft,* Sonderheft 26.

———. 1987. *Der rote Fez: Über Besessenheit und Kunst in Afrika.* Frankfurt am Main: Athenaeum.

Lewis, Herbert S. 1982. "Spirit Possession in Ethiopia: An Essay in Interpretation." Pp. 419–27 in *Proceedings of the Seventh International Conference on Ethiopian Studies,* April. Addis Ababa: Institute of Ethiopian Studies.

———. 1989. "Values and Procedures in Conflict Resolution among Shoan Oromo." Pp. 673–78 in *Proceedings of the Eighth International Conference of Ethiopian Studies,* Vol. II. Addis Ababa: Institute of Ethiopian Studies.

Lewis, Ioan Myrddin. 1969. "Spirit-Possession in Northern Somaliland." Pp. 188–219 in *Spirit Mediumship and Society in Africa,* ed. J. Beattie and J. Middleton. London: Routledge and Kegan Paul.

———. 1989 [1971]. *Ecstatic Religion: A Study of Shamanism and Spirit-Possession.* London: Routledge.

———. 1991. "Zar in Context: The Past, the Present and Future of an African Healing Cult." Pp. 1–16 in *Women's Medicine: The Zar-Bori Cult in Africa and Beyond,* ed. I. M. Lewis, A. Al-Safi, and S. Hurreiz. Edinburgh: Edinburgh University Press for the International African Institute.

Natvig, R. 1988. "Liminal Rites and Female Symbolism in the Egyptian Zar Possession Cult." *Numen* 35: 57–68.

Palmisano, A. L. 1996. "Sein and Mimesis." In *Law, Life and the Images of Man: Modes of Thought in Modern Legal Theory: Festschrift for Jan M. Broekman,* ed. F. Fleerackers, E. van Leeuwen, and B. van Roermund. Berlin: Duncker and Humblot.

———. 2000. "On the Theory of Trance: The Zar Cult in Ethiopia." *Kea* 13.

———. 2001. "Presenza, assenza e rappresentazione nelle trance rituali." In *La tarantola fra scienza e letteratura.* Atti del Convegno sul Tarantismo, San Vito, 28–29 maggio 1999. Nardo: Besa Editore.

Reminick, Ronald A. 1974. "The Evil Eye Belief among the Amhara of Ethiopia." *Ethnology* 13: 279–91.

———. 1975. "The Structure and Functions of Religious Beliefs among the Amhara of Ethiopia." Pp. 25–42 in *Proceedings of the First United States Conference on Ethiopian Studies, 1973.* East Lansing: Michigan State University.

Translating Gamk Notions of Dream, Self, and Body

"Making Sense of the Foreign"

Akira Okazaki

Translation involves making sense of the foreign. But what does it really mean to "make sense of the foreign"? Walter Benjamin (1969, 75) wrote: "All translation is only a somewhat provisional way of coming to terms with the foreignness of languages." "Like translation," Vincent Crapanzano (1986, 51) says, "ethnography is also a somewhat provisional way of coming to terms with the foreignness of languages—of cultures and societies." Then he points out a paradoxical problem peculiar to "making sense of the foreign": "Like Benjamin's translator, he [the ethnographer] aims at a solution to the foreignness, and like the translator (a point missed by Benjamin) he must also communicate the very foreignness that his interpretations (the translator's translations) deny, at least in their claim to universality. He must render the foreign familiar and preserve its foreignness at one and the same time" (ibid., 52). Does this not mean that the notion of "making sense of the foreign" is itself a contradiction?

The fact is that to "make sense of the foreign" usually means only to "render the foreign familiar," rather than to "preserve its foreignness" in translation. Lawrence Venuti distinguishes two kinds of translation strategies, fluency and resistancy: the former is "a domesticating method, an ethnocentric reduction of the foreign text to target-language cultural values, bringing the author back home," and the latter is "a foreignizing method, an ethnodeviant pressure on those values to register the linguistic and cultural difference of the foreign text, sending the reader abroad" (Venuti 1995, 20). He argues that the dominance of fluency in English-language translation since the seventeenth century has almost eliminated translation strategies that resist the hegemony of transparent discourse, "closing off any thinking about cultural and social alternatives that do not favor English social elites" (ibid., 43). So, he claims, foreignizing translation in English can be "a dissident cultural practice" (ibid., 148) as well as "a form of resistance against ethnocentrism and racism, cultural narcissism and imperialism, in the interests of democratic geopolitical relations" (ibid., 20).

Likewise, James Clifford recognizes two antithetical attitudes in anthropology: familiarizing and defamiliarizing, or what he calls "anthropological humanism and ethnographic surrealism": "anthropological humanism begins with the different and renders it—through naming, classifying, describing, interpreting—comprehensible. It familiarizes. An ethnographic surrealist practice, by contrast, attacks the familiar, provoking the irruption of otherness—the unexpected" (Clifford 1988, 145). Then he argues that the "surrealist elements of modern ethnography tend to go unacknowledged by a science that sees itself engaged in the reduction of incongruities rather than, simultaneously, in their production" (ibid., 147). In fact, most of the mainstream Anglo-American anthropologists who took a transparent style for granted have little appreciated such a defamiliarizing element. So, like foreignizing translation in English, defamiliarizing ethnography can be a form of resistance against the regime of fluent domestication of otherness.

Importantly, Venuti suggests that "the 'foreign' in foreignizing translation is not a transparent representation of an essence that resides in the foreign text and is valuable in itself, but a strategic construction whose value is contingent on the current target-language situation" (Venuti 1995, 20). In other words, it is because of "the hegemony of transparent discourse in English language culture" (ibid., 305) that the foreign has to be constructed as a form of resistance. Similarly, otherness in defamiliarizing ethnography is not an essence that is valuable in itself but a strategic construction against the regime that would smoothly render the foreign familiar, providing a reader with the "narcissistic experience of recognizing his or her own culture in a cultural other" (Venuti, 1992, 5, as quoted in Richardson 1999, 276–77).

In this paper, I shall try to translate Gamk notions of "dream," "self," and "body," and "make sense of the foreign" by "rendering the foreign familiar and preserving its foreignness at one and the same time." I would suggest that it is necessary to question the assumptions "we" take for granted in order to deal with the paradox peculiar to "making sense of the foreign."

Dream

The Gamk people (of whom there are roughly 45,000) live in the Ingessana Hills, located in the border region between northern and southern Sudan. The Gamk language is, according to Bender (1983, 338), "a relatively 'pure' remnant of a declining East Sudanic presence in an area undergoing rapid Arabization." They have been, in fact, oppressed, exploited, discriminated against, and marginalized by outsiders, mainly by northern Sudanese Arabic speakers (such as government officials and traders) but sometimes also by southern Sudanese (such as rebels). Elsewhere (Okazaki 2002), I have discussed how the Gamk use dreams as a means of resistance to domination.

Dreams are of great concern to the Gamk people. Dreams can reveal to them potential threats from various powers, including those operating in the current civil war. While I had no special interest in dreams when I began my fieldwork, my field notes were rather disproportionately filled with data on their dreams, including discussions about dreams, the social action taken on account of dreams (such as healing rituals), and the playful activities of a special group of clowns that are given the name *caalk* "dreams" (odd though this naming may sound).[1] The fact is that dreams enable people to make sense of the situation, transform it by ritual means, and so overcome the uncertainties and hardships of life in the borderland.

Among the Gamk, in village life, dreams are talked about on many occasions: at any ad hoc casual gathering such as dance or drinking sessions; at communal work parties; at water places; or at any formal meetings such as weddings, healing rituals, or divination sessions. On such occasions, dreams are talked about just like news of actual happenings in the village. Where the dream is regarded as frivolous or a "mere" dream, as in our daily settings, we may well talk about a dream as a joke. But I have never witnessed a Gamk villager treating a dream as a joke. The dreamer is expected to recount a dream seriously. And there are always people around ready to listen seriously to other people's dreams.

Dreams are put into two categories: insignificant dreams *(caalk tal eel wa)* and significant dreams *(caalk tal saage)*. The former is a dream that people regard as unworthy of serious treatment. Some villagers recognize that a child may cry in dreaming at night after he has experienced a fearful event during the day. But the idea of the "causal" connection between one's experience during the day and dreams during the subsequent night, which is familiar to us, is not taken for granted by the Gamk. Especially in the case of "significant dreams," such an idea is usually dismissed. These dreams are said to visit different people in a similar form so as to suggest a publicly significant event, which is invisible to people's senses by daylight although it is in progress in the world. These are the dreams that deserve careful examination.

Significant dreams are usually quite distinct. Moreover, most of the dreams narrated at rituals have not only distinct but also strikingly similar plot patterns.

For instance, dreams of a dead person are likely to fall in the typical plot pattern consisting of the following sequence of events:

1. The dreamer [P1] sees a dead kinsman [P2].
2. P2 asks P1 for something to eat, or just appears hungry and keeps silent.
3. P2 shows a problem in progress among the living.

And, in the case of the dreams of a demon:

1. The dreamer [P1] encounters a person or demon [P2].
2. P2 demands from P1 his life or that of an animal.
3. P1 refuses, or bargains with P2 about it.
4. P2 threatens P1, throws stones at P1, or simply disappears.
5. P1 sees people killing an animal or an animal lying on the ground.

Although not all dreams comply with such patterns, the dream that even partially suggests such a pattern is regarded as a significant dream. Then one may wait for another, more distinct dream, to come. If one is in great anxiety, then one must consult the seers (diviners).

These prescribed plot patterns and shared concerns regarding the identity of the figure in dreams no doubt play an important role in dream recollection among the Gamk. Usually, dreams are not kept to oneself for very long (and, of course, no Gamk writes down his dreams) but are immediately narrated to someone else—usually, to family members. The dreamer's precise report of his dream experience is of paramount importance, but, because both dreamer and listener(s) are familiar with the plot patterns and share the concerns, the dreamer is naturally encouraged to narrate some details much more precisely than others. Therefore the dream is dialogically and intersubjectively shaped as it is initially narrated. Here there is scarcely room for the dream to remain a "subjective" matter. At this initial stage the dream is shaped into the form in which everyone will renarrate it later as a "fact."

The Gamk villagers' dreams may well contain anecdotes and imagery as vague, evanescent, incoherent, and inarticulate as ours. But because the Gamk share distinct plot patterns of dream narrative, they are able at first to distinguish the significant part from the insignificant part of everything that happens in a dream, and then clarify further details within the significant part according to familiar plot patterns. This seems to explain not only why their dreams appear to resemble each other but also why they can narrate dreams lucidly without being perplexed by obscure elements. Comparatively, we may well argue, in theory, that we can memorize and describe our dreams in much greater detail than the Gamk because we are less "biased" toward any particular part of our dreams. In practice, however, we tend readily to forget dreams, while the Gamk are much more able to recall them. It is, therefore, not because all dreams are meaningful to them but because there exists a socially recognized distinction between significant and insignificant dreams that they are able to recollect dreams lucidly and even to share them with others.

The Gamk attitude toward dreams is in striking contrast with the Freudian treatment of dreams, and this disparity is worth noting here. Since Freud, all dreams have become significant for psychoanalyst and patient. Even a dream that a patient finds difficult to remember is explored by the psychoanalyst so as to reveal the nature of the "repression" functioning tacitly within the patient. In this way, every detail of dreams has increasingly become meaningful for therapeutic purposes, and even the "failure" to remember or the "distortion" of dreams has become meaningful. This is parallel to the process in which selfhood has been redefined in the West. That is, the definition of human intention has been, so to speak, widened, including much wider and formerly involuntary mental movement (such as dreaming), and hence the self has become responsible for a much wider conduct.[2] Now, one can "have" or even "make" a dream, as in French *je fais un rêve.*

Among the Gamk, on the other hand, a dream is not something that a person can have or make and, therefore, be personally responsible for. Instead it is an event that one becomes responsible for publicly reporting and sharing. Linguistically, too, dreams are described as externally occurring events rather than internally produced mental sensations within the self. It is indeed impossible to phrase "I dreamed" as "the subject plus the verb" because there is no Gamk verb "to dream," but only a noun. In addition, a Gamk verb "to have" *(bel)* can never be used to say "I have a dream." While it is possible to say "I saw somebody in dreams," the commonest expression is "dreams ate me" *(caalk namsa).* Dreams are unpossessable, and the dreamer is even the object of dreams that act upon him from without.

For the Gamk, the dream has nothing to do with personal pleasure. On the contrary, they say, they dislike the dream because "it is a trouble" and "it wearies me." The villagers, except for seers and a few elders, even try not to "be eaten" by too many bad dreams. For this, it is generally considered better not to sleep too early. In addition, the dream that "eats" a person who sleeps in the daytime is likely to be colorful and terrifying, and is to be avoided. In fact, I rarely saw a villager sleeping in the daytime.

Only the seer is willing to expose himself to the dream. Because of this, seers are sometimes regarded as being "brave/strong" *(seger)* and are often called "bulls." In other words, whereas we sometimes try to avoid facing "stark-naked reality," ordinary Gamk villagers try to avoid facing "dream reality."

Nevertheless, no one can stop dreams from visiting or "eating" oneself. One must sometimes admit the problem shown in dreams. This means to expect imminent danger and put oneself in the state called *ta kor* (which means "with the word" or "a serious problem to be solved"). Under such pressure and anxiety, one may well become more prone to fall ill or, at least, discover ominous signs everywhere. But, as I have mentioned, not all dreams are immediately taken seriously. Usually people do not draw a hasty conclusion from a single dream without cross-checking other dreams. Moreover, there are often conflicting views about the seriousness of the situation and also about the identification of the images involved. Therefore, a long negotiation period may sometimes be required before the final action will take place. As a result, it may be discovered that some cases have not been dealt with soon enough and end in someone's death.

Let me introduce one case (see Okazaki 1997, 10–11) in order to illustrate how dreams actually affect people.

> *Kujiba, an elder, reported, "A dream visited ('ate') me last night. In the dream, I met a very old man who asked to kill a white goat that was obtained from the man who had chopped down the fruit of baobab trees (ufuk)." The news circulated rapidly among villagers. Following this, Mansuur, a young married man, fretfully argued in public: "It is a lie! Kujiba spread his dream story around only because he wants the meat to eat!" Mansuur was working hard to obtain a second wife. He often climbed baobab trees to chop down fruit, which he packed for selling to northern Sudanese traders. But this is considered dangerous, and few people had dared to do it until recently, when the fruit became marketable. These baobab trees are not personally owned, so fruits should be shared by all the villagers.*
>
> *Kujiba's dream report seemed to Mansuur to suggest that he was the person who had to provide a goat. Some of the elders took the report seriously, but other villagers appeared indifferent to it. In such a situation, people often wait for another dream to come, or consider whether or not these dreams and someone's illness or accident are related. If the case is really serious, Mansuur himself must be so informed in his dreams. In any case, this gives him*

"anxiety" (ta kor, "with the word," see above), which may, in due course, decrease or increase to the extent that he feels it necessary to kill a goat.
Mansuur disregarded the dream warning. The following morning, he climbed the trees as before. After a while, people seemed to have forgotten this dream warning. Many days later, Mansuur came to ask me to put ointment on his leg. He said, "I had an accident at work," but I didn't ask him about the details of his injury. A few days later, he came to ask for a place to sleep, because he said he had to give up his bed for visitors. He looked a bit tired from his daylong work. Early the next morning, the cold woke me up. When I tried to make a fire, I saw him speaking in his sleep with a pout: "Ufuk! Ufuk!" The Gamk word ufuk means baobab trees. Suddenly, the dream warning flashed across my mind. More than three weeks had passed since the initial dream was first reported and then almost forgotten. I hoped that Mansuur would agree to kill a goat before it was too late.

What interests me is that this case was initiated by one dream visiting Kujiba and concluded by another dream visiting Mansuur. This shows how dreams are socially significant among the Gamk. Or, to be more precise, this shows how arguable our assumption about the distinction between the social and the mental is.

Mansuur's case may also be concerned with the dilemma between the personal or selfish economic pursuit introduced by the external market, on the one hand, and the importance of sharing the resources in the hill among the villagers, on the other. If the dream is a kind of revelation to the Gamk, its power and value lie not only in what it reveals but also in the extent to which it can relate many other problems. Thus, first of all, the dream operates as a touchstone for people to reflect on past experiences, present moral concerns, other dreams, divinatory results, symptoms of illness, and disunity among the villagers. Second, the dream suggests a clue to a missing link between these problems, so one may manage to weave otherwise fragmented, and seemingly unrelated, problems into an intelligible and sharable narrative.

The Gamk view of the dream appears incompatible with the modern European assumption that dreams are quintessentially personal experiences. However, the point in saying this is not to represent the Gamk view as exotic but to call our assumption into question. Shifting notions of dream and self in European epistemological history between Descartes and Freud suggest that we can today ignore the social significance of dreams, not because the dream is a personal or illusory experience in the first place, but because the dream has drastically and incessantly been marginalized, internalized, desocialized, personalized, psychologized (see Rose 1996 for psychology as an individualizing technology), and physiologized according to the dominant discourses in place that shaped European knowledge of the self and the world (for example, neurological theories of dreaming may be products of the elimination of subjective [psychological] and intersubjective [social] elements from the total human dream experience). Nevertheless, dreaming is seen as a common human physiological process that happens to every individual in a similar way. In other words, dreaming is almost always taken for granted, if not a priori. But the fact is that, even historically, European dream theories have undergone tremendous changes, to the extent that what one recognizes as dream experience today is quite dissimilar to what another did a few centuries ago.[3]

Self

A difficult problem arises from the Gamk notion of dream—namely, the problem of representations of the experience of the self. To the Gamk, it would be absurd to argue that dreams are internally produced mental sensations within the self. Events in dreams, they insist, happen externally. Thus, in Gamk one cannot say, "I had a dream," or, "I dreamed." "Dreams ate me" *(caalk namsa)* is not merely a matter of a figure of speech. Besides the expression of dreaming, this reversal of grammatical subject and object is frequently employed when emotional states are verbalized in Gamk—for example: "anger ate me," "hunger beat me," or "shame seized me." Moreover, not only in verbal expressions but also in actions at rituals is it evident that what our psychology would describe as internal processes—such as bad memories or "trauma," as well as "anger" and "pleasure"—are treated as something that affects people from outside as if they are experiencing a kind of power acting from without.

Geertz says, "We cannot live other people's lives, and it is a piece of bad faith to try. We can but listen to what, in words, in images, in actions, they say about their lives" (1986, 373). Yet it is not easy to "listen to what they say," because we tend to take such an expression as "dreams ate me" as "I dreamed," and so readily to read into it our own configuration of experience rather than that of the Gamk people. Some may even maintain that such an expression is only "a dead metaphor" that should not be taken "literally." But this could preclude the possibility of exploring alternative configurations of experience and result in mistaking one's own experience for the universal. Thus, in order to "listen to what they say," it is necessary to suspend such an easy "fluent" translation and, instead, listen not only to what they say but how they say it as well. This should be, at the same time, an attempt to excavate our assumptions about reality and selfhood that are embedded in language and that do not simply give shape to our experience of the self but may also preclude the possibility of understanding another form of experience. That is what Lienhardt has attempted rigorously in his study of Dinka religion (1961, 147–70). I quote his argument at great length not only because it touches the heart of the matter but also because it has received various kinds of criticism. His argument and the criticism are both useful in dealing with the Gamk case.

> The Dinka have no conception which at all closely corresponds to our popu-
> lar modern conception of the "mind," as mediating and, as it were, storing up
> the experiences of the self. There is for them no such interior entity to appear,
> on reflection, to stand between the experiencing self at any given moment
> and what is or has been an exterior influence upon the self. So it seems that
> what we should call in some cases the "memory" of experiences, and regard
> therefore as in some way intrinsic and interior to the remembering person
> and modified in their effect upon him by that interiority, appear to the Dinka
> as exteriorly acting upon him, as were the sources from which they derived.
> Hence it would be impossible to suggest to Dinka that a powerful dream
> was "only" a dream, and might for that reason be dismissed as relatively
> unimportant in the light of day, or that a state of possession was grounded
> "merely" in the psychology of the person possessed. They do not make the
> kind of distinction between the psyche and the world which would make such
> interpretations significant for them. (ibid., 149)
>
> It is perhaps significant that in English usage [as Collingwood sug-
> gests] we have no word to indicate an opposite of "action" in relation to the
> human self. If the word "passions," passiones, were still normally current as
> the opposite of "actions," it would be possible to say that the Dinka Powers
> were the images of human passiones seen as the active sources of those pas-
> siones. (ibid., 151)

While Lienhardt admits that he "can discuss only inadequately" such "a difficult question of differences between Dinka and European self-knowledge" (ibid., 149), his argument is extremely rigorous. He does not easily, or smoothly, translate the Dinka experiences of the self into modern English equivalents. His "translation" is so uncompromising that it cannot but historicize, and almost deconstruct, modern European assumptions about reality and selfhood that are embedded in language.

Despite, or perhaps because of, his subtly provocative and highly imagina-tive account (though Ryle's skepticism about "the concept of mind" [1963 (1949)] is detectable), it has been (mis)interpreted at times and referred to as evidence for an evolutionist argument (Hallpike 1976, 259, quoted in Heelas 1981, 55), as a typical example of the mistake often made by anthropologists about selfhood (e.g., Cohen 1994, 171) or as a highly distorted view of African conceptions of the person (Morris 1995, 146–47). To these critics, Lienhardt has merely described the Dinka as a "mindless" people. In my view Lienhardt has not given a "distorted" or exaggerated account of Dinka self-knowledge. Rather, he has argued that some of the representations of European self-knowledge are exaggerated. He would not have been able to give a "fuller" account of Dinka struggles against human existential situations if he took "our popular modern conception of the 'mind'" for granted. In order to make my point, it is necessary to examine carefully his use of the Latin word "passiones."

His use of the Latin "passiones" as the opposite of "actions" is crucial in elucidating the inchoate configurations of human experience that still maintain "a link between moral and physical experience" (Lienhardt 1961, 148). Importantly, the term is used to express what we cannot express in modern English: a form of experience that is not grounded in psychology but that reveals itself when "the kind of distinction between the psyche and the world" is blurred. What is more important, this does not mean that the Dinka have no concept of "action," but simply that "we [modern Europeans] have no word to indicate an opposite of 'action' in relation to the human self"—hence, a "fuller" account as I said. Nevertheless, Heelas, for example, takes his argument rather technically and uses the term "passiones" to classify "indigenous psychologies" (1981, 41). On the other hand, Kramer rightly argues that "*instead* of being content, like Horton, with the concepts from our present-day psychologies, he [Lienhardt] reverted to a Latin word in order to denote a mode of experience and of conceiving of experience for which there is no longer a word in modern languages" (1993, 58):

> When Lienhardt reverts to the concept passiones in order to "translate" an African mode of belief into European language, this tacitly reflects a far-reaching change within Europe, and not, as Horton presumes in his own analogous scheme, some difference between African and European codes. The decisive boundary is not one which divides African and European conceptions of the social and individual constitution of the subject, but rather one which divides cosmology from psychology in their entireties. (ibid., 59)

This suggests that those who condemn Lienhardt for his description of the Dinka as a "mindless" people are completely missing the point. Because they take modern European popular psychology of "mind" for granted, they are unable to recognize

Dinka self-knowledge as a possible configuration of human experience of the self unless it is described in modern European categories. In this respect, Needham has perhaps not overstepped the mark in saying (in a different context): "The preju-dice . . . is that human nature is essentially the same everywhere, and that inner states, dispositions and capacities have already been adequately discriminated by psychological vocabularies of Western languages" (1981, 67).

But from a different perspective, Lienhardt's account has been questioned. Crapanzano, referring to the account, admits that "[m]uch of what is articulated in the West as within the individual may be articulated as outside the individual in those societies in which the spirit idiom is current." But he warns, "We must distinguish carefully here between the phenomenology of experience, including the experience of the self, and the articulation of experience, including the ar-ticulation of the self. The effect of the latter upon the former must always remain hypothetical. The difficulty of keeping the phenomenology separate from the articulation results from the necessity of suspending disbelief in our everyday encounters with others in our world" (Crapanzano 1977, 12). Also Jackson, quot-ing the above passage from Lienhardt's book, notes "a view widely held among Africanists, that Africans tend to exteriorize and bestow social and bodily identity upon processes which Westerners tend to see as abstract and intrapsychic." He makes similar remarks:

> [O]ne may be misled into thinking that empirical and epistemic levels of understanding are identical. However, the lack of emphasis on interiority in Dinka and Fulani thought does not necessarily reflect a modality of self-experience wholly different from our own; it may simply represent a different ideological representation of experience. My own view is that the relation between human experience of the world and ideological representations of the world is nonisomorphic and indeterminate. . . . [Their] emphasis on community makes it appropriate for them to see "psychic" phenomena as functions of social relationships. (Jackson 1989, 47, 48, original emphases)

Thus both critics argue that we must distinguish representations from experience. My comment on these critiques is that it may still be ethnographically proper, if phenomenologically awkward, to explore the relation between them. Certainly, "conventional modes of explaining phenomena should be seen not as descrip-tions of lived experience but as interpretations and rationalizations that reflect the exigencies of the sociopolitical order" (ibid., 48). But the fact is that the people themselves do not usually see their own representations in this way. For them, these are neither interpretations nor rationalizations. This is also the case with us.

While Jackson briefly contrasts these society-oriented representations with "the strongly individualistic ethos of the Western world," which "entails a conception of the person . . . with a unique inner life that is not reducible to social processes" (ibid.), Westerners do not normally regard the representations of their "internal" experience "simply" as ideological (hence, false) representations. On the contrary, "inner" states are often taken for granted or as true experience, or even as universal.[4] That is to say, the distinction between representation and experience is less clearly drawn by those who use it than by those who analyze it. In other words, to the former, representations can be part of their experiences. Their "lived experience" does not seem entirely separable from their expressions.

Smith argues, though in a different context, that it is important to explore the complex effect of representation upon experience: "How people construe themselves and how their constructions are culturally phrased should interest us not only because they are humanly interesting for their own sake . . . but also because as reflexively conscious creatures people are influenced by their self-conceptions. Their metaphors of selfhood become in part self-fulfilling prophecies" (Smith 1985, 84). What is emphasized here is the inseparability of experience from representations or the constitutive aspect of representations. That is to say, by representing the experience of the self, one can "actualize" (Bruner 1986, 7) or even "achieve" (Goodman 1968, 8) it rather than simply represent, or copy, it either short of or in the fullness of its properties. This theory also suggests that the self should be seen not as the essential and static entity that may be represented or distorted in various ways but as itself being constantly constituted and reconstituted by the parameters and possibilities of expression (see Parkin 1991, 205).

I have suggested that Lienhardt has not given an exaggerated account of Dinka self-knowledge, but rather has contended that some of the modern European representations of the self are exaggerated. Of course, he never spoke explicitly of "exaggeration." Instead, he made it reveal itself in and through comparative understanding, by translating Dinka experiences of the self so rigorously that modern European assumptions about selfhood embedded in language are forced to deconstruct themselves, as I have argued. There is a particular area of experience that requires rigorous comparative understanding because of a striking conflict of representations. Compare, for instance, the French expression "I make a dream" with the Gamk one, "a dream ate me"; or English "I caught a cold" with the Gamk "a cold caught me." Experiences such as art, love, laughter, anger, anxiety, pain, hunger, shame, memory, or dreams that one cannot easily control are likely to be represented in European languages in reverse order. That is, whereas these experiences are described as something that affects people from without in Dinka and Gamk expressions, modern European languages often describe them as something that occurs internally, as if one can create, contain, and control them by oneself, or as if something like a much deeper self or "unconscious" mind acts upon the "surface" self. I am not arguing here that Dinka and Gamk expressions are more "natural" or "truer" to "real" experiences, but simply that such persistent reference to "I" and the "inner" self in European expressions certainly serves to make the active and self-contained subject look more "natural" and "truer."

Jameson argues that the "individual autonomous subject" is "a philosophical and cultural mystification" (1985, 115). Mary Douglas regards "the unitary, indivisible person" or "subjective agency" as "part of the jurisprudential definition of reality which has to exclude dreams and visions and occultism so as to protect our civil liberties" (1995, 93). But although such an extremely autonomous form of subject may never really exist, the idea itself has been persistently imposed upon people in the areas of juridical, medical, educational, moral, and economic practices in the West; as a result, such a form of human person is almost taken for granted. The irony is that autonomy is not "autonomously" formed within the individuality of the person but imposed upon him/her by external discourse in a way that one cannot control. Thus Strathern rightly argues that "prescriptive individual*ism* displaces the individuality of the person" (1992, 149, original emphasis). All this suggests that it is not our knowledge of the self but the power to shape our knowledge of the self that makes it possible to accept such a form of subject as "true" (Hutton 1988, 135). Thus, the question to be asked is not whether we are autonomous subjects, but how this discourse of self works.

The model of autonomous selfhood serves various ends. Since this form of self is independent from its environment or context, it is able to maintain the "anaphoric potential" of the "I"—that is, the "I" that, once it is registered in discourse, is the referent for all subsequent invocations of the "I" (Kondo 1990, 32). Obviously, this is fundamental to the modern juridical system. Without presupposing a unitary form of self (and rejecting any claims of the multiple forms of self), it would be difficult to hold an individual person responsible for his own doings and intentions, a theme that Douglas has extensively discussed in relation to her theory of the accountability system (1982, 1992).

Yet such an individual subject would not properly be maintained even by the disciplinary power of various institutions unless people tried to discipline themselves with a strong will to internalize experience. Although the question of whether people are shaped by others or shape themselves may seem insoluble, they do not want to see themselves as disciplined or shaped by others. What is evident here is that this form of self is no longer regarded as solely imposed by these institutions, but as being acquired by one's own "choice," even by a "spontaneous" action, so that each individual becomes totally responsible for the choice and its consequences. To return to the problem of representations of the experience of the self, all this indicates how the self is "actualized" and "achieved" rather than simply represented by representations.

Body

Another problem concerns the lack of a Gamk word equivalent to the English word "self." The word *iing,* the only Gamk term that may be glossed as "body," may also be used to refer to "self." I will translate it as "body/self." It does not, however, make sense in itself unless it is used as a reflexive pronoun (or as a reflexive emphatic pronoun); for example: *nar iing* ("he curses himself/body") "he swears," *goth iing* ("he opens himself/body") "he becomes well or recovers," *as iing* ("he becomes himself/body") "he is arrogant." In addition, the term is a compound of the possessive prefix plus the stem and always undergoes vowel harmony; that is, *a + (ii)ng = aang,* "myself/body," *uung* "yourself/body," or *iing,* "herself/body." So it always takes the form of "myself/body," "yourself/body" or "herself/body" but not the form of "the body" as an independent noun detached from the person. In other words, the Gamk notion of "body" is always already inscribed in the notion of self in such a way that the former cannot make sense without the latter.[5]

Therefore it is scarcely surprising that it is impossible to render into Gamk the concept implicit in the English term "body"—that is, "corpse" or "carcass." I suspect that the body-corpse equation becomes imaginable only when the body, regardless of living or dead, can be thought of as an objective entity detachable from a human person. Does it follow that the human body is inconceivable to the Gamk? I think that, if it is difficult for us to understand the Gamk notion of "body/self," the reason has to be sought not in the Gamk notion but in the European notion of body, which has been deeply entangled in the "body/mind" dichotomy. In fact, when translating local terms concerning selfhood, anthropologists have been careful about using their own terms such as "mind" or "soul." But the term "body" has usually been used without the slightest hesitation. If the body/mind dichotomy is problematic at all, is it not one-sided to put only the notion of mind under comparative scrutiny?

The European notion of "the body" is no more universal than those of "inner states" that are, according to Needham, "preponderant concerns only in certain civilizations" (1981, 77). In the area of politico-medical practice, for instance, we are now familiar with the fact that, in the West, the body itself, as well as the notion of body, has been subjected to control, discipline, training, shaping, manipulation, and torture (Foucault 1977), as well as with the argument that the notion of the body as an object of positive knowledge emerged from the eighteenth-century medical experience of opening up corpses and from the experience of individuality that was bound up with the experience of death (Foucault 1973, 1977).

Thus it is not surprising that there is a counteractive tendency to liberate the body from such suppression. In fact, "the body" today seems to be even more "fashionable" as a subject of study (as well as an object of possession and obsession) than "self" or "person," which Andrew Strathern calls "mentalistic" subjects. He then argues that "the shifts from a mentalistic to a bodily focus has been accompanied by a determined effort to reconceptualize the mind/body relationship itself" (1994, 44). Nevertheless, "a bodily focus" seems to obscure, rather than elucidate, the problem involved. The recent overheated attention to the body itself indicates not only how historical and political the body is but also how the power to control the body (and the self through the body) operates in an ever more invisible way.[6]

The European notion of the body is, therefore, not only complex but has probably been too manipulated to be used to understand notions of body in other, less industrialized, politically less centralized societies.[7] In any case, the Western dissociation of "mental" from "physical," or of "thinking" from "feeling," may involve a more complicated process than it is popularly thought. The precise question to elucidate the issue should be asked from the viewpoint of critical historicism.[8]

What is significant for the present consideration is, however, not the extent to which the European conception of the body can be revealed or criticized, but rather the fact that the body/mind dichotomy has already so profoundly infiltrated our (European) language that it even seems impossible to describe the Gamk experience of the "body/self" without being implicated in the dichotomy (as so many "anti-Cartesian" thinkers seem to unwittingly speak in a quite Cartesian way). In the circumstances, there is always a danger of reinventing a familiar Cartesian agent in the borderland village if we translate Gamk notions of "self" and "body" in a smooth and fluent way.

Making Sense of the Foreign
by Sending the Reader Abroad

At the start I suggested that it is necessary to question our assumptions in order to deal with the paradox peculiar to "making sense of the foreign"—that is, to "render the foreign familiar and preserve its foreignness at one and the same time." I have tried to keep questioning and defamiliarizing European assumptions about the human person.

The result shows, I hope, that, in the process of making sense of the foreign, what is important is not so much to preserve the foreignness of Gamk notions as to render our familiar notions foreign and strange by comparison with Gamk. This suggests that the foreign in defamiliarizing ethnography should be strategically constructed in order to provoke a defamiliarizing effect—that is, rather than to make another people strange or exotic others, to make a reader (and what he or she takes for granted) stranger than others or, to use Venuti's words, "to send the reader abroad." In other words, it is necessary to make a reader admit *Je est un autre,* as Rimbaud said, in order to undermine his or her cultural narcissism.

Clifford argues that familiarization and defamiliarization, which are anthropology's antithetical attitude, presuppose each other (1988, 145). Importantly, only defamiliarization enables people to think the unthinkable and know the unknowable. In the process of familiarization, on the other hand, the unthinkable, the unknowable, and anything strange are simply presupposed or smoothed away. Thus it is highly likely that the entire process of familiarization is closed and therefore serves only to eradicate otherness and establish sameness.

According to Foucault, "[m]odern thought is advancing towards that region where man's Other must become the Same as himself" (1970, 328). Likewise, William Desmond says that, in Western philosophy, otherness is always subsumed within a dialectical *Aufhebung,* yielding diversity within unity, difference within identity, otherness within sameness. "Otherness thus seems to be both saluted and domesticated within a larger overarching totality" (1987, 1). In other words, Western dialectic is in fact a dialogical monologue. This is why we need more openness to otherness and more resistance against the regime of fluent domestication of otherness.

Notes

1. For details of Gamk clowns, see Okazaki (in press).

2. This is also parallel to the process of shaping of a private realm by introspection at penitential confession: "Examine diligently, therefore, all the faculties of your soul: memory, understanding, and will. Examine with precision all your senses as well. . . . Examine, moreover, all your thoughts, every word you speak, and all your actions. Examine even unto your dreams, to know if, once awakened, you did not give them your consent" (*L'Instruction du penitent* by Segneri 1695, quoted in Foucault 1978 [1976]).

3. See Okazaki 1997 (Appendix 2: "The History of Dreams in Europe") for details.

4. Jackson himself seems to take "inner states" for granted (ibid., 48). Needham says that there is a persistent tendency "to interpret exotic psychological obser-vations as the varied expressions of [natural] universal inner states." He regards this as a kind of essentialism, or "a craving for ultimate particulars," characteris-tic of "Western epistemology" (1981, 76).

5. This kind of inseparability is not unique to Gamk; see Lienhardt (1980, 78) for a Dinka word *gwop* ("body," "self") and Evans-Pritchard (1956, 156) for Nuer words *pwony* ("the whole creature," "the individual," "the self," or "the total organism") and *pwonyda* ("myself").

6. In a newspaper, an art critic wrote about the irony suggested by a sculptor who presented an objet d'art entitled "fashionable fitness body-building equipment." It is in fact a wooden replica of a modern "bench press style multi-gym," but it is so ancient-looking that it closely resembles a set of traditional instruments of torture.

7. How exotic the Western idea of the body is may be illustrated by "a famous in-cident that occurred to the missionary and ethnologist Maurice Leenhardt (*sic*) in New Caledonia. Asked whether he finally understood the Christian concept of the soul, one of Leenhardt's disciples replied, 'No, Reverend Leenhardt, it was the idea of the body that you brought to us; we have always known the soul'" (Napier 1992, 11).

8. For example, see Asad (1988, 84) for the medieval monastic conception of *gestus*, which "brings together what later centuries were to separate sharply: cognition and affect. "

References Cited

Asad, Talal. 1988. "Towards a Genealogy of the Concept of Ritual." Pp. 73–87 in *Vernacular Christianity: Essays in the Social Anthropology of Religion*, ed. W. James and D. H. Johnson. Oxford: JASO.

Bender, M. Lionel, ed. 1983. *Nilo-Saharan Language Studies*. East Lansing: African Studies Center, Michigan State University.

Benjamin, Walter. 1969. *Illuminations*. New York: Schocken.

Bruner, Edward M. 1986. Ethnography as Narrative. Pp. 139–55 in *The Anthropology of Experience*, ed. V. W. Turner and E. M. Bruner. Urbana and Chicago: University of Illinois Press.

Clifford, James. 1986. "Introduction: Partial Truths." Pp. 1–26 in *Writing Culture*, ed. J. Clifford and G. Marcus. Berkeley: University of California Press.

———. 1988. *The Predicament of Culture: Twentieth-Century Ethnography, Literature, and Art*. London: Harvard University Press.

Cohen, A. P. 1994. *Self Consciousness: An Alternative Anthropology of Identity*. London: Routledge.

Crapanzano, Vincent. 1977. "Introduction." In *Case Studies in Spirit Possession*, ed. V. Crapanzano and V. Garrison. New York, London: John Wiley.

———. 1986. "Hermes' Dilemma: The Masking of Subversion in Ethnographic Description." Pp. 51–76 in *Writing Culture*, ed. J. Clifford and G. Marcus. Berkeley: University of California Press.

Desmond, William. 1987. *Desire, Dialectic, and Otherness: An Essay on Origins*. New Haven and London: Yale University Press.

Douglas, Mary. 1982. *In the Active Voice*. London: Routledge and Kegan Paul.

———. 1992. *Risk and Blame: Essays in Cultural Theory*. London: Routledge.

———. 1995. "The Cloud God and the Shadow Self." *Social Anthropology* 3: 83–94.

Evans-Pritchard, E. E. 1956. *Nuer Religion*. Oxford: Clarendon.

Foucault, Michel. 1970 [1966]. *The Order of Things*. London: Tavistock.

———. 1973 [1963]. *The Birth of the Clinic*. London: Tavistock.

———. 1977 [1975]. *Discipline and Punish*. London: Penguin.

———. 1978 [1976]. *The History of Sexuality. Vol. I: An Introduction*. London: Penguin.

Geertz, Clifford. 1986. "Making Experiences, Authoring Selves." Pp. 373–80 in *The Anthropology of Experience*, ed. V. W. Turner and E. M. Bruner. Urbana and Chicago: University of Illinois Press.

Goodman, N. 1968. *Languages of Art*. Indianapolis: Bobbs-Merrill.

Heelas, Paul, et al., eds. 1981. *Indigenous Psychologies: The Anthropology of the Self.* London: Academic.

Hutton, Patrick H. 1988. "Foucault, Freud, Technologies of the Self." In *Technologies of the Self,* ed. L. H. Martin, H. Gutman, and P. H. Hutton. Amherst: University of Massachusetts Press.

Jackson, Michael. 1989. *Path Toward a Clearing: Radical Empiricism and Ethnographic Inquiry.* Bloomington: Indiana University Press.

Jameson, Fredric. 1985. "Postmodernism and Consumer Society." In *Postmodern Culture,* ed. H. Foster. London: Pluto.

Kondo, Dorinne K. 1990. *Crafting Selves: Power, Gender, and Discourses of Identity in a Japanese Workplace.* Chicago: University of Chicago Press.

Kramer, Fritz W. 1993. *The Red Fez: Art and Spirit Possession in Africa,* trans. M. Green. London: Verso.

Lienhardt, Godfrey. 1961. *Divinity and Experience: The Religion of the Dinka.* Oxford: Clarendon.

———. 1980. "Self: Public, Private; Some African Representations." *Journal of the Anthropological Society of Oxford* 11: 69–82.

Morris, Brian. 1995. *Anthropology of the Self: The Individual in Cultural Perspective.* London: Pluto.

Napier, A. D. 1992. *Foreign Bodies: Performance, Art, and Symbolic Anthropology.* Berkeley: University of California Press.

Needham, Rodney. 1981. "Inner State as Universals: Skeptical Reflections on Human Nature." Pp. 65–78 in *Indigenous Psychologies: The Anthropology of the Self,* ed. P. Heelas et al. London: Academic.

Okazaki, Akira. 1997. *Open Shadow: Dreams, Histories and Selves in a Borderland Village in Sudan.* Ph.D. dissertation, University of London.

———. 2002. "The Making and Unmaking of Consciousness: Two Strategies for Survival in a Sudanese Borderland." Pp. 63–83 in *Postcolonial Subjectivities,* ed. R. Werbner. London: Zed.

———. In press. "Defamiliarizing Ourselves: Clowning, Dreaming and Anthropology in a Sudanese Village." In *The Games of Gods and Man: Essays in Play and Performance,* ed. K. P. Koepping. Hamburg: LIT Verlag.

Parkin, David. 1991. *Sacred Void: Spatial Images of Work and Ritual among the Giriama of Kenya.* Cambridge: Cambridge University Press.

Richardson, Michael. 1999. "Translation as a Means of Cultural Transmission." Pp. 267–86 in *Crossing Cultural Borders: Towards an Ethics of Intercultural Com-*

munication, ed. S. Inaga and K. L. Richard. Kyoto: International Research Center for Japanese Studies.

Rose, Nikolas. 1996. *Inventing Our Selves: Psychology, Power, and Personhood.* Cambridge: Cambridge University Press.

Ryle, Gilbert. 1963 [1949]. *The Concept of Mind.* London: Penguin.

Smith, M. B. 1985. "The Metaphorical Basis of Selfhood." In *Culture and Self: Asian and Western Perspectives,* ed. A. M. Marsella, G. DeVos, and F. L. K. Hsu. New York and London: Tavistock.

Strathern, Andrew. 1994. "Keeping the Body in Mind." *Social Anthropology* 2: 43–53.

Strathern, Marilyn. 1992. *After Nature: English Kinship in the Late Twentieth Century.* Cambridge: Cambridge University Press.

Venuti, Lawrence. 1992. *Rethinking Translation: Discourse, Subjectivity, Ideology.* London: Routledge.

———. 1995. *The Translator's Invisibility: A History of Translation.* London and New York: Routledge.

Translating the Pain Experience

Jean Jackson

 10

The Introduction to this volume speaks of translation in terms of processes of appropriation and recontextualization, noting that translation presupposes a mobility of meanings under new sets of interpretive conditions. This essay utilizes this broad definition to address the issue of cognizing and communicating the chronic pain experience. The tighter meaning of translation—translating a text in a source language into a target language—is used here metaphorically.[1]

The essay proceeds as follows: I first address the difficulties that inhere in attempts to talk about one's pain, and follow with a note on the issue of intentionality behind pain behavior, both verbal and nonverbal. I then consider the issue of how one translates an embodied pain experience into concepts, and into verbal and nonverbal behavior interpretable by others, beginning with a discussion of why communicating about pain is so difficult. Objectification and subjectification, two processes involved in cognizing the pain experience, are then explored, as well as the question of whether empathy can be considered a kind of translation. The final section, on interpretive competence, asks two questions: Who is talking, the self or the illness? and, Whose translation is the most authoritative, the sufferer's or another's, in particular the clinician's? The biomedical discourse on chronic pain translates pain-related behavior into a set of technical, text-based assertions. By definition this discourse is engaged in by persons who are not speaking out of their own pain; in fact, having the experience oneself is thought to potentially hinder the translation. We will see that many sufferers complain that much of what their pain means to them is "lost in translation," so to speak, during this particular process of appropriation and recontextualization.

This essay is based on a year (in 1986) of ethnographic fieldwork with sufferers of severe chronic pain in an inpatient pain treatment facility in the United States, which is here called the Commonwealth Pain Center (CPC).[2]

Five preliminary caveats about how this essay conceptualizes pain need to be established. The first is succinctly stated by Loeser, a pain specialist: "Pain is not a thing; it is a concept that we impose upon a set of observations of ourselves and others. It . . . cannot be measured directly" (Loeser 1996, 102). The second is that pain is an experience felt in the body.[3] Third, if emotionally caused pain is experienced physically, it *is* physical pain, no ifs, ands, or buts. Fourth, the reader should remember that "pain" here refers to chronic pain.

The fifth caveat concerns an issue occupying a large space in the philosophical literature: to what degree can one's pain be communicated to others? One position—the phenomenological one—holds that another's pain is unknowable. A more or less opposite position, associated with Wittgenstein, holds that pain is extremely knowable because our experiences are socially informed, and a great deal of cultural meaning and importance is assigned to pain. The position taken here holds that, however a person experiences a given pain and whatever meanings it holds for him, that experience and those meanings derive from language and culture, which are shared (i.e., even preobjectified pain is not precultural)—and that a given sufferer's experiences of pain cannot be anyone else's unmediated experience.[4]

Intentionality

Although translation can be said to occur at every stage of the pain process,[5] I focus here on consciously intended (discursive) translations of pain into concepts and communications. (Note that the interlocutor can be oneself.) According to our definition of pain as conscious experience, cries and screams under properly administered anesthesia are not examples of pain being communicated.[6] Because we have ample evidence that, should a sufferer so choose, even severe pain can be undergone with no accompanying pain-related behavior,[7] we can conclude that communicating about the presence of chronic pain usually involves some degree of intention. I do not deny that at times behavior resulting from a pain experience lacks such intention; for the most part, people reacting to torture do not intend the behavior they exhibit. But *chronic* pain's natural language, verbal and nonverbal, is silence; as Morris and others have pointed out, after a while, such pain constitutes a radical assault on language: "There is simply nothing that can be said."[8]

Translating the Embodied Experience of Pain
Difficulties

⌢ Although we speak and think from an embodied perspective, there turn out
to be numerous reasons why chronic pain sufferers say they have difficulty formu-
lating concepts about their pain, either to assist their own thinking or to communicate about the pain to others. For example, one impediment is that envisioning
severe pain that lasts and lasts is nearly impossible; Hilbert, a sociologist, states
categorically that chronic pain is "meaningless" in this respect (1984). Another
source of difficulty for some pain sufferers is their lack of a comprehensive psychological vocabulary. However, inadequacies in the language cause problems for
all sufferers trying to conceptualize or communicate their pain, regardless of their
degree of psychological sophistication. Sufferers also complain that their communications about pain, despite being well formed, even eloquent, are often not
correctly received, and that their messages are interpreted in ways not intended by
them. For example, a sufferer grappling with enormous amounts of pain will find
that the more she communicates her pain, the greater the risk of its being seen as
illegitimate, for she will very likely be seen as inappropriately using the body to
accomplish goals of the mind. A related difficulty derives from how Western ideology holds that a sufferer of "real" pain (pain having organic causes) is much more
entitled to it than one who suffers embodied pain due to emotional causes, if it
lasts and lasts. Knowing this, CPC patients focused a great deal of attention searching for ways to demonstrate that their pain had physical causes. However, they
found that an adequate description of their pain required a more comprehensive
semiotics than one limited to cause. Trying to reconcile this requirement with the
threats to self-esteem posed by more psychologically comprehensive discourses
on chronic pain often resulted in inarticulateness and silence that were, ironically,
eloquent communications about an important feature of the experience.

In general, as Scarry notes, pain "resists language" (1985, 4). In the first place,
the mind/body division in Western culture sees language as belonging to the mind,
not the body. Bodily communications, whether within the body (the body's reactions to external stimuli—for example, a horror movie—or to inner states such as
hunger or sexual arousal) or using the body to send a message ("body-language"),
are seen as prelinguistic.

In severe pain, embodied communication is clearly taking place; we could
call this communication the language of pain, but so antithetical is it to ordinary
natural language that "antilanguage" might be a better label. When communicat-

ing its messages, pain not only resists, but also can obliterate, everyday language. The expression "seeing stars" suggests the quality of this erasure.

Pain not only resists linguistic treatment, it resists all attempts at representation. One cannot reproduce a given pain (or other experience) in media such as painting or music; one can only elicit an observer's memories of a pain or produce a new pain that is perceived to be connected in some way to the original pain. Artistic productions that depict pain by producing a new pain are often seen as successful because they engage empathic processes that produce the sense that one is feeling what the other feels. Whether or not these are to be considered translations is discussed below.

Pain also resists language because it is invisible, and cannot be measured or ascertained apart from the sufferer's affirmation of its presence. We can determine very little about a pain (absent any other signs) when the affected individual can make only nonverbal responses, as happens with infants and animals. With more information about the cause, or about the body's and mind's reactions to a pain, we can begin to treat it linguistically by giving it a name and describing its characteristics. But without such information, pain, like other bodily based feelings, resists verbal description.

Language allows distance from experience, and while we may benefit from this feature when we try to gain control over aversive experiences, language does not reproduce the link between the experience and the "me" undergoing it. We intellectualize with language; we see it as distinct from the body, and we privilege it—often stripped of the emotional (see Rosenberg 1990, 165)—over the body. Since pain is experienced in the body, is almost always aversive,[9] and contains much that is indeterminate and inchoate, it is often poorly served by language. Kirmayer (1992, 324) questions whether we can ever say the body is a certain way when that knowledge is worked out through a language that imposes its own structure on experience and thought. For these reasons, attempts to translate the language of the pain-full world are understandably never very successful. *Traduttore, traditore* ("the translator betrays") definitely applies here.[10]

Note that although language has trouble describing lived experience, eloquence often emerges when metaphor is allowed—the interlocutor's attribution of eloquence probably due to his empathetic response to the metaphor. Metaphors of pain most often refer to either agency (e.g., a knife) or bodily damage. Some CPC examples: "My back feels like it's an S, twisted." "It's like a pimple that took a long time to develop and finally abscess, and I'm at the abscess point." "*That* pain is a heavy, dull ache, the other is like a flash of lightning—all I can think of is the 4th of July." "It was one solid mass of tension, they're like huge fists." "It's like a blowtorch aimed at you." "Like Joan of Arc at the stake, a burning, burning, burning, and they never stop." "And underneath it is so hypersensitive that if I step on a pebble it feels as if someone ran a dagger through my foot and up out of my shoulder." "It whips me, it really whips me." "Like an anvil on my shoulder." However, in general, despite attempts to describe one's pain, despite even eloquent metaphors, one's extremely real chronic pain often remains unreal to others.[11]

Translating Pain from Experience to Cognition: Objectification

⌢ When a pain draws our attention, we usually respond by foregrounding and objectifying it, most often to understand and control the difference between painful and painless states. CPC patients spoke of their pain as an object in this sense, as well as in the sense of being "out there": "physical," "real" pain.[12] They also spoke of their bodies as objects that "had" pain. Many felt that such pain could be measured, a notion that confounded tissue damage (nociception, the alteration in the body that produces the onset of pain) with pain. Thus, the results of a CT scan might be spoken of as if they showed the pain itself. But patients found that pain would not submit to being thus constrained, leading to many complaints about how difficult it was to think about or speak of a pain that permeated, infused, dominated, and merged with their lived reality—in short, possessed their bodies and, at times, their minds.[13]

Brian, a pain sufferer interviewed by Byron Good, describes his body as being taken over by pain. For him, "the pain has agency. It is a demon, a monster—Pain is an 'it'" (Good 1992, 29). Pain sufferers speak of an intruder that invades the body and, if the pain lasts, invades the self as well, changing both substantially. The pain literature is full of sufferers' descriptions of their alienated bodies, perceived as much more distinct from the experiencing and acting self than prior to the onset of pain. In addition, severe, long-lasting pain changes the world surrounding body and self; Good, describing Brian's world, shows how the building blocks of his perceived world—time and space—have begun to dissolve. Our usual relationship to the body is that of nonexperience—Leder's notion of "the absent body" (see Leder 1990). However, sufferers of severe chronic pain find that they participate in a relationship with their bodies characterized by obscenely intensive and extensive interaction.

Another reason CPC patients experienced difficulty translating pain into concepts or speech was that language robs pain of some of its preobjective quality.

To speak of preobjectified pain would result in something like, "I combine with pain, I include pain." Merleau-Ponty talks about a painful foot as a "pain-infested space" (1962, 140). The awkward language here reveals the difficulty of using referential language to describe the experience of pain. When fully experiencing severe pain, we simply are "in pain," we are "pain-full," and in this state there can be no appropriation, no recontextualization, and hence no translation.

Not wanting to remain in this state, CPC patients were highly motivated to translate their pain by objectifying it, as Good puts it, "to reverse the deobjectifying work of pain by forcing *pain itself* into avenues of objectification" (Good 1992, 29). But they realized that because such objectification distorted the experience, in a sense betrayed it, their translations were defective. Ironically, although speaking about pain automatically robbed it of at least some of its preobjective, "pure" experiential quality and resulted in the translation difficulties patients reported, they persisted in their efforts. In a sense they wanted both an accurate representation *and* the distortion, for they hoped the latter would somehow reduce the aversiveness of the experience. If a text is aversive in both form and content, and if it is inscribed on a would-be translator's body, she will be ambivalent about producing a "faithful" translation. Patients at CPC searched for objectifying language that would provide a better label for their malady, or more information behind the diagnosis they already had, or a new prognosis—anything that would provide a return ticket to the pain-free world. However, they continued to find that language failed to represent their lived reality, and that meanings that seemed to hold promise turned out to be siren-meanings that neither helped them in their quest to be understood as pain-full beings, nor helped them return to a pain-free state.

Despite our notions about language as communicating, clarifying, enhancing, and creating experience (as in the case of performative language),[14] referential language inadequately conveys ongoing subjective experience because it must objectify, and in so doing inevitably restrict, distort, and mystify. But given that CPC patients lived an abominable reality, in a sense hell itself, despite this misrepresentation they continued to long for a language that promised distance, control, and abstraction precisely *because* representation is not coterminous with experience itself. Every time they chose to speak or groan or remain silent, and were disappointed (at times a disappointment approximating despair) at how their communications were lost in translation, they compellingly illustrated the incommensurability between embodiment-as-lived and embodiment-as-represented. This is why, paradoxically, patients both pursued everyday language—answers, names,[15] definitions, meanings that promised reassurance and cures—and avoided it. Kirmayer refers to this problem when he opposes the order of the text and the order of the body, questioning how meaning and value can be sustained when consciousness is constricted, degraded, and defiled by pain (1992, 323, 324). Although patients reported feeling profoundly misunderstood and pigeonholed by referential language, because they passionately wanted to escape their reality, they felt compelled to pin their hopes on it.

CPC patients saw how language misrepresented their pain, and saw how, to an equivalent degree, their pain replaced and transformed referential language, distorting and trivializing its messages. If a patient made an effort to temporarily leave the pain-full world—for example, to concentrate on a relaxation audio-tape—he would then return to the pain-full world and find that what he had just worked so hard to absorb now resembled Jabberwocky.

Some patients tried to rethink pain's objectlike quality and the degree to which it was "out there." Edward Valliant, a CPC patient nearing the end of his stay, spoke of how he had come to reconceptualize his pain, saying that, although the level of pain was the same, there was "less felt pain." The awkward language he was forced to use resulted from the paltry number of concepts and lexicon available to him, leading him to wonder whether his comment made sense. We can explain what he meant if we accept that, in daily life, we seldom become objects to ourselves (see Csordas 1990; also Leder 1990). In describing the recontextualization he has achieved, Edward begins with a preobjective and prereflective experience of his body and finds less "felt pain." Yet when he objectifies himself and his body he finds, in fact, no decrease in pain. Although patients found it difficult to express this idea, I recorded many similar remarks; another patient spoke of "less noticed pain." Fred Hardy, another patient, said "the pain's the same severity, but it doesn't hurt as much." Similar examples can be found in the pain literature. In a Public Radio International broadcast, the writer Reynolds Price stated that, while the level of pain from a tumor had remained the same, in a kind of "oriental, mystical" way his mind had ceased worrying about it: what was once a "huge bonfire" has turned into a "small campfire" about a hundred yards away (Public Radio International n.d., 11).

Although pain sufferers find they cannot eliminate pain—at least very few CPC patients found they could—some of them report achieving "less felt pain." Edward's and Reynolds's characterizations illustrate what takes place during such a recontextualization of perception. These sufferers' comparisons of the original and translated pain experiences show some features that changed and some that held constant (e.g., "the pain's the same"; even Reynolds's "huge bonfire" and "small campfire" share some features). Reynolds's metaphor situates the self at a greater distance from the perception, and diminishes its size and significance. Edward speaks of his pain as remaining the same, but says the impact of the perception has decreased. In the same radio broadcast Reynolds also provides an image of a rotary switch that, when turned down, helps decrease consciousness of a part of the body; here, presumably, the object remains the same (painful body part), but the perception is affected by altering one's consciousness of it, a process more similar to what happens with Edward. All these images describe how the context changes by increasing distance, or decreasing impact or awareness. Such changed conditions permit, first, changes in interpretation, and, second, changes either in how the text is read (perception of pain), or in the perceiver: another pain sufferer quoted in the radio broadcast said, "So it's sort of like another me, almost, that has this pain, but the real me of course doesn't."

A number of discourses can be employed to analyze what has occurred (see Damasio 1999; Loeser 1991).[16] The one I have chosen, drawing on the metaphor of translation, looks at the effects of a rereading of a bodily experience while it is happening. Like Siamese twins, the original and translated pains must co-occur in some fashion. Patients either described two co-occurring pain experiences or described experiencing two selves. The translation is a recontextualization of the perception, but it does not replace the old perception. If a total substitution were to happen, once the new pain had entirely supplanted the old, it would exist only as a memory, and we would no longer have a translation. But this has not happened in the instances discussed here.

Interestingly, if we explore the relationship between the two pains, we find that, despite sufferers' assertions about a "pain that's the same," the original pain is necessarily experienced differently as well (as in "the real me, of course, doesn't"). Both new and old pains have become objectified and lost some of their "pure" experiential quality simply by being compared with each other. Although using the metaphor of translation is often tricky, the hermeneutic work these sufferers do resembles translation in that the pain experience that remains "the same" cannot be the same; the new experience existing alongside it has altered it.

Such a codependency between original and translated pains recalls a phenomenon that occurs with translations of written texts discussed by several literary critics. Benjamin (1968, 71) speaks of an "organic" relationship between original text and translated text: "[By] virtue of its translatability the original is closely connected with the translation."[17] Crapanzano notes that "anyone who has read [Lowell's translation of Racine's *Phaedre*] will never be able to read the original again without recalling the raw violence that Lowell has uncovered in Racine's courtly alexandrines" (2000, 116). These critics argue that while a translated written text would seem to be separable from the original—would seem to stand by itself if the reader could not access the original (it has disappeared or is in an incomprehensible language)—in some important respects it would no longer be a translation, because the relationship has been severed.

Another parallel between translating a pain text and translating a written text lies in the nature of the mystification of just what the text consists of. Yes, a text is a material object, analogous to the chemical and electrical activity that produces a pain experience. But, as Iser (1978) and others have pointed out, texts do not exist without readers, and each reading to some degree is unique. In similar fashion, Edward and Reynolds seem to have discovered that if they rethink their pain as something unstable, as in fact not so "out there" and objectlike, they can read it in significantly altered fashion, and even control the disposition of the new reading to some extent. They have discovered that the unchanging aspects of the pain object (chemical and electrical activity that continues to occur in peripheral tissue and the brain) have been mystified as the essence of the experience, and this insight has allowed them to correctly see that the material object is merely a necessary precondition for a reading to occur.

Subjectification: The Impossibility of Translation

〜 Chronic pain sufferers at CPC had found that body, self, and pain were linked in numerous and intricate ways. Pain was seen to be a part of self because it was a feeling, was inside their body, and dominated their lives. Many CPC patients reported that their self-concept had changed radically over the years. A sufferer of intractable chronic pain finds that, to a great extent, her pain-full body has determined the self she has acquired. Although unwanted, this altered self is, like the altered body that accompanies it, the only one she has. Here we can speak of pain appropriating the meaning of self and assigning a new one: the pain-full self. Those sufferers like Edward and Reynolds who reported achieving less suffering spoke of transforming the relationship that had developed between self, body, and pain. Although these individuals described the transformations in numerous ways, in general it was a process in which pain became more incorporated into their selves. They came to see pain as less threatening and more approachable, and spoke of negotiating, arguing, and drawing up contracts: CPC patient Terry Kaplan said, "My God! I can talk to it!" We can speak of this process as subjectification in the sense of strengthening the link between the pain and the experiencing subject, the self.

A related, but negatively valenced, way of speaking about subjectification concerns processes in which the self is forced to combine with the pain-full body to become the "pain-full me." At times CPC patients identified the self with pain: Terry said outright, "The pain is me." In extreme cases, at times phenomenologically one *is* pain; one's selfhood and one's pain-full body combine. When it claims so much attention from the self that it is experienced as absorbing the self—the "me"—pain is subjectified in this unwanted way, and the self finds itself subject to the rule of pain. Roy Deleo, a machinist who had loved his job and had become very bitter following a needless work-related accident that forced him into retirement, said, "If this is retirement, you can have it. I guess the only thing keeping me alive is the pain." Here the pain is seen to control whether he lives or dies. I collected many similar statements: pain that subjected the experiencer to torture, for example, or subjected the sufferer to suicidal ideation. For some, like Brian, such subjection increased as pain progressively destroyed their world. Unlike other subjectification processes, for instance, a fervently sought merging with the Holy Spirit, merging with pain was unwelcome, a terrifying process sometimes. Teresa Gilman, a young woman at CPC with severe back pain, spoke of becoming "psychotic with pain." Less than a month after this interview she killed herself. When such extreme subjection happens, no translation of the pain experience is possible, because the translator has merged with the text.

These quotations illustrate that acquiring a new, pain-full self involves extensive recontextualization and meanings that have been *very* mobile, so much so that we have to ask, Who is the actor doing the appropriating, the self, the body, or the pain? These are slippery issues, because pain is both subject and object, both "me" and "not-me." It is not unique in this respect: people speak of many kinds of feelings as being both "me" and "not-me." All-powerful, overwhelming feelings have this property: by requiring the experiencer to leave the everyday world, the experience of self is transformed, so that the "me" and "not-me" converge in some ways, or at least have different boundaries.

Some CPC patients tried to work with this notion of "subject" pain—pain merged with the self. However, they found that deobjectifying their pain transformed it into "all in your head" pain. Imaginary pain cannot be an object "out there" (note that "out there" can refer to inside the body). Patients sometimes said, almost always in jest, that they would welcome finding out that their pain was of this subject/subjective nature because, even though it is stigmatized, a pain that "doesn't exist" would be less threatening, less horrible. Good's interviewee Brian, for example, wants to "explain it away . . . say that it's all just imaginary, it's a figment, it really doesn't exist" (Good 1992, 40). Mary Rourke, a CPC patient, spoke of how she would look in the mirror and argue with herself: "This can't be as bad as I think it is," followed by, "You're imagining it, it's really not as bad." Brian's and Mary's efforts illustrate the hoped-for transformative role of increased agency that accompanies such subject/subjective pain. They are hoping to alter an experience by altering the interpretive conditions within which it is conceptualized, an attempt, in fact, somewhat similar to Edward's attempt to achieve "less felt pain." Imogene Felice, also a CPC patient, tried the same strategy: "I tried willing it away. 'Well,' I figured, 'if I did it to myself, I can get rid of it.' And I kept telling myself, 'I don't want you, get out of here.' Didn't work." To be sure, she is speaking of the pain as an "it" and so objectifying; however, the distance between pain and the subject, the self, is far less when pain is seen as imaginary. The slide from "myself" to "it," then back to "myself," and then to "you" in the quotation is telling. She is trying to set up new interpretive conditions that will change the pain experience's meaning and bring about a change in the experience itself. However, the message was not successfully sent—the translation "didn't work" for her, just as it didn't work for either Mary or Brian.

Patients who tried to deobjectify their pain by boldly labeling it imaginary found that such an exercise did not bring peace of mind. For one thing, if something so horrible is imaginary, they would have to conclude that they were seriously delusional. Most of these patients found that such reasoning simply did not succeed: their attempts at linguistic (de)representation, deobjectification "didn't work" because the goal of changing experience through the performative effects of translation was not achieved. Neither Reynolds nor Edward, nor patients like them who reported success, saw their pain as something they "did" to themselves. Rather than deny that their pain was "there," their translations involved changed perception ("less felt pain")[18] or changed self-concept (noticing that there was both a "me" and a "real me"). In general, self-blaming discourses did not bring about successful recontextualizations.

Of course, there is no such stark division between "real" and "imaginary" pain, but for many CPC patients, "imaginary" was the meaning that resulted from attempting to translate "object" pain into an experience occurring inside the brain and mind (as opposed to, for instance, in a tooth), for that made it "in your head" pain. Everyone knew the potential hazards of seeing their pain as "in your head," for this came close to saying the head was involved in producing it.

The above examples of the varying degrees of success following the translation attempt reveal some sources of difficulty in achieving the goal of altered experience of pain. The successful efforts recontextualized the pain experience and allowed a translation of the self's conceptualization of itself experiencing the pain, which, simultaneously allowed a back-translation, as it were, of the actual experience, changing it.[19] Not by eliminating pain, nor by denying its existence, the process split either the experience or the self, and thereby allowed the original to exist side by side with the translation, resulting in a successful translation, though hardly a faithful one.

Empathy Rather than Translation?

We have explored some reasons why the pain experience is difficult to define and describe, whether to oneself or to others. We saw that metaphor can help represent the pain experience, and that sometimes, by altering the metaphor, one can alter the experience. Such metaphorical representations also can produce powerful reactions in others, resulting in what often seem to be successful communications, at least in some respects. Are such communications translations?

CPC patients reported feeling frustrated when trying to talk about their pain "on the outside," but said they felt understood "for the first time" by their fellow patients. They reported something akin to joy at being in a community of fellow-sufferers, even though prior to admission some had dreaded the prospect, and they talked of a sense of shared experience and shared identity, of feeling comfortable, of finding it much easier to talk about many problems connected to chronic pain. Patients did disagree with one another sometimes, but about the cause of each other's pain, about what kind of pain behavior was appropriate, and about proper treatment. When they were effusive about how well they understood one another, they were talking about the experience itself. Interestingly, they also said they didn't have to talk: "We have something in common, it's sort of a bond between people. No one says anything to complain, not any more." "They know when you don't grimace that you aren't necessarily free of pain." Given the difficulty communicating about pain, and given that their principal message ("I am in pain and I realize you are in pain") was sent and received early on, why continue to talk, or communicate nonverbally, about pain? They knew from having experienced pain's preobjective and prelinguistic quality that attempts to provide more information about it would most likely be unsuccessful.

Perhaps the reason patients felt that only their CPC fellows really understood their preobjective, preabstracted pain experience, and came to feel comfortable with minimal communication about it, was precisely that the shared understanding they reported did not depend on translation. In a community of sufferers like CPC, all members met the preconditions for understanding *bodily lived* meaning, which allowed them to bypass the objectification that translating experience requires.

I have mentioned the possibility that pain can be successfully communicated by producing a pain in the interlocutor. A great deal of ritual, music, and other forms of expressive culture works this way.[20] The interlocutors will make connections between a pain they begin to feel as a result of the communication, and respond empathically. However, while experiencing an elicited pain or an embodied comprehension of another's suffering may indicate that a communication about pain has been successfully sent, has translation occurred? One can argue that empathy is not translation. Any similarity between the original and the new pain is inferred by the interlocutor; perhaps in actuality no resemblance exists at all.[21] Clearly, eliciting a pain empathically associated with another person's pain does not depend nearly as much on creating a likeness as would an attempt to accurately describe a pain; rather, empathy depends on the interlocutor experiencing something she understands to be a representation *in some way.* Indeed, she might know that the two experiences are incommensurable, yet report a successful communication because she has been so powerfully moved. Hence, if we still want to consider the production of empathetic pain as translation, we must allow that the nature of such a translation differs significantly from translations that attempt to appropriate an original pain and represent it with some degree of verisimilitude. Applying Jakobson's notion of translation as involving two equivalent messages in two different codes to such cases of empathetic pain production would be a stretch (Jakobson 1959, 233). The nature of the appropriation is different, as is what makes it a successful communication.

To conclude: perhaps sufferers of severe chronic pain like those at CPC feel they understand one another's pain precisely because no one's pain has been translated. Rather, by remembering his own pain, or by feeling a new pain, an interlocutor finds he is successfully connecting to the other's pain. Ironically, abandoning attempts to translate a pain experience may constitute a step toward successfully communicating what the experience is like.

Interpretive Competence

〜 We have seen that chronic pain sufferers sooner or later find out that everyday language can be a serious stumbling block to communication, because it requires objectifying, and therefore distorting, the experience. In addition, many CPC patients felt that not only was language inadequate, it also was the handmaiden of the medical establishment. Good's interviewee Brian complains that "the professionals" have their own answers and solutions, which do not match his (Good 1992, 40). Pain sufferers' anguished search for meaning arises out of their desire to escape from inauthentic, imposed, inadequate meaning. In particular, those patients whose diagnoses are inadequate in some way, resulting in their feeling anxious about whether the medical establishment will ultimately legitimize their pain with a proper diagnosis, have special reason to be suspicious of the clinical language being employed. CPC staff members engaged in medico-scientific, psychotherapeutic, and, occasionally, holistic-medicine discourse about pain, but although all patients granted at least some authority to these approaches, for the most part they "didn't work"—or at least didn't work well enough.

Who's Talking?

〜 We saw above that not only is pain conceptualized as an object, an "it," but it is also described as having control and wanting to dominate. Pain sufferers spoke of feeling possessed, of being forced to speak the antilanguage of pain. In an aptly titled essay, "The Sick Who Do Not Speak," Basil Sansom reports a somewhat similar idea of illness taking over the body, pushing the self aside, among Australian Aborigines in the fringe camps of Darwin. It is not actually the case that the sick do not speak; rather, when they speak they are seen as making no sense, because the illness has taken charge and has the floor. Even lucid, well-constructed sentences are wholly discounted: "That not Long Billy talkin. Thatta sickness talkin" (Sansom 1982, 191). In the West a similar assumption that the sufferer's rational faculties have been suppressed lies behind the at times rather automatic discrediting of a patient's ability to speak authoritatively; here, as well, a person deemed to be truly sick may be seen to lack "any capacity to yield up a volitional statement" (ibid., 190).[22] In fact, those who are granted authority to interpret—to translate—are by definition not firsthand experiencers. What is interesting in Darwin is that people who have been ill can *never* speak of their illness; only the community that helped the sick person get well has the authority to do so. In the West the formerly sick are permitted to speak about their ailment (and at times hold forth in a manner requiring great forbearance on the part of their audience). However, in some respects they also continue to be denied speaking privileges, for the real story of an illness is contained in the medical record, similarly owned, as it were, by the community that brought the sufferer out of his painful state.

Sansom argues that the "sickfella caan talkin" rule snatches the ill "out of the world of inter-subjective understandings to become patients—that is, human beings who will have to endure objectification for the period of their suffering. This objectification begins with diagnosis. It is a relegation to impotence, based not on enunciated complaining, but grounded instead in the ability of unaffected third parties to read signs" (ibid., 190–91). Hence, in a sense, CPC patients who report feeling possessed have analyzed their situation correctly; the pain monster has indeed taken over, for the self has been transformed into a *patient,* whose illness authoritative observers must examine directly, without the self mediating. An example is provided by Keefe and Dunsmore, two pain specialists: upon perceiving nonverbal communication about pain to be a conscious effort, clinicians become "enraged," for nonverbal pain behavior should be "unintentional" (i.e., prosodic) pain communication, presumably a far more reliable source of information about "the pain sensation" than discursive speech.[23]

Kleinman describes the process of authoritative speech shifting from the sufferer to the clinical community in this way:

> [B]iomedicine presses the practitioner to construct disease, *disordered biological processes, as the object of study and treatment. . . . The patient's and family's complaints are regarded as* subjective *self-reports, biased accounts of a too-personal somewhere. The physician's task, wherever possible, is to replace these biased observations with* objective *data: the only valid sign of pathological processes, because they are based on verified and verifiable measurements. . . . This is a view from a depersonalized nowhere. Thus, the doctor is expected to decode the untrustworthy story of* illness as experience *for the evidence of that which is considered authentic,* disease as biological pathology. *In the process, the doctor is taught to regard experience—at least the experience of the sick person—as fugitive, fungible, and therefore invalid.* (Kleinman 1995, 32, emphases in original)

The main reason why many chronic pain sufferers occupy an especially liminal, suspect space in the world of the sick is that pain itself cannot be observed without the participation of the sufferer's self. As Kleinman indicates, biomedical practitioners have trouble dealing with inner states. Clinicians speak of many kinds of unconscious motives that hinder a sufferer's ability to know what is actually going on inside his body, and therefore impede his ability to speak authoritatively about it to others—which means that a systematically distorted translation can never be ruled out. Primary, secondary, and tertiary gain are clinical phrases describing such unconscious motives.[24] For these and other reasons, despite the fact that no one can authoritatively describe another's experience, clinicians speak with far greater authority than pain sufferers do, an authority generally granted to them by the pain sufferers themselves.

Clearly, an important reason behind sufferers' difficulty translating the chronic pain experience is their exclusion from the list of approved-of translators. Those who can produce authoritative translations—the members of the Language Academy, so to speak—not only are, by definition, nonexperiencers, but, in addition, their job is to eliminate the experiential qualities of whatever malady lies behind the pain symptoms and replace them with observed, objective data—with signs rather than symptoms. Even though pain sufferers attempt to learn the professionals' language, they will never be seen to speak it fluently, precisely because they experience pain.

~ Employing the metaphor of translation to describe cognizing and communicating pain is challenging because of the need to shift from defining pain in terms of material processes to defining it as a text to be read, which requires postulating a merged body and mind in a way that many Westerners find difficult to apprehend. Pain is usually seen as something that is just felt, caused by tissue damage or organ malfunction. This essay has argued that seeing, cognizing, and communicating the pain experience as a translation process can be useful precisely because of the effort needed to recontextualize—translate—the concept of pain. Seeing pain as more unstable than conventionally supposed, as capable of being "read" in more than one way, and as never being quite the same experience, allows us to fruitfully analyze pain sufferers' statements that at first seem contradictory, for they speak of two simultaneous pains, or two perceiving selves. That original and translated pains must exist side by side in some fashion reminds us of Benjamin's notion of an "organic" relationship between original and translated text. The metaphor of translation also helps us to understand the instability of self and body during objectifying and subjectifying processes. Self, body, and pain at times appear to be distinct, but at other times seem to merge.

We can say that while both patients and clinicians seek to "force pain itself into avenues of objectification," pain sufferers also protest that what they feel are inauthentic and imposed meanings that result from certain attempts at objectification on the part of "the professionals." Patients live out the paradox of wanting to convey the nature of their pain-full world, to produce an accurate, authorized translation, while at the same time wanting to produce a distorted translation that, in its very misrepresentation, would performatively alter their experience of that world, rendering it less horrible.

⌒

Notes

Author's note: Research was funded by NIMH Research Grant MH41787, and sabbatical funds from the Massachusetts Institute of Technology. My deepest thanks to the staff and patients at CPC for supporting the study in so many ways, and to Tullio Maranhão and Bernhard Streck for organizing the conference and making this volume a reality. Also thanks to Vincent Crapanzano and Cheryl Mattingly for comments on earlier drafts.

1. De Man provides a conventional definition of translation: "a species of extended metaphorical equivalent in another language of an 'original' text" (1986, 73–105, as cited in Crapanzano 2000, 114). If we employ Jakobson's tripartite scheme (1959), his third type of translation, "intersemiotic translation or *transmutation*," comes closer than the conventional meaning of interpretation of verbal signs by means of some other language (ibid., 233).

2. See Jackson 2000. Patients' names have been changed.

3. The International Association for the Study of Pain defines pain as: "an unpleasant sensory and emotional experience associated with actual or potential tissue damage, or described in terms of such damage" (IASP 1979). The cause of a pain (e.g., a herniated disc) should not be conflated with the experience itself. Like virtually everything else in this field, the definition of pain is contested. Damasio distinguishes *pain* and *emotional reactions to pain* (1994, 266–67; 1999, 71–76) because he is interested in the neurobiology of pain and, to some extent, its evolution. He presents convincing examples of cases of neurological pathology in which patients report "the pain's the same" but do not experience the usual emotional responses to pain. For my purposes, however, defining pain as something that can occur when the individual is unconscious is not useful. A

neurological model of pain that accounts for all instances and all etiologies is not available at present.

4. In her discussion of how we manage to move out of the "inexpressible privacy and suffocation of [our] pain," Das (1997, 70) refers to Wittgenstein's notion of a "language game," which Kirmayer describes as "a metaphor . . . to explicate the different ways in which knowledge is acquired and used. It roots meaning in social interaction and technique or praxis" (1992, 338; see also Sullivan 1995). According to Das, in this game, a statement like "I am in pain . . . makes a claim asking for acknowledgment, which may be given or denied. In either case, it is not a referential statement that is simply pointing to an inner object" (1997, 70). As many linguists have pointed out, speech acts are rarely simple communications about referential information, something especially true about pain-sufferers' speech about pain—one reason why Wittgenstein devised the notion of a "game" using the example of pain (the other reason is pain's reputation as the quintessentially private inner state). Wittgenstein wished to remind philosophers of the intersubjective and social nature of all inner states.

5. Fields, a pain specialist, argues that pain is always "virtual"—that is, occurs in the form of cerebral representations, even at the molecular level. Apparently, like the proverbial turtle in the tale, pain turns out to be representations "all the way down" (Fields 2000).

6. Note that some pain researchers would say that pain is being communicated when the individual is unconscious.

7. There are, to be sure, physiological indicators of the probable presence of pain (e.g., a foot jerking spasmodically, an X-ray), but these imply pain; we base our inference either on observed responses to nociceptive stimuli (i.e., stimuli that bring about the onset of pain) or on observed physiological *responses* to pain. The absence of such physiological responses can help validate the absence of pain, as when a man undergoing a religious ordeal, who looks as though he ought to be experiencing pain (he is chewing glass or sticking a sword through his side), says he is not, and his claim is supported by a remarkably small amount of bleeding. But the bottom line is that, since pain is an inner state, people must use some kind of communication—speech or gesture—to communicate that they are feeling pain. As pain persists, communicating its presence in order to inform others is seen to be less and less necessary, bringing about an accompanying decrease in the legitimacy of such communication.

8. Morris (1991, 73). He also comments that "[as] one medical treatment after another fails, chronic pain becomes an experience about which there is

increasingly nothing to say, nothing to hope, nothing to do. It is pure blank suffering" (ibid., 78). The writer Reynolds Price notes that *King Lear* contains these lines: "The worst is not / So long as we can say 'This is the worst.'" He concludes that at the actual worst, "presumably, we'll be mute as rocks. Or howling, wordless, or humming nonsensical hymns to any conceivable helper" (1995, 160). Also see Das's discussion of the "fractured relation to language" documented for the many survivors of prolonged violence "for whom it is the ordinariness of language that divides them from the rest of the world" (1997, 76). Finally, the medical historian Roy Porter, discussing nonsufferers' choices of language to write about pain, notes:

Indeed, the very notion of a syntax of pain has been culturally and morally problematic. Over the centuries, it has often been argued that physical outrages or emotional injuries may be so terrible that to translate them into words may obscenely traduce and degrade them; we talk after all of "unspeakable" atrocities. Silence may be more eloquent than speech. "The rest is silence": great playwrights like Shakespeare have recognised that the dramatic presentation of tragedy is readily trivialised by descriptive vocabulary. In the depths of his pain, the words King Lear utters are "Howl, howl, howl, howl, howl." (Porter 1994, 108)

9. See endnote 4: whether aversiveness is to be seen as an emotion depends on one's definition of pain.

10. Adams notes that while this "trite and timeless" Italian proverb is true, it is also true "of any man who opens his mouth . . . to 'say what he means.' He isn't going to, because he can't" (1973, 6). A nonpain example of a translation of experience is Oliver Sacks's (1984) description of "musicking" himself down a cow path after an injury.

11. However, as many authors point out, this is not the whole story. Cademenos notes: "Pain is paradigmatic of all human intersubjectivity, and its recognition cuts across all cultural barriers. We are more certain of its reality in others than of anything else in them" (1981, 73). He notes that "[e]ven the most abhorrent forms of torture are based on the torturer's ability to apprehend the exquisiteness of the pain he is inflicting upon his victim" (ibid.).

12. On "real" pathology, see Good (1994, 10) and Kirmayer (1988).

13. In the words of one sufferer: "It is impossible to define physical pain, one cannot describe it; it is only a matter of experience. One cannot speak of pain with a capital P. It is a succession of seconds, a succession of minutes, and this is what

makes it so hard to withstand" (quoted in Morris 1991, 16, who cites Herzlich and Pierret 1987, 87).

14. See Das's moving discussion of men inscribing slogans on "enemy" women's bodies during the partition of India and Pakistan (1997, 83–85). She also describes a novel in which a father's speech gives life to his horribly violated daughter: "and though she may find an existence only in his utterance, he creates through his utterance a home for her mutilated and violated self" (ibid., 77).

15. Note that I am including here individuals at CPC who suffered severe chronic pain from well-known causes. Although in one sense they already had a "name"—a diagnosis of arthritis, for instance—they still searched for words to describe their condition more comprehensively, the words that would account for why they, unlike some other arthritis sufferers, suffered *so much.*

16. The contributors to Cohen and Campbell, eds., 1996, collectively illustrate the range of approaches to treating pain.

17. Compare "[No] translation would be possible if in its ultimate essence it strove for likeness to the original. For in its afterlife—which could not be called that if it were not a transformation and a renewal of something living—the original undergoes a change" (Benjamin 1968, 73).

18. Elsewhere Edward speaks of "a turnaround in how I perceive the pain," adding that if you looked at the pain as being a horrible, terrible thing, then it was indeed going to do horrible, terrible things to you. But if you looked at it as being a neutral thing—as just *there*—it lost a lot of its power.

19. The pain literature contains a vast number of studies of how imaging changes experience, including perception of pain, some of it arguing that physiological processes are altered as well.

20. See Schieffelin (1976) for a striking example of pain used in ritual for this purpose.

21. An example is Bill Clinton saying, "I feel your pain." Interestingly, scholars' analyses of poetry translations sometimes approach this point when considering "untranslatable" colloquial styles. The "key" for conveying such styles is radically different, yet the translation works. See Leighton's discussion of Chukovsky's "signal devices" when translating Kipling, Burns, and Whitman into Russian (1984, xxii).

22. See Hahn 1995, 234–61, for a discussion of the way in which the authority of patients who are themselves physicians is discounted by their fellows who are treating them. These afflicted physicians, troubled and surprised, sometimes refer to this phenomenon as "shunning."

23. As cited in Sullivan (1995, 11).

24. Benefits from being ill are spoken of as "gains." Primary gain diverts the patient's attention from a more disturbing problem; secondary gain occurs if the patient is exempted from difficult or tiresome duties or receives sympathy and care; tertiary gain involves persons other than the patient receiving a benefit from the illness (Hahn 1995, 26).

References Cited

Adams, Robert M. 1973. *Proteus, His Lies, His Truth: Discussions of Literary Translation.* New York: Norton.

Benjamin, Walter. 1968. *Illuminations,* ed. H. Arendt, trans. H. Zohn. New York: Schocken.

Cademenos, Stavros. 1981. "A Phenomenological Approach to Pain." Ph.D. dissertation, Brandeis University.

Cohen, Mitchell J. M., and James N. Campbell, eds. 1996. *Pain Treatment Centers at a Crossroads: A Practical and Conceptual Reappraisal.* Seattle: IASP Press.

Crapanzano, Vincent. 2000. "Transfiguring Translation." *Semiotica* 128 1/2: 113–36.

Csordas, Thomas. 1990. "Embodiment as a Paradigm for Anthropology." *Ethos* 18: 5–47.

———. 1993. "Somatic Modes of Attention." *Cultural Anthropology* 8: 135–56.

———. 1994. *The Sacred Self: A Cultural Phenomenology of Charismatic Healing.* Berkeley: University of California Press.

Damasio, Antonio. 1994. *Descartes' Error: Emotion, Reason, and the Human Brain.* New York: Avon.

———. 1999. *The Feeling of What Happens: Body and Emotion in the Making of Consciousness.* New York: Harcourt Brace.

Das, Veena. 1997. "Language and Body: Transactions in the Construction of Pain." Pp. 67–92 in *Social Suffering,* ed. A. Kleinman, V. Das, and M. Lock. Berkeley: University of California Press.

Fields, Howard. 2000. "Setting the Stage for Pain." Paper presented at Houghton Conference on "Pain and Its Transformations," Harvard University, May 18–20.

Good, Byron. 1992. "A Body in Pain—The Making of a World of Chronic Pain." Pp. 29–48 in *Pain as Human Experience: An Anthropological Perspective,* ed. M.-J. DelVecchio Good et al. Berkeley: University of California Press.

———. 1994. *Medicine, Rationality, and Experience: An Anthropological Perspective.* Cambridge: Cambridge University Press.

Hahn, Robert A. 1995. *Sickness and Healing: An Anthropological Perspective.* New Haven: Yale University Press.

Herzlich, Claudine, and Janine Pierret. 1987. *Illness and Self in Society,* trans. E. Forster. Baltimore: Johns Hopkins University Press.

Hilbert, Richard A. 1984. "The Acultural Dimensions of Chronic Pain: Flawed Reality Construction and the Problem of Meaning." *Social Problems* 31: 365–78.

International Association for the Study of Pain. 1979. "Pain Terms: A List with Definitions and a Note on Usage." *Pain* 6: 249–52.

Iser, Wolfgang. 1978. *The Act of Reading: A Theory of Aesthetic Response.* Baltimore: Johns Hopkins University Press.

Jackson, Jean. 2000. *"Camp Pain": Talking with Chronic Pain Patients.* Philadelphia: University of Pennsylvania Press.

Jakobson, Roman. 1959. "On Linguistic Aspects of Translation." Pp. 232–39 in *On Translation,* ed. R. A. Brower. Cambridge: Harvard University Press.

Kirmayer, Laurence J. 1988. "Mind and Body as Metaphors: Hidden Values in Biomedicine." Pp. 57–93 in *Biomedicine Examined,* ed. M. Lock and D. R. Gordon. Boston: D. Reidel.

———. 1992. "The Body's Insistence on Meaning: Metaphor as Presentation and Representation in Illness Experience." *Medical Anthropology Quarterly* 6: 323–46.

Kleinman, Arthur. 1995. "What Is Specific to Biomedicine?" Pp. 21–40 in *Writing at the Margin: Discourse between Anthropology and Medicine.* Berkeley: University of California Press.

Leder, Drew. 1990. *The Absent Body.* Chicago: University of Chicago Press.

Leighton, Lauren G. 1984. *The Art of Translation: Kornei Chukovsky's A High Art.* Knoxville: University of Tennessee Press.

Loeser, John D. 1991. "What Is Chronic Pain?" *Theoretical Medicine* 12: 213–25.

———. 1996. "Mitigating the Dangers of Pursuing Care." Pp. 101–8 in *Pain Treatment Centers at a Crossroads: A Practical and Conceptual Reappraisal,* ed. Mitchell J. M. Cohen and James N. Campbell. Seattle: IASP.

Merleau-Ponty, Maurice. 1962. *Phenomenology of Perception,* trans. C. Smith. London: Routledge and Kegan Paul.

Morris, David B. 1991. *The Culture of Pain.* Berkeley: University of California Press.

Porter, Roy. 1994. "Pain and History in the Western World." Pp. 98–119 in *The Puzzle of Pain.* Reading, UK: Gordon and Breach.

Price, Reynolds. 1995. *A Whole New Life: An Illness and a Healing.* New York: Scribner.

Public Radio International. n.d. "Gray Matters: Pain and the Brain." Typescript of radio broadcast.

Rexroth, Kenneth. 1964. "The Poet as Translator." Pp. 29–50 in *The Craft and Context of Translation,* ed. W. Arrowsmith and R. Shattuck. Garden City, NY: Doubleday.

Rosenberg, Daniel V. 1990. "Language in the Discourse of the Emotions." Pp. 162–85 in *Language and the Politics of Emotion,* ed. C. A. Lutz and L. Abu-Lughod. Cambridge: Cambridge University Press.

Sacks, Oliver. 1984. *A Leg to Stand On.* New York: Harper and Row.

Sansom, Basil. 1982. "The Sick Who Do Not Speak." Pp. 183–96 in *Semantic Anthropology,* ed. D. Parkin. London: Academic.

Scarry, Elaine. 1985. *The Body in Pain: The Making and Unmaking of the World.* New York: Oxford University Press.

———. 2000. "Physical Pain and the Ground of Creating." Paper presented at Houghton Conference on "Pain and Its Transformations," Harvard University, May 18–20.

Schieffelin, Edward L. 1976. *The Sorrow of the Lonely and the Burning of the Dancers.* New York: St. Martin's.

Schutz, Alfred. 1971. "On Multiple Realities." Pp. 207–59 in *Collected Papers,* Vol. 1, *The Problem of Social Reality.* The Hague: Martinus Nijhoff.

Sullivan, Mark D. 1995. "Pain in Language: From Sentience to Sapience." *Pain Forum* 4: 3–14.

Translation as *Pontificium*

Bernhard Streck

 **11**

Και ειπεν κυριοσ Ιδου γενοσ εν
και ξειλοσ εν παντων,
και τουτο ηρξαντο ποιησαι,
και νυν ουκ εκλειψει εξ αυτων παντα,
οσα αν επιτωνται ποιειν.
Δευτε καταβαντεσ συγξεωμεν
εκει αυτων την γλωσσαν,
ινα μη ακουσωσιν εκαστοσ
την φωνην του πλησιον.

AND THE LORD SAID, BEHOLD, THE PEOPLE IS ONE,
AND THEY HAVE ALL ONE LANGUAGE;
AND THIS THEY BEGIN TO DO;
AND NOW NOTHING WILL BE RESTRAINED FROM THEM,
WHICH THEY HAVE IMAGINED TO DO.
GO TO, LET US GO DOWN,
AND THERE CONFOUND THEIR LANGUAGE,
THAT THEY MAY NOT UNDERSTAND ONE ANOTHER'S SPEECH.
—Genesis 11:6–7

What translators in Alexandria in the second century B.C. had to understand as a curse that would burden humanity to the end of time, they themselves knew how to turn into a blessing. Through translation into the Greek lingua franca, the law of Moses became accessible to the entire civilized world, even though the proper way of reading it and its meaning have been disputed ever since. The art of translation initially overcame the curse, only for controversy to return over the text. The work on the Babylonian tower continued: translators joined the architects, engineers, and building workers. Without them, nothing else was possible, though they also created great difficulties.

George Steiner has summarized the Babylonian problems of translation in his frequently translated book, *After Babel* (1975), which deals with the totality of mankind, in which each individual is already faced with problems of understanding. Steiner surveys the whole spectrum, from the professional translator with his belief in accuracy to the imitative artist with his right to form things freely, from the comparative linguist to the cultural hermeneut and historian, from the scribe to the newspaper reader and everyday speaker. All of these have patterns they repeat, interpret, decipher, vary, and especially encode, for the business of the translator is without end. Even the person who speaks only one language puzzles over the meanings of his forefathers and clothes his thoughts and feelings in metaphors, since his innermost being cannot be conveyed to the outside in any other way.

Speaking is translating, and translating is repeating: only the distance between the original and the copy varies. In interpreting music, sovereignty is accorded to the pattern, while the restorer feels quite a different sort of obligation toward the original. Yet each is working on a past worth reviving. The copy and the translation are always more recent than the original: it is always a matter of bridging time. Each culture consists of a number of such chronological and spatial bridges. If every speech act performs the task of mediating something, the act of translation does this potentially, mediating between mediations, or being, as Friedrich Schlegel has expressed it, in the service of "understanding of the understanding" *(Verstehen des Verstehens)*. In this sense, Pieter Breughel the Elder had all the details right in his painting of the Tower of Babel of 1563: whether interpreted as a ruin or a building site, the gigantic structure of world culture consists of a confusing wealth of arches, pillars, and stories linked with one another. As the Old Testament assures us reproachfully, but the cuneiform scripts in an affirmative manner, the whole structure was intended as a bridge: *etemenanki*, the "foundations of heaven and earth," were to link the two poles of existence of the world under and above (Klengel-Brandt 1982, 172).

Both in their cultures and between cultures, human beings are all pontifices, or bridge-builders. This was the meaning of the title of the priest in heathen Rome; the functionaries of the Catholic religion of mediation also bore it; and in this paper it is used in a democratized fashion as the task of everybody, though intensified in the cultural, historical, linguistic, and social sciences that are brought together under the notion of the humanities. Building bridges creates equality.

Adults who want to make their children understand them stoop to their level; children who want to please their parents temporarily express themselves "precociously." Different genders, classes, statuses, subcultures, speech communities, and home defense groups not only stress their characteristics and boundaries, but they are also concerned with adjustment and accommodation with the outside.

The humanities became differentiated in the nineteenth century, though at the start of that century the understanding was of people and society as a community of communication and translation in the sense of Humboldt and Novalis. The nineteenth century then became the great period of epigonality in which art was understood as an attempt at reconstruction and the dark pastimes were translated into the present. However, the obsession with seeking original forms and origins, for the pure and genuine, belonged also to this general time-translationism known as historicism. This may have been the price that had to be paid for the high degree of consciousness concerning what was mediated and mixed together. In this process of becoming humanities, the pontifices longed for the starting points or, in technical language, the abutments of their structures, which they then naively translated into the industrial present. Anthropology, the first world understanding with a strong feeling for differences, arose in this milieu. However, for a long time these differences were technically linked to the work of *homo faber* on an objectified nature as a model.

In the twentieth century, "modern art" blocked this readiness to translate in its search for untranslatability, originality, uniqueness, and shock effects. According to Steiner, literature set itself against language, painting against pictures, atonality against music. The revolution was aimed at the past, on which no one wanted to work any more. In art, the *pontificium* ceased, however much gallery-owners, feature-writers, and art teachers tried to awaken the public's understanding. Only the humanities held fast to the old task: the century of catastrophe and of broken models was that of the commandment to mediate and translate. The understanding of alien cultures had never come closer than in the period of imperialist and technical globalization.

The Question of Translatability

In the Bible, Babel is seen as the second fall. In any case, for the humanities this had a greater impact than the first fall, which was caused by eating from the tree of knowledge. Then nakedness and hunger were revealed. This time, confusion imposed as a punishment brought doubt and strife, for example, over the original language that made translation possible at all to begin with. The Jewish critics of the Jewish Greek translation of the Old Testament invoked Hebrew as the original language: the language of God could not be translated, only corrupted. This was later repeated by Muslims, whose God—whose written revelations in the *qur'ân* are considered "inimitable" (Arabic *i'gâz*, from *mu'giz*, wonder)—spoke Arabic. However, in the thirteenth century Roger Bacon said that a *grammatica universalis* was the basis of translatability. In German mysticism, conversely, silence was the language of divinity: "nothing and more than nothing" *(Nichts und Übernichts)*. Angelus Silesius wrote the following verses in 1657: "Go where you cannot; see where you do not see; hear where nothing sounds or rings; then you are where God is speaking."

With Herder too, the translatability of songs and dances certainly had a basis in God, though his thoughts were ultimately beyond examination and as many-sided as the peoples, his creations. Only in the catastrophic twentieth century did Walter Benjamin postulate the *logos* as the original language and Noam Chomsky discover the generative grammar that made learning and understanding possible across linguistic boundaries. In this way, the modern bases for a renewed belief in all-round translatability were laid, and psychological or pathological causes sought for the doubt and misunderstanding found on the Babel building site. Thus the twentieth century ended in the rebirth of earlier heydays of translatability, such as those brought about by Hellenism after the fall of Babylon, and later, the Renaissance.

These famous historical periods all rejoiced in the increase in linguistic and cultural mixing. Human beings dressed up and changed their costumes, and above all wore different speaker masks that they could change. It was less truth that was sought in the word than beauty. Gestures in speaking came to prevail over content. Rhetoric alone could promise well-being, and what triumphed were applications and ornaments, formulas and set phrases, costumes and scenery of a world theater grown self-aware. In these mixed times, media always prevail over the message, perhaps because each time a new medium was invented: in Babylon cuneiform, in Greek the alphabet, in sixteenth-century Europe printing, and at the end of the twentieth century electronic data-processing.

George Steiner has examined the giants of Western intellectual history for their views on the problem of translatability. There have been strong skeptics, like Benedetto Croce and Ortega y Gasset, for whom speech is a unique creation that cannot be repeated or even transferred. (The translation of holy texts was continually prevented with similar arguments, and their epigonality, once they had been translated, freely denied.) Then Hölderlin and Novalis enthused over the equation between poetry and translation, Pushkin spoke of the translator as the "courier of the spirit," and Franz Rosenzweig saw himself as a translator on the path to deliverance. Conversely, Nietzsche called the translations of the Renaissance "conquests," and, in the same spirit, the German Romanist Karl Vossler spoke of translation as linguistic imperialism. We are thus confronted with a shining act making possible the rebuilding of the Tower of Babel, comparable with the controversial ethics of the plan itself.

At this point, Steiner offers a four-phase model that makes the different assessments of the art of translation understandable, and simultaneously makes our metaphor of translation as a bridging operation technically comprehensible. The hermeneutic process is then introduced as an act of trust in which foreign terrain is recognized as accessible in principle. Without this assessment of translation as doable, no strategy for understanding the other can be set in train: the bridging materials remain in the warehouse. According to what was said above about the situation regarding belief in translatability, it is clear that this preliminary examination can turn out quite differently. In this respect, anthropologists are professional optimists: even where linguistic knowledge is meagre, they take on the challenge of the darkest themes and translate them into known terms.

The second phase Steiner calls, psychologically or politically, aggression. The bridging operation begins; the previously prepared apparatus is deployed. Construction follows according to plan and regulations, until the opposite bank is reached, thus making the river between the banks, which had earlier separated them, harmless. The soldiers of understanding cross the engineers' bridge safely and proceed directly to the third phase: incorporation. A bridgehead is constructed on the opposite bank to secure the bridging operation. Says Steiner bluntly, "The translator forces his way in, steals, and makes off." Only the fourth phase offers a certain reconciliation that Steiner calls "compensation." To continue with our metaphor of military technology, this could explain that the new bridge can now be crossed in the opposite direction too. Linguistic and cultural goods can freely spread hither and thither. However, Steiner's meaning is somewhat different.

In the fourth phase, "After Babel" means especially the harvest of the translation. The effort has proved its worth when the translated work experiences a wider distribution, as with the seventy Jews of Alexandria, whose law was able to achieve world currency through translation. Certainly the substance has suffered through the act of conquest, since every encoding entails a reduction in quality, and the commercial law of value takes offense at any dissemination of preciosities. Yet for Steiner dissemination is an acceptable return for the reduction in substance: Moses in the Brazilian rain forest, Shakespeare in the *Wehrmacht* soldier's knapsack, Goethe in Japan, Borges in Leipzig, Mohammed in London.

World culture is the result of many such conquests of foreign land. As said before, Steiner did not refer his notion of reciprocity to a settled balance of trade. No comparable return gift followed the dissemination of the Septuagint; Solon's Laws remained mostly unnoticed in Jerusalem, and Hammurabi's were rediscovered only in the nineteenth century. Steiner's "reciprocity" serves solely to reconcile the work with its translation. It is now dressed in different clothes, an insult compensated by the fact that it can now travel to other countries. Translation widens its effectiveness or, in military or political terms, the area of influence. Does this process go so far that ultimately translation is no longer necessary?

Toward Untranslatability

⌒ In his contribution to the collection entitled *The Translatability of Cultures* (Budick and Iser, eds., 1996), the Heidelberg Egyptologist Jan Assmann has recon-structed the ancient world as a peak time for translations in which even the most holy beings, the gods, could be transferred across boundaries without problems (J. Assmann 1996). From the start Babylon was multilingual, and thus the gods were known by different names. Accordingly, the gods of neighboring cities and states were recognized as trusted powers whose names could be translated into one's own language without difficulty. This was also a precondition for both peaceful and warlike interaction. Agreements made sense only if they were concluded be-fore authorities who were believed in by all parties. The same went for the break-ing of agreements, whenever that was felt to be sinful.

In heathen antiquity, religion—which, in the period of the "clash of civilizations" (Huntington 1996), tends to represent intolerance, missionary expansion, and jealousy—was an ideology of bridging. When entering a foreign city or country, the foreigner was happy to learn that "there are also gods here." And even commanders who had come as conquerors showed respect to the city gods, since they were like their own—that is, multiform. As is well known, the Romans deported conquered gods to Rome—the so-called *evocatio*—because in the center of the world they had to feel better than in the remote provinces (Cancik 1988).

The Jewish Yahweh-alone movement caused a revolution in this world of translatability of a sort that, according to the studies of Max Weber, could be produced only in a minority situation. Assmann has called this "'counter-identity' against the dominating system." In the religion of the Jewish covenant that arose in opposition to the Babylonian world of the gods, translatability was denied. The gods were not equal, but rather the enemies of Yahweh, and later they no longer even existed. One must follow a religion of this new type, with its own formless god, in full consciousness: one enters it as a convert and leaves it as an apostate.

According to Assmann, who draws a sharp boundary between belief in translatability and a belief in truth that allows no falsification: "As long as there is the possibility of translation, there is no need of conversion" (1996, 31). In the heathen world, gods claimed to be this and that and ultimately everything. Yahweh said, "I am who I am," and denied all bridges to other gods. Monotheism desires no further enrichment or improvement to the world of the gods, but their replacement, the radical devaluation of the many gods in favor of the one God. Zeus may not be worshipped in the temple of Yahweh, though Yahweh communities formed in many cities of the Mediterranean and Middle East. The heathens and the Jews, and later also the Christians, talked past each other, even when they mastered the same language. Experience teaches the interchangeability and ubiquity of the gods, while belief demands the uniqueness and veracity of the one God.

Between Hellas, the "eye of the world," and Israel, the "ear of the world" (Taubes 1991 [1947]), no mediation was possible. The heathen world of translatability reacted helplessly against the weapons of mission and conversion of Jewish and later Christian monotheism. The experience of the eternal return all around the world was overshadowed by a belief in the deliverance of the world. The traditional ontology had to make way for the new eschatology. The internal troubles that the seventy translators in Alexandria had to struggle with are understood: the law and the prophets, the charter of the holy alliance between Yahweh and Israel, were to be translated into a world language that thought completely differently. Here the split was produced between the Yahweh universalists (the Christians) and the Yahweh particularists (the Jews), determining the religious history of the next two thousand years.

In the volume edited by Budick and Iser, Almeida Assmann, the scholar of literature, reminds us of the solution that the universalists found for the problem of translatability, which in the tradition of the Church is associated with the event of Whitsun. In the so-called outpouring of the Holy Spirit, the Babylonian confusion of tongues was lifted. The followers of Jesus who were assembled in Jerusalem

certainly continued to speak different languages, but they understood one another
without translation. They grasped the belief in the untranslatability of Yahweh
in such a way that linguistic problems of understanding could be skipped. Just
as Babel stood for diversification, so, according to Almeida Assmann, Jerusalem
stood for universalization. The Holy Spirit, which until then had spoken only
Hebrew and from whose translation into Greek many Jews distanced themselves,
now became multilingual. For deliverance seemed near, and "any language turned
into a messianic language" (A. Assman 1996, 92).

On the one hand, the victory of monotheism brought to an end the heathen
culture of translation. In place of the named and translatable gods came the sole
god without a name. Ideas of truth and purity and of the uncorrupted original
had an impact far beyond the boundaries of the Jewish communities, even though
the prohibition on images could only partially be transferred. In the view of Jewish orthodoxy the word of God had to suffer all too many losses and too much
dilution in the hands of the Christian masses. As a result, Bible translations were
initially very difficult, and every attempt to make one caused divisions. Hierony-
mus had to defend his "vulgarization" of the seventies' Bible and the evangelists
with their having come into existence under the conditions of hermitage and divine inspiration. Over a thousand years later, the English Bible translator Tyndale
was executed and Martin Luther outlawed. Only in the modern period defined
by Protestantism did the Bible translator achieve a really high position, but at the
same time apocalyptic pressure: the Gospel, which for so long had been reserved
for the successively sanctified languages—Hebrew, Greek, Latin, and, in Eastern
Europe, also the Slavonic of Cyril and Methodius—now had to be translated into
all the thousands of living languages for, according to the revived belief in Whitsun, no one might any longer be left aside, while the coming of the Lord, Yahweh's
son, was expected immediately. "O that I had a thousand tongues" (*Oh, daß ich
tausend Zungen hätte*—Johann Mentzer 1704), sang the evangelical communities
now, since praise of the one and same God could never be heard in enough languages.

Almeida Assmann draws a line between the events at Whitsun, in which
everyone praised the same God, and postmodernism, in which the otherness of
everyone is sanctified. Does the circle close at this point with Babylon, which
has already cultivated the acceptance of difference in its all-embracing culture of
translation? This means disregarding the fundamental gulf between polytheism
and monotheism. In postmodernism, it is not the heathen multiplicity of Babylon that is returning, but rather the multivocality of Jerusalem. This no longer

required translation in the Babylonian sense because, although there were many tongues, there was only one spirit. For the same reason, the postmodern ethic does not require any translation either. As indicated above, this is something it has in common with modern art. Derrida's "altarity" consciously renounces attempts at mediation or flattening into "alterity." In this way postmodernism, like the Whitsun community, also involves talking at cross-purposes, but in one and the same spirit—love in Jerusalem, tolerance in San Francisco.

Toward Translatability

Why did people doubt the translatability of the truth for so long? Because it cannot be pluralized? Because it cannot stand any variation? Because it is as jealous as its God, who was discovered in the Babylonian exile and has developed from this to being the Lord of a world that He rejects and wishes to redeem from itself? In this difficult context, Jan Assmann has separated "the energetic dimension of language" from its functional aspect. The latter is readily translatable, the former not. The power of a language, perhaps also its aura, cannot be translated. All the sacred languages of the world depend on this fact, including Hebrew, which the Yahweh-alone movement used to establish itself within an Aramaic-speaking population. Even oral societies use archaic formulas in important rituals, formulas that hardly anyone understands but that are held to be important and constitutive. Does the untranslatability of the truth lie in their incomprehensibility?

In his book *Translation and Taboo* (1996), Douglas Robinson constructs a history of the development of translatability according to which old cultures believed in mysteries that lacked a rational meaning. These were imagined in rituals that cultivated the mysterious. Religion consisted of taboos that were not spoken of, forget about in an unauthorized manner. In his *Das kulturelle Gedächtnis* (1992), Jan Assmann develops the distinction between oral mystery religions, which have refused to reduce their sacred texts to writing, and "bookkeeping" religions. It has already been indicated what problems the latter have with translations. Mystery cults were not translated even in the periods of their decay and of mass conversions—for example, in late antiquity after the old gods were banned in A.D. 391–92, or under European colonialism and heathen mission. This depressing situation concerning sources inspired mythologists' fantasies and has burdened the present-day anthropology of religion.

Robinson's running historical leitmotif is the painful, step-by-step detabooing of the sacred, marked by setbacks. First, the usual words are not used in speaking of taboo: in the case of a textual religion, the books are considered sacred. This stage of "grapholatry" (Jack Goody) was characteristic of the history of the churches for centuries and is nowadays still represented worldwide by book-owning communities of believers: "Illiterate Christians in the Middle Ages see the veneration with which the Bible is treated in church and learn not to go near it, not to touch it, not to try to read it, let alone translate it, even if they later go to school and learn Latin—and their fear is still with us today. Taboos do not die easily" (Robinson 1996, 24). For a thousand years, dealing with the sacred text in this way on the other side of the choir screen was practiced prefiguratively; then the reformers conquered access for themselves and their communities through translations into common languages, though reserving to themselves the right of interpretation. In the pietistic community of brothers, with their lay apostleship, this was democratized further, although, in accordance with the Pauline law, it remained in the hands of men. Only in feminist theologies of the late twentieth century were new interpretations hazarded, which, to the disgust of all three book religions, resembled heathen dogmas once again and sometimes removed worshippers from Christian services.

Regardless of the change in content, however, the belief in the inexpressible (in Greek, τα αρρητα), extended into reverence for the sacred word, maintained for almost two thousand years. Neither was negotiable; discursive language remained excluded from the history of religion, though Robinson recognizes certain advances. Initiations, whether into ancient mystery cults or age classes and secret societies in contemporary ethnic groups, lead into darkness, not into the light of the religions of redemption. Therefore, even less can be discussed regarding the former than the secrets of the religions of revelation, even though children in Bible, Talmud, or Koran schools repeat the sacred words like incomprehensible mystery formulas.

Robinson stresses the flourishing translation activities that were happening in this basically translation-unfriendly world. Thus Babylonian culture was translated from the Sumerian, Greek from the Egyptian, and Roman from the Greek. We recall that Assmann, from a totally different perspective, stressed translation as the characteristic of heathen antiquity and, especially in the area of the sacred, of the gods themselves. Obviously the two authors do not share the same understanding of translation. Robinson is pursuing the path from taboo to ethics, made possible by a step-by-step freeing of human reason through translation. Assmann is pursuing the path from the interchangeability of truths to the one sole truth, no longer able to tolerate translations. Both have in view the genesis and dissemination of the Judeo-Christian world view as the precondition for the Western, modern mode of thought.

The process of rationalization—that all the humanities thematize and that Max Weber raised to the status of the leitmotif of his newly founded sociology—introduces reason into contexts that, according to Robinson, were governed by "unreason"—that is, by feelings or experiences that were not reflected upon. This creation of meaning occurs through transparency, to which also belongs the proposition that any meaningful sentence can be expressed in a foreign language. This is the basic assumption of translatability in general: "Hence we have the rationalist notion of absolute translatability, the belief that anything that can be said in one language can be said in another. Related is the reductive method for achieving this absolute translatability: reducing a text to a stabilized semantic object, a decontextualized and detexturalized <message>, stripping the text of its sensual or carnal aspects, the sound and feel of it, none of which ever translates" (Robinson 1996, 36). Here the demand for translatability brings with it an increase in clarity, but also an impoverishment of reality, and thus Robinson's and Assmann's perspectives converge again. The old gods stood for passions that occur in any culture. Thus they were related to one another and exchangeable. Yahweh embodies that meaning in history that can tolerate no other meaning. Thus the sacred text assembled by the Jews combated the old translation culture of sensuality and passions, permitting new translations only under the strict supervision of reason.

⌒ Robinson calls the two models of understanding the other, "other as mystery" and "other as reason." Humanities disciplines are well advised not to look at things in just one way, but to keep both eyes open. Certainly the rationalistic perspective and its belief resemble the "identity in difference" of the hope of Whitsun invoked by Almeida Assmann: many languages, but one spirit. This emerges with the universal claim and ultimately provides for transparency: unbounded translatability, yet still only within a particular spirit. The structuralist Jean Pouillon refers to it in the following formula: Meaning is what to say in another way, what is translated into another language: what a translation permits (1984, 71, my translation). Now, however, there are many humans who have not taken part in the wonder of Whitsun, and still today there are many cultures that can be understood only in the reverse formula—that is, "difference in identity." Anthropologist of art Ingrid Kreide-Damani has referred to this boundary of translatability with respect to culture and language: [We] must come to terms with the fact that there are word pictures in other languages without an equivalent in our language and world of ideas (1992, 68; my translation). Neither anthropology nor, indeed, other humanities, can cope with Robinson's idea of translation—that is, with the reduction of reality to what is meaningfully expressible and thus translatable. The cultures they study are dominated mostly by passions, which resemble the worlds of the gods of antiquity more than the "religion of reason from the sources of Judaism" (Cohen 1988). It may be that attempts at translation in this area of "unreasonable" qualities are condemned to fail, like the link between heaven and earth that the tower of Babylon is supposed to have created. Nonetheless they must be undertaken; otherwise there will be no tower of Babylon consisting of a multiplicity of bridges, even those that create no meaning at all.

The task of the humanities thus consists more of a multiple pontificium than of reduction to one spirit. Scholars in the humanities are also scholars of spirits, and have to do with spirits—spirits of the times, folk spirits, local spirits, spirits of the dead. Only monotheists are able to bring all this together as the nonspirit of superstition. For others, the work of translation remains, which must sometimes mediate via violent precipices that are chronological, spatial, or rational. The latter are becoming more and more visible even in modern society, and they invite anthropologists, who otherwise specialize in exotic worlds, to study and comment on them. Here too, their special task is the undermining of privileges that claim particular traditions of reason and hierarchies that belong to the Western tradition, though not absolutely to a critical science. Translation activities in the humanities also call into question the Eurocentric, chronocentric, and logocentric bases of our scientific tradition and, with all the efforts of methods and discursiveness, work more at a type of polyprovincialism, and in any case at an "end to arrogance" (Lepenies 1981). Translation between the spirits—the Babylonian principle—is permitted to claim the same right as translation in one and the same spirit—that is, the Jerusalem principle.

In the old Jewish communities, a strict distinction was made between original text rolls and Aramaic translations, the so-called *targum*. He who read out the original text might not come to the aid of he who read out the translation, lest the impression arise that the translation was already being included in the original text (Leipoldt and Morenz 1953, 76). As in Egypt, in old Babylon the translator *(targummannum,* Sumerian *eme-bal)* enjoyed a higher reputation. The same was true of the *dragoman* in the Ottoman Empire, from whom, in a marvelous way, the

German *Dolmetscher* (interpreter) can be traced (Assmann 1996, 28). The paths leading from the Arab *tardjemâm* to the Catalan *torsimany* and the French *truchement* are clearer (Steiner 1994, 269). These are all pontifices who, however, carry out their profession not like machines but like human beings or like diplomats, the virtuosi of politeness and disguise. Thus the abutments of their bridges are not the same. The Tower of Babel consists not of facsimiles of the truth but of variations, modulations, and interpretations that explain as much as they conceal and must for their part be re-explained. The pontificium is a system maintaining and reproducing itself without end. The ancient Greeks called the passion of joining and committing Hermes, the god of activity, of lie, and theft, who, as the messenger of the gods, mediated between the immortals and the mortals. This is the founding myth of the humanities practicing hermeneutics.

$\sim$

References Cited

Assmann, Almeida. 1996. "The Curse and Blessing of Babel; or, Looking Back on Universalism." Pp. 85–100 in *The Translatability of Cultures*, ed. S. Budick and W. Iser. Stanford, CA: Stanford University Press.

Assmann, Jan. 1992. *Das kulturelle Gedächtnis: Schrift, Erinnerung und politische Identität in frühen Hochkulturen.* Munich: C. H. Beck

———. 1996. "Translating Gods: Religion as a Factor of Cultural (Un)translatability." Pp. 25–36 in *The Translatability of Cultures*, ed. S. Budick and W. Iser. Stanford, CA: Stanford University Press.

Benjamin, Walter. 1995 [1921]. "Die Aufgabe des Übersetzers." Pp. 50–64 in *Sprache und Geschichte: Philosophische Essays*. Stuttgart: Reclam.

Bolz, Norbert, and Willem van Reijen. 1991. *Walter Benjamin.* Frankfurt am Main and New York: Campus.

Budick, Sanford, and Wolfgang Iser, eds. 1996. *The Translatability of Cultures: Figurations of the Space Between.* Stanford, CA: Stanford University Press.

Cancik, Hubert. 1988. "Religionsaesthetik." Pp. 121–54 in *Handbuch der religionswissenschaftlichen Grundbegriffe*, vol. 1. Stuttgart: Kohlhammer.

Cohen, Hermann. 1988 [1919]. *Religion der Vernunft aus den Quellen des Judentums.* Wiesbaden: Fourier.

Derrida, Jacques. 1972 [1968]. "La différance." In *Marges de la philosophie*. Paris: Éditions gelilée.

Huntington, Samuel. 1996. *Clash of Civilizations.* New York: Simon and Schuster.

Klengel-Brandt, Evelyn. 1982. *Der Turm von Babylon: Legende und Geschichte eines Bauwerks.* Leipzig: Koehler and Amelang.

Kreide-Damani, Ingrid. 1992. *Kunstethnologie: Zum Verständnis fremder Kunst.* Cologne: Dumont.

Leipoldt, Johannes, and Siegfried Morenz. 1953. *Heilige Schriften: Betrachtungen zur Religionsgeschichte der antiken Mittelmeerwelt.* Leipzig: Otto Harrassowitz.

Lepenies, Wolf, ed. 1981. *Geschichte der Soziologie.* 4 vols. Frankfurt am Main: Suhrkamp.

Pouillon, Jean. 1984. "Die mythische Funktion." In *Mythos ohne Illusion,* ed. J-P. Vernant and C. Levi-Strauss. Frankfurt am Main: Suhrkamp.

Rahlfs, Alfred, ed. *Septuaginta.* 2 vols. Stuttgart: Privilegierte Württembergische Bibelanstalt.

Robinson, Douglas. 1996. *Translation and Taboo.* DeKalb: Northern Illinois University Press.

Steiner, George. 1994. *Nach Babel: Aspekte der Sprache und des Übersetzens.* Frankfurt am Main: Suhrkamp (orig. English: *After Babel: Aspects of Language and Translation.* 1975/1992).

Taubes, Jacob. 1991 [1947]. *Abendländische Eschatologie.* Munich: Matthes und Seitz.

Weber, Max. 1923 [1921]. *Das antike Judentum.* Vol. 3 of *Gesammelte Aufsätze zur Religionssoziologie.* Tübingen: Mohr.

Wehr, Gerhard. 1977. *Angelus Silesius: Der Cherubinische Wandersmann.* Vol. 3 of *Zeugnisse christlicher Esoterik.* Schaffhausen: Novalis.

List of Contributors

ELLEN B. BASSO is Professor of Anthropology at the University of Arizona. Her research has emphasized narrative discourse and ritual communication in central Brazil. Her published works include *A Musical View of the Universe* (1986), *In Favor of Deceit* (1987), *The Last Cannibals* (1995), and "The Neologistic Imagination: A Review of Some Recent Books on Translation," in *Reviews in Anthropology* 3 (December 2002).

VINCENT CRAPANZANO is Distinguished Professor of Comparative Literature and Anthropology at the City University of New York. Among his books are *Tuhami: A Portrait of a Moroccan* (1980), *Hermes' Dilemma and Hamlet's Desire: On the Epistemology of Interpretation* (1992), and *Serving the Word: Literalism in America from the Pulpit to the Bench* (2000). His latest book, *Imaginative Horizons: An Essay in Literary-Philosophical Anthropology,* will be published in the fall of 2003.

VOLKER HEESCHEN is Professor of Ethnolinguistics in the Institute of Ethnology at the University of Munich. He has published on language philosophy (Wilhelm von Humboldt), the evolution of speech (and speech act theory), metalinguistic awareness, texts, grammar, and the language and culture of communities in the mountains of West Papua.

JEAN JACKSON is Professor and Chair of Anthropology at the Massachusetts Institute of Technology. She has been examining social and ethnic identity in the Northwest Amazon since 1968 (*The Fish People: Linguistic Exogamy and Tukanoan Identity in Northwest Amazonia,* 1983), as well as gender, small-scale societies, indigenous rights, new social movements, and the epistemology of ethnography. For the last ten years she has been concerned with the anthropology of chronic pain. She is editor, with Kay B. Warren, of *Indigenous Movements, Self-Representation and the State in Latin America* (University of Texas Press, 2003).

TULLIO MARANHÃO was Professor of Anthropology and Education at the University of St. Thomas. He authored *Therapeutic Discourse and Socratic Dialogue: A Cultural Critique* (University of Wisconsin Press, 1986). His work focused on Amerindian Amazonia and questions of alterity in dialogue and translation.

WALTER D. MIGNOLO is Professor of Literature, Cultural Anthropology, and Romance Studies (Latin America) and Director of the Institute for Global Studies in Humanities at Duke University. He has published on semiotics, literary theory, colonial cultural history, and postcolonial theories. His books include *Writing without Words: Alternative Literacies in Mesoamerica and the Andes* (coeditor, 1994) and *The Darker Side of the Renaissance: Literacy, Territoriality, Colonization* (1995), as well as *Local Histories/Global Designs: Coloniality, Subaltern Knowledges and Border Thinking* (1999).

MARK MÜNZEL is Professor of Ethnology in the Institute for Comparative Cultural Research at the University of Marburg. His wide-ranging research interests and publications cover personhood and identity and ritual exchange and healing among Amerindian groups. He has developed numerous museum exhibits on Amerindian artists and the photographic representation of South American Indians.

AKIRA OKAZAKI teaches intercultural communication and anthropology at Kanagawa University, Japan. He has conducted fieldwork among and written about the Maasai of Kenya and the Gamk of Sudan and has written on world music. He was elected to the first Evans-Pritchard Lecturership, All Souls College, Oxford University.

ANTONIO LUIGI PALMISANO is Professor of Anthropology at the University of Trieste, and he has done research in the Horn of Africa. His main interests include the anthropology of religion and ritual.

RICHARD ROTTENBURG is Professor of Anthropology at the MLU Halle, Germany. His main research interests are the anthropology of objectivity and the ethnography of organizations, technology, and the state. His main geographical areas are Africa and Europe. His latest publication is *Weit hergeholte Fakten: Eine Parabel der Entwicklungshilfe* (2002).

FREYA SCHIWY has a Ph.D. in Spanish from Duke University and is Assistant Professor of Spanish in the Modern and Classical Languages Department at the University of Connecticut. She has published articles on indigenous video production in Spanish and English and has coedited the book *Indisciplinar las ciencias sociales: Geopolíticas del conocimiento y colonialidad del poder. Perspectivas desde lo andino* (Abya-Yala, 2002). Her research interests include contemporary Latin American literature and film, postcolonial theory, and gender studies.

BERNHARD STRECK is Professor in the Institut für Ethnologie at the Universität Leipzig. His research interests include the history of anthropology, the ethnography of Northeast Africa, Gypsiology, and the Rhetoric of Culture. Among his publications are *Sudan* (Dumont Buchverlag, 1982), *Wörterbuch der Ethnologie* (Peter Hammer Verlag, 1987 [2000]), *Die Halab* (Peter Hammer Verlag, 1996), *Fröhliche Wissenschaft Ethnologie* (Peter Hammer Verlag, 1997), and *Ethnologie und Nationalsozialismus* (Escher Verlag, 2000).

Index